D0501571

# The Game before the Money

# The Game before the Money

## Money

*Voices of the Men Who Built the NFL*

JACKSON MICHAEL

University of Nebraska Press
Lincoln & London

All photographs in the text are courtesy of the author unless otherwise noted.

A portion of the sales of this book will be donated to the following football-related charities:

Lone Star Paralysis Foundation, Doug English, President. "The mission of the Lone Star Paralysis Foundation is to cure paralysis from spinal cord injury by funding research, recovery therapy, and community outreach. We call it our three "Rs:" Research, Recovery, and Recreation. We are working to move the clock forward on a cure." http://www.LoneStarParalysis.org/

Retired Players Association, Carl Eller, President. http://www.NFLRetiredPlayersAssociation.org/

Pro Football Hall of Fame Enshrinees Assistance Foundation.

Library of Congress Control Number: 2014943025

Set in Lyon Text by Renni Johnson.

*When you leave, you got your friends and your memories.*
*That's it. Hopefully, you cultivated both of them.*

WALT GARRISON, Dallas Cowboys

# CONTENTS

# ILLUSTRATIONS

Before free agency, professional football was generally an unstable, unpredictable job, paying roughly a middle-class wage. It was seasonal work providing minimal retirement benefits and guaranteed to be temporary.

The game also offered an excitement and competitive challenge few occupations could match, not to mention hordes of cheering spectators, television coverage, and the accompanying notoriety. On the other hand, a career could end at any moment, outside of one's control.

Football first topped Gallup's poll as America's favorite sport in 1972, but baseball has long held the market on nostalgia. A delight in the personalities that played the grand old game—from Stan Musial's charm to Ty Cobb's sourness—cultivates baseball's endearing timelessness.

Football history, however, is rarely presented in such fashion. Many writers simply depict football players in gladiator-like stereotypes that are frequently inaccurate. Often the athletes' off-field demeanor stands in contrast to the gridiron's stoic image.

*The Game before the Money* is simply a book by a fan who dreamed of having a book like this upon his own bookshelf. I was frustrated by the dearth of pro football history presented in an authentic, genuine fashion, beyond the typical sportswriter angles of iron, blood, and guts. I wished to know these men beyond stereotypes, learn about their lives, and celebrate their contributions to both the game and our country's culture.

When sports artist Robert Hurst heard my idea to do an oral history of pro football, he invited me to attend Bob Lilly's annual golf tournament at the Texas Sports Hall of Fame. That kick-started the project and led to interviews with Ken Houston, Elvin Bethea, and Walt Garrison.

I put my professional music career on hold and brainstormed a four-page dream list of players I hoped to interview. My good friend Karl Anderson tossed in a few vintage football cards of the players for good luck. Remarkably, I wound up contacting a large percentage of the names on the list. Meanwhile, I started working full time in a mailroom to pay the bills.

Assembling this book was a tremendous privilege. My objective was to document both football history and the individuals who played the game while conveying what it's like to be a pro football player. To get a range of perspectives, attempts were made to include stars as well as journeymen and players who only played a few seasons.

These pages contain the life stories of NFL legends, a history of football from their perspective, backstories to classic game moments, and glimpses into NFL life by those most capable of offering them–the men who created that history, lived those backstories, and experienced the NFL firsthand.

These men have won the Super Bowl and the Heisman Trophy. They've collected All-Pro and All-American honors and had their numbers retired by major universities and pro football teams. Several have earned spots in the Pro Football Hall of Fame; the majority are in the College Football Hall of Fame. Many have been featured on the covers of *Time* and *Sports Illustrated*. All have tremendous stories to tell.

I expected to learn a lot about football while compiling this anthology. I also unexpectedly learned a great deal about life.

Virtually every one of the players discussed here tied some sort of valuable life lesson to his story, either in a purposeful or an indirect way.

A grand set of elders spinning yarns speckled with wisdom is a wonderful gift. As you prepare to enter the locker rooms of Vince Lombardi and Tom Landry and step onto the field with Bronko Nagurski, Walter Payton, and Terry Bradshaw, know that in the hearts and minds of many of these men, success in football, business, and life are all connected.

# The Game before the Money

# FIRST QUARTER

*Players Whose Careers Began before 1950*

Before the 1950s, the single-wing formation dominated football, pro players were usually paid per game rather than annual salary, and All-Americans like Al Wistert worked their way through college. African Americans were barred from the NFL between 1933 and 1946, an unwritten policy generally attributed to Redskins owner George Preston Marshall, although racial restrictions were standard at every level of competition throughout athletics. Many college stars eschewed pro football. Virtually every pro player worked a job outside of football, a trend that continued into the 1980s. Like starving artists, many risked professional and financial futures to pursue football.

World War II impacted young men's dreams of pro and collegiate careers. Pro players left their NFL coaches for drill sergeants; college athletes enrolled in the armed services rather than spring semester classes. Draft notices trumped scholarship offers in the mailboxes of high school graduates, replacing gridiron action with combat on the battlefields of Europe and the Pacific.

### Pro Football before the 1950s Timeline

1920    American Professional Football Association forms in Canton, Ohio.

1921    Fritz Pollard becomes first African American head coach.

1922 American Professional Football Association changes name to National Football League.

1925 Red Grange signs with the Chicago Bears. Grange receives percentage of gate receipts, later claims having received $50,000 for one game and $35,000 for another.[1]

1933 No African Americans appear on NFL rosters for the first time in league history.

1935 Bidding war pushes Stan Kostka's rookie contract to $5,000—similar to established star Bronko Nagurski's. Philadelphia owner Bert Bell suggests a player draft, limiting players to one pro football employment option.[2]

1936 NFL conducts its first player draft, Jay Berwanger being the top selection. He chooses a higher-paying career in the foam-rubber industry. Second-overall pick Riley Smith signs for $250 per game.[3] Average annual income for Americans working full time: $1,184.[4]

1939 World War II begins; 638 pros end up joining war effort, 21 killed in action. NFL regular season attendance tops 1 million for first time.[5]

1946 Pro football reintegrates with four African American athletes. All-American Football Conference (AAFC) begins play. NFL expands west; Cleveland Rams move to Los Angeles.

1947 Leveraging competition between rival leagues, Charley Trippi negotiates $100,000 four-year contract. Red Grange publicly declares contract as "playing for peanuts."[6] NFL makes first-overall draft pick the "Bonus Pick," and team selecting is randomly determined.

1949 The NFL drafts African American athletes for the first time.

# Notes

1. Charles Chamberlain, "Red Grange Says Trippi, Who Is Scheduled to Sign $100,000 Pact with Cards, 'Playing for Peanuts,'" *Florence Times*, January 18, 1947.

2. David J. Berri and Martin B. Schmitt, *Stumbling on Wins: Two Economists Expose the Pitfalls on the Road to Victory in Professional Sports* (Upper Saddle River NJ: FT Pearson Education, publishing as FT Press Delivers, 2010).

3. William Povletich, *Green Bay Packers: Trials, Triumphs and Tradition* (Madison WI: Wisconsin State Historical Society, 2012), 43.

4. George Thomas Kurain, ed., *Datapedia of the United States: American History in Numbers*, 3rd ed. (Lanham MD: Bernham Press, 2004), 121.

5. NFL Communications Department and Seymour Siwoff, *2012 NFL Record and Fact Book* (New York: Time Inc. Home Entertainment, 2012), 533.

6. Chamberlain, "Red Grange Says."

# 1

## Chuck Cherundolo

Center/Linebacker

Penn State University

Undrafted

Cleveland Rams, 1937–1939

Philadelphia Eagles, 1940

Pittsburgh Steelers, 1941–1942, 1945–1948

3 All-Pro seasons

I went out for the high school team as a freshman and didn't make it. The shock of my next football season was when we pulled up and they said, "You're going to be a center."

No more carrying the ball than the man on the moon. My forte wasn't offense, though. Defense was what I liked, and I could really play it. You got a chance to hit somebody, and they couldn't hit you back. Offense is just the opposite: you hit somebody, and they'd hit you back.

I used to love that defense.

There was a Goody Lawless in Scranton. He came down to see me all the time and encouraged me to attend Penn State.

They didn't have scholarships. School cost about $17 a month. Now you spend that much for breakfast. My dad was a coal miner and paid for it.

We didn't have that good of a team. Our record was lucky to break even.

I thought I'd love to play professionally but never realized I'd be in it that long. I started with the Cleveland Rams. One of the coaches was a good friend of mine and talked me into it. At that time my reputation wasn't that good either. [*Laughs.*] He just said, "Why don't you come with me?"

I said, "Heck yeah, I'll go with you."

I was only a kid at the time, about twenty years old. I was just glad to make the team.

I remember my first game. Who was that big back from the Bears? Nagurski. They used to tell me how great he was and all that crap. He came through the line and I tackled him. Boy, did it all come back. I knew what they were talking about. When you hit him, he'd hurt you. It never worked that way, you know? With him it would.

He knocked me around every time I hit him. At that time I only weighed about 185 pounds; he weighed about 220. He was at the end of his career, and I was just beginning mine. He was so great, I'm glad I wasn't around before that. He's the best football player I saw during my career, especially from that position.

When you were hurt, you wouldn't play, but you *had* to be hurt. There were no prima donnas then. They didn't have that many players. I think one year we went through with seventeen players. I played nine games in a row without coming out. I was beat up, stiff. Boy, you'd be stiff, but it was a great life. I wish I had it to live all over again.

I later played with Pittsburgh. I used to make $150 a game. The last couple years I did pretty good. I didn't set the world on fire, but I'd make $12,000–$15,000 a year. I was also a wine salesman and worked on commission for fifteen cents a case.

The Steelers didn't pass much. We never had a great quarterback. Bobby Layne was the first one; that was after my time.

We had good runners. Bill Dudley was one of the best backs I've ever seen. What made him so good was his attitude. If he was hurt, he'd play. He was that type of kid. At that time he was a kid compared to me. He never cursed, never did anything bad. A real religious kid, and everybody respected him. A guy like Bill Dudley, he'd probably make about $500 a game.

When the war came, I enlisted in the navy. There was nothing much you could say, and I just left the Steelers. [Steelers owner] Art Rooney said, "Go ahead."

We had football teams in the service and played other teams in the military camps. Our team had a guy with a great reputation as a football player. He was our quarterback and captain. He played for Duquesne, a college in Pittsburgh. I wish I could remember his name. I used to remember the signals; why can't I remember stuff like that? I was thinking of him the other day.

I was in the service sixteen months: two seasons. I went back to playing center and linebacker with Pittsburgh.

On offense, I'd rather play center than any other position on the line. You start everything and you're right in the center of the action.

They tried to change how I threw the ball back on punts. Once you learn it, you're not going to jag over here or change it, and I had it down pretty good. I can't ever remember making a bad pass on a punt. They said, "We need more speed, more spiral."

I'd laugh because it's not easy. Very few people can do it.

The big thing is, when you grab that ball with your right hand, you got to almost squeeze the ball. That's the one that's controlling it. A lot of times, the left arm's just guiding it. I'm talking about a right-handed thrower, now. If you're left-handed, it's just the opposite.

You got to continuously do it and get the arms in that rhythm of going back, going back, going back. You got to throw it so many times you almost get dizzy, but that's the only way to learn.

Take and stick your fingers the way you hold the ball; everybody holds it different. I squeezed it with my right hand. I'd even do exercises to keep my right hand inspired.

After the snap, the guy is going to work on you, trying to knock you down. Once you learn that, though, you'll get that under control pretty good. You can get it off fast and get ready for him. Throw the ball back, come back on your heels, and you're ready for anything. The big thing is being ready for someone to hit you.

The coaches helped, but it just came natural. You can't teach what I knew from just being coached. They tell you how to do it, but the way you react is something different.

You see a guy in sports that has ability but never shows it. They try to coach him to do this and do that, but he still goes back to the same stuff. That's the difference between the fortunate and the unfortunate. The unfortunate never get it, whereas the lucky guy, you tell him once and he remembers. He reacts to it when it occurs.

Back then, you got to know the sportswriters, and you'd go out drinking with them. There's no better way to get to know a guy than to get drunk with him.

The team used to go down to Duquesne Brewery around the end of the season once a year. We'd get together and we'd have a helluva time. Drinking for free; that's what football's like, brother, to get in free. I'm so glad I lived that life. That was better than being a millionaire.

I went into coaching after playing, mostly with Pittsburgh. Then the Redskins with Bill McPeak, and the Philadelphia Eagles with Nick Skorich. They were good friends of mine. They needed a line coach, and there I was. It's tough on your kids because you're there two years and then you get fired or move on, and they have to leave all their friends behind.

That first year coaching, I thought I knew everything, and I didn't know anything. After two or three years, you learn that stuff. You learn how to use it too. That's the big thing. After five or six years, it was just like going back to school.

If I had the choice to go back to live in Pittsburgh, I'd never go. The weather's terrible there. That's why the people are so great. Boy, they got great people there. Really down to earth. They just keep you going.

The Rooney family was one of the best families I've met, especially the old man. If I needed any money, all I had to do was call them, and they'd send it to me. They treated me like a son. That's why I played so long.

My nose was broken five times. I can reach up and slide it around. It never stopped growing, though. It's so big it's in the way.

The injuries I have now are just the ones I've caused myself. [*Laughs.*] Right now, I'm running around with this aluminum crutch. I got heavy shoes, and the left leg kicked the right ankle and broke the ankle. You get real clumsy when you hit that big 9-0. Never expected to, I'll tell you.

The bad thing about it, I'm losing my memory. I tried to say the Hail Mary the other night, and I forgot it. I didn't forget the whole thing, but I got to the third part, and I couldn't remember it to save my life. I said to myself, "Somebody's mad up there at you, fellow; get going."

You got to take life different than that. You start feeling sorry for yourself, and the first thing you know, you start acting sorry. I figure every time I start feeling like that, I think, "You got this far, you're lucky to be this far, so let it go at that." Nobody pays attention when you're complaining anyway.

Life is great; enjoy it, that's the big thing. Don't let anything get you down. Which is tough to do, but do it. Make up your mind that you're going to do it. I'm not kidding you; you can do it. You probably think you can't, but you can.

Don't let anybody talk you out of it either. If they get you once, they get you twice. If they get you twice, they got you forever. That's why when I say, "No," they finally get to know what I mean by "no." That's what you have to do. Just don't wear heavy shoes and fall down. [*Laughs.*]

I enjoyed it; it was a great life, and I thank the Lord every night that He let me have it. That's why I played so long.

CHUCK CHERUNDOLO

# 2

## Joseph "Buddy" Lex

Tailback

College of William and Mary, 1946–1949

Set NCAA single-season touchdown pass record, 1949

## Clarence "Ace" Parker

Tailback, defensive back, quarterback

Duke University

Drafted, 1937 (2nd round, Brooklyn Dodgers)

Brooklyn Dodgers, 1937–1941

Boston Yanks, 1945

New York Yankees, 1946 (AAFC)

5 All-Pro seasons

NFL Most Valuable Player, 1940

Pro Football Hall of Fame inductee (1972)

[Buddy Lex discusses "Ace" Parker and his own story.]

Ace was all set to go to college at Virginia Tech; VPI we called it back then. A Duke alumnus in Ace's hometown of Portsmouth, Virginia, asked Ace if he would mind going to Durham to talk to Duke's renowned coach, Wallace Wade. Ace got down to Duke University and went into Coach Wade's office.

Coach Wade said, "Clarence, I understand that you're all set to go to VPI."

Ace said, "Yes, sir."

Coach Wade said, "I think you're making a wise decision

because if you came here to Duke, I don't think you could make the ball club."

As soon as Coach Wade said that, Ace made up his mind that he was going to Duke to show Wade he could make that ball club. Coach Wade used a little reverse psychology and it worked.

Ace was a single-wing tailback, just like I was. He was at Duke University from 1933 through 1936 and was an All-American.

The sportswriter for Norfolk's *Virginian-Pilot* wrote an article on one of Duke's football games in the 1930s, back when Duke was big time. In it he said, "If Duke University needed four yards or eight yards or ten yards, they would give it to Clarence Parker. He was like an ace in the hole."

That's how he got the name "Ace," and it sticks with him to this day.

Ace could do anything. He and future Masters Champion Sam Snead were in high school at the same time. They held a longest-drive contest at a golf tournament, and in that contest Ace came in first and Snead came in second.

In track, Ace did the high jump in high school and at Duke.

From Duke he went to the Brooklyn Dodgers, one of only eight NFL teams back then. In 1940, Ace was the Most Valuable Player in the NFL. When he was named that, he said, "If I'd known I was this good, I'd have asked for more money."

Ace also was an outstanding baseball player and wanted to play pro baseball rather than football. He went right from college to the Philadelphia Athletics and hit a home run in his first major league at bat. He played for the Athletics for a few years but broke his ankle sliding into second. He wore a little boot and played football on that cracked bone the year he was MVP.

After his football career, Ace managed the Durham Bulls and the Portsmouth Cubs. Both were in the Piedmont League, a Class B league when the minors were AAA AA, A, and B.

Later he was a backfield coach at Duke University. He then scouted for over twenty years with the San Francisco 49ers and St. Louis Cardinals. He retired in his seventies, well respected.

At ninety-nine, he's the oldest living member of the Pro Football Hall of Fame, but he's slipping. Ten months ago he was still playing nine holes of golf, could have talked to you and answered questions, but now he can't hardly talk. His birthday is May 17, so he's got a few more months to make one hundred. [Ace turned 101 on May 17, 2013, and passed away on November 6, 2013.]

As for me, I was a pretty good athlete. In 1943 I made All-State in basketball and All-Southern in football. I graduated from high school in June of 1944, after I had turned eighteen. World War II was in the midst of everything, and I got drafted in August. I then went to Camp Blanding, Florida, for sixteen weeks of basic training. I was lucky to get Christmas Eve, Christmas Day, and five more days at home right afterward. From home I went to Camp Kilmer, New Jersey, and boarded the *Queen Elizabeth*, one of the fastest ships afloat.

The *Queen Elizabeth* was so fast the German U-boats could not zero in on it, so we didn't need an escort. We crossed the Atlantic in four and a half days. I landed in Glasgow, Scotland, and took a train to Southampton, England. From there they ferried us across the English Channel to Le Havre, France. From Le Havre I rode in a boxcar to a replacement center in Verviers, Belgium. An army truck took us to the front lines, where I was assigned to the Ninety-ninth Infantry Division. This was the Battle of the Bulge, and snow was probably three feet deep in the Ardennes Forest.

We were dropped off around five o'clock at night, and it was just getting dark. One of the boys around my age started crying and wanting his mother. They took him back, and I never saw him again.

We saw three dead German soldiers lying on the ground. This was all weird to me because I'd never seen anything like this. One of the Germans had a gold tooth. Another had a ring on his finger, and the other had two rings, one on each hand. The next morning when we woke up, the gold tooth was gone, and the fingers were cut off. That's what some of our GIs were doing.

On my nineteenth birthday, February 23, we went back to R&R at a convent in Belgium. We had been living in the woods in foxholes to survive. We'd worn the same clothes for weeks, everybody had dysentery, you had crapped in your britches and everything else. I had jock itch down to my knees and ringworm from my elbow almost down to my hip. My hands and my face were black as soot. People don't understand what these frontline soldiers had to go through.

When the war was over, you got points to come home from length of service and battle stars. I didn't have enough points to come home, so I stayed. I got to play some ball over there and traveled all through Germany. I finally got home in June of '46.

I didn't know where I wanted to go to college. I had about twelve or fourteen scholarships before narrowing it down to Norte Dame, William and Mary, and Duke.

I wanted to go to Duke when I was growing up because of Ace Parker and Eric Tipton. Tipton was the tailback in 1941, when Duke played in the Rose Bowl. They moved the Rose Bowl Game for that season to Durham, North Carolina, after the Pearl Harbor attack.

My dad wanted me to stay close to home. I grew up in Newport News, Virginia. William and Mary was only thirty miles away, in Williamsburg. William and Mary had already enrolled my brother—who was not an athlete—and said they'd give him a half-scholarship if I would go there. Wake Forest offered the same thing.

I chose William and Mary, and it was the best thing that

ever happened to me. I thoroughly enjoyed it; I met my wife there, and my brother graduated from there as well. Eric Tipton was my backfield coach, and Marvin Bass was my line coach. Coach Bass later was a head coach at William and Mary and South Carolina, where he was Dan Reeves's college coach.

Nowadays, Lord knows what they're getting under the table, but I got everything paid and $20 a month spending money, and my brother got that half-scholarship. I got two suits of clothes a year and all the meal tickets I needed. When my wife, who was a cheerleader, ran out of meal tickets, I'd go to Coach Rube McCray and tell him I needed another one. I would then give the ticket to her. [*Laughs.*]

We played in the Southern Conference. There wasn't an Atlantic Coast Conference then, and teams like Maryland, Clemson, NC State, Duke, and Wake Forest all played in the Southern Conference. We had about twenty teams.

When I was in high school, everyone ran from a single-wing or what they called a short punt. By the time I came back from the war, I would say 70 percent of the college teams were still running the single-wing. William and Mary and a few others stayed with it, though by my senior year only about 25 percent of college teams were running from the single-wing. All of the pros had gone to the T formation.

In the single-wing the tailback stood about four yards behind the center and would get a direct snap. The fullback was next to him on the right—about three yards back—and would also get a direct snap. A blocking back started about a yard behind the line of scrimmage and never touched the ball. To his right would be the wing back, and the only time he'd touch the ball was on a reverse. Most everything was geared to the right. Very seldom did we run to the left.

The quick kick was really a weapon. We utilized it quite a bit, and I was classified as one of the best quick kickers in the country. You'd line up about four yards behind the center,

14                                                     FIRST QUARTER

and just before the snap you rocked back about a step. You then caught that ball and punted it. The rocker step is the key.

My junior year, North Carolina was ranked second in the nation, and they had All-American tailback "Choo-Choo" Charlie Justice. We went down to Chapel Hill to play them, and I quick kicked twelve times that day. Every time we'd get that ball, whether we were on our 20-, 30-, or 40-yard line, I would quick kick. Even on first or second down. The ball would go over their heads, and it'd roll down to the 5-, 8-, or 15-yard line. Carolina stayed in the hole the whole game, and we ended up tying them, 7-7. Really, they tied us because we scored first. That was the only mar on Carolina's record in 1948.

Carolina went and played Oklahoma in the Sugar Bowl, and we played Oklahoma A&M [now Oklahoma State] in the Delta Bowl. There wasn't but eight bowl games back then: the Sugar, the Cotton, the Orange, and the Rose. You also had the Gator, the Sun, the Dixie, and the Delta. That was it.

My senior year, I led the nation in touchdown passes with 18. Those 18 touchdowns were a national record in 1949. Vito Ragazzo, my favorite target, caught 15 touchdown passes that year, a national record that stood until 1965.

In '49 against Pittsburgh, we got beat 13-7. We got penalized on first down and had second-and-fifteen on our 8-yard line. We decided to quick kick, but the center snapped the ball over my head. I went back, picked it up in the end zone, and got creamed. I was knocked out cold and fumbled. I had a concussion and didn't play anymore that half, but I went back in during the second half and threw a touchdown pass to Ragazzo.

We had won at Houston 14-13 the week before. We were ahead 14-0 before the heat slowed us down.

Heat really slowed us my freshman year against Miami of Florida in the Orange Bowl. We led that game 3-0 at halftime but lost 13-3 because the heat was devastating and wore us down.

They gave us very little water. They'd give us a little bite of orange, maybe half a Coca-Cola, and a salt pill, which was the worst thing in the world.

For a little school, William and Mary had an awful lot of talent. We had a big tackle named Lou Creekmur. Lou was about 235 pounds, agile and fast. Back then if you weighed over 230, you didn't play much because most guys that big were too slow.

In the Delta Bowl, one of our guys, Bull McDowell, hit Oklahoma A&M's quarterback, and the ball popped straight up. Creekmur parted with it on the fly and ran 70 yards for a touchdown.

We also had All-American fullback Jack Cloud, who was in the same graduating class as me. Our sophomore year, he got his knee banged up in the Dixie Bowl and wasn't the same afterward. He didn't play much his junior and senior years. Because of Cloud's injury, we started passing the ball more. That's the reason we led the nation in passing and I threw those 18 touchdown passes.

We were only 6-4 my senior year, so we didn't go to a bowl game like the previous two years. Cloud, Creekmur, George Hughes, and I ended up playing together for Texas coach Blair Cherry in the Blue-Gray Game.

All three of those other boys went on to the pros. Cloud went with Green Bay, but he didn't play a whole lot and ended up coaching the next year. Creekmur went to the Detroit Lions, made All-Pro several years, and was inducted into the Pro Football Hall of Fame. He played on the Lions during the 1950s, when Bobby Layne was their quarterback and either they or the Cleveland Browns won the championship every year for several years. George Hughes was co-captain of the Pittsburgh Steelers as an offensive guard. The problem with the Steelers was they ended up in the cellar every year. He didn't get a whole lot of publicity. The Steelers were the last pro team to run from the single-wing.

I could have signed with the Chicago Bears or the New York Yanks in the All-American Conference. Instead, I took an appointment to the FBI Academy and became an FBI agent. I made more money as an FBI agent than I would have with the Bears.

I don't regret not playing in the pros. I'm beat up enough. I had a knee replacement on the knee I hurt in a game against Boston College. I got knocked out twice, the other time being against North Carolina one year. I had to have my hip replaced five years ago and had my nose broken four times.

I ended up wearing a nose guard [facemask] my senior year because my nose had been broken so damn much. The nose guards we wore weren't like those light plastic straps they have now. Ours were made of hard rubber around chicken wire and heavy as hell. It made your helmet weigh twice as much as a regular helmet.

We still wore leather helmets my freshman year in college. They were made of hard leather on the outside with a lot of cushion on the inside. I think you get just as many concussions now because the plastic helmet is so damn hard. If you hit somebody with a plastic helmet, on the side of the head where you don't have full protection, you're going to end up with a concussion. I think the plastic helmets do more harm than good sometimes.

It's like with Lou Creekmur. In his final years he had dementia. I guarantee you it was from banging heads, from high school to college to eight years in the pros. It's bound to have an effect. [The Boston University School of Medicine posthumously diagnosed Creekmur with chronic traumatic encephalopathy (CTE), a condition induced by repetitive head trauma that deteriorates brain tissue.]

I also played with Knox Ramsey for two years before he went in the pros. His older brother was William and Mary's first All-American, Garrard "Buster" Ramsey. The last ten years of his life, Buster was in a wheelchair, crippled with arthritis from being beat up in football.

I'll be eighty-six in February. I'm still playing tennis every Saturday and Sunday morning, and I play golf about four days a week. I shot a 76 today. I hit the ball pretty good. [*Laughs.*] I also play doubles tennis on soft courts. There are ten of us who rotate, and the nine other guys are all in their fifties or sixties. I'm hanging in there with them pretty good.

I'm lucky I got good genes, but I got a wife that cooks right. I think that's part of it, her taking good care of me. I gotta give her credit.

# 3

## Al "Ox" Wistert

Offensive and defensive tackle, guard

University of Michigan

Drafted, 1943 (Philadelphia Eagles, 5th round)

Philadelphia/Pittsburgh "Steagles," 1943

Philadelphia Eagles, 1944–1951

2-time NFL champion (Philadelphia Eagles, 1948, 1949)

8 All-Pro seasons

1 Pro Bowl

1940s NFL All-Decade Team

We were a very athletic family. My two brothers, three sisters, and I were very interested in sports. I guess that started out with my dad, who was a Chicago policeman. He was shot and killed when I was six years old. That's a tough way to start.

I grew up mainly in Chicago, and then I went off to college at Michigan. I wasn't recruited because I didn't play football in high school. I never played football until I got to the University of Michigan.

One day my freshman year, assistant football coach Wally Weber said, "Wistert, I've been watching you run. You run fast but too long in the same place." [*Laughs.*] It sounds like a ridiculous statement, but he was right. He said, "I'm going to put you with the track coach and have him teach you how to run."

The track coach said I should take larger steps—as large a step as I could—and reach out with my toes as far as I could. Also, I had my arms too close to my body. He taught me I should get those arms swinging out there, pulling me along.

Then lean forward. So take a long stride, use your arms, and lean forward. Those techniques helped me pick up speed and become a very fast runner. Wally Weber was the guy responsible for that.

My time at Michigan was wonderful. It's a great institution. You can't help but do well there because the atmosphere is entirely attuned to being a good student. Academics were very important to me. Academics and athletics were tied right together.

Bob Stenberg, one of my Michigan teammates, gave me the name "Ox." The way I played the game, I guess I impressed him with being as strong as an ox. It stuck, and I've had it ever since. I didn't do a lot of weight lifting; I was just naturally strong.

In 1942 we played Notre Dame and beat them [32-20]. It was a big thrill to play against them, but to go out there and beat them—that was an extra big thrill. The game was at Notre Dame Stadium, which had been built to duplicate our stadium at Michigan.

Francis "Whitey" Wistert was the first of us brothers to play football at Michigan. I was the second, and Alvin was the last one. There are two Als: Alvin and Albert. I'm Albert. We all wore number 11. Three brothers, all at the same university, all at the same position, all wearing the same number—it's the only situation like that in history, anywhere. Our number 11 is one of only five numbers that have been retired for eternity at Michigan. That's as good an honor as you can have.

Because I wasn't on scholarship, I had four or five different jobs that I worked in order to earn my way through school. I did whatever I could to earn the money to pay for college.

Although I graduated during World War II, I was never in the service. I had broken my left wrist, and because of that broken wrist I was rejected from military service. It ended up as a blessing in disguise because it helped me do what I really wanted to do: play pro football.

Harry Thayer, the manager of the Eagles, signed me to play for the Eagles. What he didn't tell me was that the Eagles and Steelers were combined that year. I didn't know anything about that until I got to Philadelphia.

We had an outstanding coach, Earle "Greasy" Neale. He was a fine man, and he and I got along famously. I felt sort of like he was my substitute father because my father was shot and killed. He helped me succeed as a player.

That speed of mine also helped me to become an outstanding player. On kickoffs and punts I was always the first one down there and usually taking the first shot at the guy bringing the ball back. I was first-team All-Pro for several consecutive years, both ways, as an offensive and defensive tackle.

I most always would play the whole game, sixty minutes, and never come off the field. I wanted to play the whole game, and there were no rules that would prevent me from doing that.

We played in the 1947 NFL Championship against the Chicago Cardinals. We lost the game 28-21. I weighed about 215, and the guy that I was playing against probably outweighed me by about fifty pounds. I just belted him as hard as I could. He had a pretty tough afternoon. [*Laughs.*]

We beat the Cardinals in '48 and the Rams in '49 to become world champions two years in a row. Both games were shutouts. To be able to shut those guys out in the championship game was really something, especially two years in a row. We're the only team in history to have back-to-back shutouts in championship games.

Steve Van Buren scored our only touchdown in the 1948 NFL Championship. [The Eagles beat the Cardinals, 7-0.] He scored it over the right tackle spot where I played. I made the block with Frank Kilroy, my teammate all the years that I played.

Our receiver Jack Ferrante scored on a long pass earlier in the game but it was called back because he was offside.

He came running back after the play and yelled, "Who in the hell was offside?"

We said, "You were, Jack." [*Laughs.*]

It was so glaring. The rest of us stayed on the line of scrimmage since Ferrante was the only guy going downfield for the pass. I guess he wanted to get a head start, and he sure got one! [*Laughs.*]

Van Buren was my most famous teammate and probably the greatest running back we ever had. It was a pleasure to block for him. He had great speed and weighed about the same as I did. He and I were born the same day, December 28, 1920. How about that?

We had a receiver by the name of Pete Pihos, and he was a great threat. He was really fast and could outrun the defensive halfbacks [cornerbacks]. We also had a good passer in Tommy Thompson.

Later on we got Chuck Bednarik. He came as a rookie in 1950. He was a young spring chicken to us, and, man, he was good. He was a doggone good blocker, and the two of us could clean things out on our side of the line.

Around that time, they replaced the leather helmets with plastic ones. I didn't like the plastic helmets. When you put them on, you almost took your ears off. It was quite an imposition to put that helmet on every day. I liked the old-fashioned leather helmets better. They were more comfortable.

I left football after the 1951 season, mainly because I got too old. You can only play for so many years.

Because I was an All-Pro and on championship teams, people sometimes ask why I'm not in the Hall of Fame. I'll tell you what the problem is there—I was never in the military. I think that's what kept me out of the Hall of Fame. It wasn't my fault; it was just a set of circumstances that I was faced with. I couldn't serve in the military.

After football, it's been quite normal, quite pleasant. I had my wife for many years; we were married for over sixty years, and that was a wonderful thing because she was a wonderful girl. When she took ill and died, that was a tough thing for me.

I guess you have to have some sadness in your life. You hit bumps in the road as you go. In other words, you have things happen, and some of them are not so good. But you have to overcome those things and go on with your life. I always felt like I was leading a charmed life, and things were happening in such a way that made me feel like I was a lucky guy.

I've always been an optimistic person and consequently always look at the sunny side of life. I feel that everything is going to be just fine, and it usually is. That started when I was a child because my dad was a very positive-thinking kind of a guy. He led the way as far as that was concerned.

I just turned ninety-two. I'm kind of proud of the fact that I'm that advanced in years. Not too many people get to live that long. I never thought about it; it just kind of happened, and here I am. [*Laughs.*]

I still enjoy life tremendously. I love all these ninety-two years I've put in so far, and I expect to be around here for a while. I would get a big kick out of reaching one hundred

# 4

## Nolan Luhn

Wide receiver, defensive tackle

Tulsa University

Drafted, 1945 (Green Bay Packers, 25th round)

Green Bay Packers, 1945–1949

When I was ten or twelve, I played a lot of volleyball. I was taller and faster than most of the kids in my class or above me. A friend of mine told me about football, and that's where it started.

After high school, I went to Kilgore Junior College and played three seasons of football before going to Tulsa University. I chose Tulsa because they offered me room, board, tuition, laundry, books, and an off-season job.

We had a good football team. Most of players were like myself and didn't get to go into the army. I think we had eighteen players that couldn't go in.

I had signed up for the Marines but didn't pass the health examination. I had a hernia, and they turned me down at the Marines station.

When I got to Tulsa in January 1943, I worked for Douglas Aircraft running a turret machine. At Kilgore Junior College, we had a shop where you learned to do those things. I just walked right on the floor and they assigned me to a machine. I helped make parts for b-29 bombers.

We played against Georgia Tech in the Sugar Bowl for the 1943 season. The next year we played them in the Orange Bowl. That Orange Bowl is where I guess I played pretty good football.

A man on the field pulled me by the arm after the Orange Bowl. He said, "I'd like to have a guy that plays pretty good football. I need a right end."

I said, "Who are you?"

He said, "I'm Curly Lambeau of the Green Bay Packers. If you don't sign with any other team, I'll draft you."

He drafted me in the 25th round, and I went to Green Bay in 1945.

I came from Tulsa to Green Bay on a train, and Don Hutson met me at the train station. The first thing he said was, "What's your nickname?"

I said, "I really don't want to tell you my nickname."

He said, "Oh, come on."

I told him that in college they called me "Nylon." During the war you couldn't buy nylon because they made parachutes out of it. The girls in Tulsa nicknamed me Nylon because I was so hard to get.

Don was our coach and player the whole time I was there. I credit a lot of my success at Green Bay to Don Hutson. He would make me stay after practice, and we'd run from goalpost to goalpost. I thought I was pretty fast, but he would outrun me by a yard and a half every time.

He taught me about getting past the linebacker and getting a good fake to get open. Also if the quarterback's in trouble, run to an opening so the quarterback can throw you the ball. We worked on things like that after practice. Lambeau would come back out and say, "Nolan, you've run enough today. Get in the shower." [Laughs.]

Clyde Goodnight had also played end at Tulsa, and we both were drafted by Green Bay in 1945. Goodnight was supposed to take Don Hutson's place. My first year, Hutson played left end and I played right end. The next year, Hutson retired and stayed on as a coach. Goodnight then played left end.

My first three years, I also played down end on defense, just like a tackle really. I weighed about 200, 205 pounds, and the people that blocked me weighed about 230, 240. You always had a guard pull out and block on pass defense, and that was a pretty good chore.

I also ran down punts and kickoffs. Some games I played sixty minutes, depending on whether we first kicked off or received. If we received, I started. If we kicked off, I didn't start but got in once we got to run down a punt or a kickoff.

Substitutions were limited my first year to one player. My second year, 1946, we were limited to three players at a time. I think around '47 they passed a rule that you could put a whole team in the field. Then you could switch offense and defense.

In 1947 we had a decent year. We changed quarterbacks somewhere in that season, and I led the Packers in receiving.

Before one game Lambeau said in the locker room that we were going to run a play called 1-19. That was to me for in-and-out and down the sideline. I beat Sammy Baugh, caught the ball, and went for about 60 yards. After that I caught a bunch of short ones. [Nolan had 140 receiving yards that day.]

Baugh also played for sixty minutes. He played quarterback and could punt, pass, and kick. He was a very good all-around football player.

I played with some injuries. I got hit in the chest with an elbow, and it cracked three ribs. I still have a wound on the back of my right leg where they had to sew it up because someone stepped on it and filled my shoe up full of blood. They taped me up and put me back in the ball game.

During another game I got hit in the face, and it broke my nose. They put me on the sideline, laid me on my back, put stents up my nose, and taped my face together. Lambeau stood over me and said, "Are you ready to go again?"

"I guess so."

He said, "Get in there!"

I went back in the game with my nose all plastered up. I didn't miss any games that season due to the wounds on my face, but I bled a lot.

You got hit in the face a lot. I once said to Lambeau, "Coach, I've been hit so many times in the face that I haven't kissed my girlfriend in six games."

You didn't have facemasks back then. I had one put on, and Lambeau kept looking at me as we were walking on the field before a game. He finally came up to me and said, "What have you got on your face?"

I said, "A facemask."

He said, "The league won't allow that."

I had to have it cut off right there; league rules.

Lambeau and I got along pretty good. One incident, I went down and out and down the sideline. The ball went over my head about one inch from my fingers. Lambeau was there saying, "Nolan, we don't drop those kinds of passes in this league."

I went back to the huddle, and the quarterback said, "What did he say?"

I said, "He didn't tell me anything. Let's run that play again."

We ran it again, and I caught the ball in the end zone for a touchdown. Lambeau was standing on the sideline with his hands on his hips, waiting for me to come by. I just stuck that football under his arm. He looked at the football, dropped it on the ground, and kicked it about 15 yards into the stands. Nine or ten thousand people stood and applauded that.

One day he called me into his office. I thought he was going to ship me out. He said, "Nolan, you're playing pretty good football. Here's a check for $1,500. There's a Chevrolet place up there."

He bought me a new 1946 Chevrolet. You couldn't just buy them in those days; you had to be on a list if I remember right.

Lambeau was always pretty good to me. When I'd come off the field, maybe for one play or whatever, he'd always stop me and ask if I was okay. He'd also tell me what he wanted me to do to get prepared. That helped me too. He'd say, "During the game you players all sit on the bench. You don't stand on the sideline. Put a coat on and you sit on the bench."

One year I stayed in Green Bay during the off-season. We had a big snowstorm, and my friend and his wife wanted to take me tobogganing. We went to the top of a hill, and I got in one of those round metal outfits. You hold on, fold your legs underneath you, sit down, and here you go. No brakes.

When I got to the bottom of the hill, there was a Cadillac waiting for me. The glass rolled down and Curly Lambeau said, "You're under contract with the Green Bay Packers. This is the last time I want to see you out here in the ice!"

That was the end of my toboggan riding.

In those days the league, coaches, and owners did not tell anybody what the other person was making. It was almost a secret, and you couldn't support yourself in the off-season on an NFL salary.

My first off-season, I worked at a Tulsa radio station, selling air time for Fred Jones Lincoln-Mercury. Then I decided I ought to stay in shape and worked in the oil field as a roughneck. I did that for the next few years.

I took off from work the first part of June and met about eight other Tulsa alums that played pro ball. We would work out twice a day for about twenty-five days. I would come back to Green Bay in pretty good shape.

We played home games at the high school stadium on the east side of town. They called it City Stadium or East High— for East High School. We worked out in the high school.

In 1945 the stadium held only about twenty thousand people. We could have had a crowd of probably fifty thousand when we played the Chicago Bears, but they didn't have that many seats.

George Halas would walk around the stadium when we were warming up before the game started. He always came to me, shook my hand, and said, "Have a nice day."

I thought that was very nice of the coach and owner of

the Chicago Bears. In fact this kid from Kenney, Texas, was real thrilled to shake a man's hand like that. George Halas was a good friend of Curly's, but when game time come, he was after you.

The Bears were our No. 1 rival even then. One time, I was walking across the street with about five other players. This car let out its grip and bumped my knee. Curly taped it up for the game, but it hurt for two weeks. The driver was from Chicago, and the FBI questioned the man who hit me to see if he'd done it on purpose. It really was an accident.

We dealt with the weather. We played one game in a blinding snowstorm that stopped by the middle of the game. We had about four inches of snow on the field; they pushed it to the side with a road grader, and we still played. The field was covered with frozen ice.

It's pretty hard to run on a frozen field. You could change cleats, short or long, so I put on real short cleats. You wore high-top shoes in those days because they supported the ankles a little more.

Speaking of shoes, we went up to Minnesota and played up there—an exhibition game against the 49ers, I believe. Curly had told me to buy a pair of new shoes that day. I bought the shoes, left them on the counter, and then got on the train. I told Lambeau about it and he said, "Well, you can't play; you don't have any shoes." One of the players had brought along two pairs of shoes, so I wore his shoes for the game. They were a little large for me, but I made it all right. [*Laughs.*]

By the end of the 1949 season jobs were beginning to get a little tough to find. A lot of soldiers were coming home from the war, and jobs were being taken up. I was afraid I couldn't get a job when I quit playing football if I played another year or two or three. On top of that I wanted a three-year contract, and Lambeau said, "I can't do that. I'm going to sell the Packers to the city next Monday," which was the second day of January 1950.

I said, "Well, I think I'll just retire."

He said, "Oh, you can't do that."

I said, "Yeah, I will."

Lambeau went to the Chicago Cardinals as the head coach. I didn't want to change coaches, and I had a job promised to me. We moved to Coffeyville, Kansas. Seven of us on the starting team of the Packers retired at the same time.

I worked for North American Car. We were rebuilding chatter cars, ice cars that hauled from Minnesota down to Kentucky. I come up as a troubleshooter and had to go and decide whether we were going to repair a boxcar or not. It was a pretty good job.

They later shut that plant, moved me to Chicago, and gave me a similar job in the Chicago office. We had twelve thousand cars on the railroad. Then North American sold, and I could see a lot of us were going to be out of a job. I moved back to Coffeyville and worked at Coop Refinery. I retired in 1983 as a supervisor.

I coached receivers and tight ends as a volunteer at Coffeyville Community College almost every year from 1978 to about 2002. Ron Springs, Mike Rozier, Mel Gray, and Brandon Jacobs were some of our players.

One day I was running practice plays with the offense, and Rozier asked me, "Coach, do you think I'll be as good as Ron Springs?"

I said, "You will if you run through the line of scrimmage and run ten yards. That's what Ron Springs did." He always ran ten yards on every practice play we ran. That helped make him a good football player.

My second-to-last trip to Green Bay, we former players lined up to be introduced one at a time. They applauded the first two or three people, and then the announcer said, "Hold your applause until the last person." I was the oldest person, so I was last. I got a kick out of going last because when I got on the field, everybody stood and applauded, and the band played real loud.

After the game, the players elected me chairman of the board to count the players on the bus. I teased the guys who made All-Pro and the Hall of Fame: "Hey, I got the applause; you didn't."

All those thrills went along with the game. I thoroughly enjoyed playing with the Packers while playing in the National Football League. Even though I got bruised around a little bit, I still liked it.

# 5

## Charley Trippi

Halfback, quarterback, defensive back, punter, returner

University of Georgia

Maxwell Award Winner (1945)

Drafted, 1945 (Chicago Cardinals, first-overall pick)

Chicago Cardinals, 1947–1955

3 All-Pro seasons

2 Pro Bowls

NFL champion (Chicago Cardinals, 1947)

1940s NFL All-Decade Team

Pro Football Hall of Fame inductee (1968)

I only weighed 165 pounds out of high school. Georgia was the only school that offered me a scholarship.

I then went to a prep school in Long Island, New York—LaSalle Military Academy. After gaining ten pounds, I made the All-Metropolitan team in New York. With that exposure Notre Dame wanted me, but I promised Georgia I would go to Georgia.

Back then it was common for players to play offense and defense. We trained on both sides of the ball. Georgia head coach Wally Butts used to say, "If you can't play defense, then you can't play offense."

We won our first eight games in 1942 and then got upset by Auburn. The tenth game was between Georgia and Georgia Tech. The Rose Bowl said the winner of that game would go to the Rose Bowl.

After that loss to Auburn we were a mad team. There's a saying in football: "Don't ever play a good football team that got upset the week before because they're mad and they'll beat you."

We beat Georgia Tech 34-0.

My teammate Frank Sinkwich won the Heisman Trophy that year. We had a scrimmage before the Rose Bowl, and Frank hurt his leg. He couldn't walk hardly. He sat on the bench during the game until we worked the ball down to the 1-yard line. We called time out, wanting Sinkwich to score the touchdown. He hobbled in from the 1 and scored. It was a tribute to Frank for the years he played at Georgia.

I played fifty-nine minutes of the Rose Bowl and was named Most Valuable Player. I gained 130 yards on the ground and did a pretty good job on defense too. [Georgia beat UCLA 9-0 in the 1943 Rose Bowl.]

After the Rose Bowl, I went into the military. We all signed up, knowing we were all going to end up in the service. I never held a rifle, never did anything but entertain the troops playing football and baseball.

I saved my military furlough to play in the College All-Star Game in Chicago. I participated five different years in the College All-Star Game. I played in four during my career as an amateur, and as a pro I played once. We beat the pros two out of the four years I played as an amateur.

I came back to Georgia after two and a half years in the service. After the '45 season I played in the Oil Bowl in Houston, and we beat Tulsa. Next year, we played against North Carolina in the Sugar Bowl. We won that game too.

I played pro baseball for the Atlanta Crackers in 1947 and hit .343. They wanted to sell me to a Major League team, but I wanted to pursue my football career.

The Chicago Cardinals had already picked me as the number one choice in the 1945 draft. I was honored. Of course, when you're the number one choice you've got good negotiating power. I signed a four-year contract, and my salary over four years was $100,000. It was a lot for back then, but I would like to be negotiating today. Boy, they make big money now.

The first thing you got to do when you're a rookie is prove yourself. I worked hard trying to convince them that I belonged there.

The biggest change is that they're all good football players you're playing against. It's not like in high school or college where some of the ballplayers are subpar. When you get to a professional climate, you're competing against the best that's available.

It's not a question of playing any harder. You try to eliminate your mistakes. See, football is a game of mistakes. If you make a lot of mistakes, you're going to lose the football game.

In the 1947 NFL Championship we beat the Eagles on a frozen field. You play in Chicago around December, and you don't know what kind of weather you're going to come across. The wind chill factor was 20 below zero. We couldn't play with cleats; we played with tennis shoes. It's the only time I've ever scored a touchdown with tennis shoes.

I scored two touchdowns in that game. One was a 50-yard run from the line of scrimmage. I also ran a punt back 63 yards for a score. The traction we got with our tennis shoes was amazing. It was a well-played game, and we beat the Eagles 28-21.

When you're playing, you don't worry about how cold it is. Your concentration is on playing football. Of course when you come off the field, you put a good hood on you, and they had heaters on the sidelines.

We played the Eagles again in the '48 championship, only this time it was in Philadelphia. The night before the game they had a snowstorm. We [the players] spent most of the time cleaning the football stadium up so we could play. As we cleaned the field, snow kept coming down. They had a tarpaulin on the field, and we all got together and pushed it off the field.

When the game started, you couldn't see the lines. The officials improvised the game; we just had to accept whatever they thought was the right thing regarding whether you got a first down. It really wasn't a home advantage because both teams struggled.

It's not a good deal playing in heavy snow because you don't get good traction with your cleats. It's more of a pushing game than a tackling game. We lost that game, 7-0.

I think the fans got cheated. They came to see a championship game. What they really should have done is postpone the game for a week, but Commissioner Bert Bell said, "Play ball!"

Jimmy Conzelman was our coach in those championship games. He decided after the '48 season to retire. Before my career was over, I played for several other coaches. Joe Stydahar was one; Buddy Parker, who ended up winning championships with Detroit, and Cecil Isbell were two others. Curly Lambeau coached for two years.

I played five years as a running back, two as a quarterback, and two as a defensive back. The other positions were natural, but quarterback had a lot of different things to adjust to. I made the adjustment, and we won several games.

The big game of the season was when we played the Bears. When you got two teams in the same city, you're fighting for the publicity. The way you get top publicity is by winning. Winning that game was a big moment.

I first had a leather helmet. Then we went to a plastic helmet, which was terrible. Ball players were getting concussions, and they had to make improvements in the original plastic helmets. They came out with a real good helmet toward the last five years I played, padded real tight on your head. You need a tight helmet when you play football.

I ended up playing with a facemask. I had a single bar because when I kicked, the double bar would split my vision. The latter part of my career, a guy got a forearm in between the single bar and my nose, busting my nose. I had to have plastic surgery to correct the damage. The double bar would have prevented that.

When you play nine years in professional football, I think you're lucky to get out sound and lucky to accomplish what you achieved. You got to get out and give somebody else a chance.

After playing those nine years with the Cardinals, I coached five years with them. I spent fourteen total years with the Cardinals. I went back to Athens and coached five years with Coach Butts on the Georgia staff.

I also got involved in real estate. I have commercial properties in Athens. I invested in real estate with monies I made playing football, and it turned out extremely well for me.

Sometimes you get lucky.

# 6

## Johnny Lujack

Quarterback, defensive back

University of Notre Dame

Heisman Trophy Winner (1947)

Drafted, 1946 (Chicago Bears, 1st round)

Chicago Bears, 1948–1951

NFL interceptions leader (1948: 8 interceptions)

NFL passing yardage leader (1949: 2,658 yards)

NFL touchdown pass leader (1949: 23 TDs)

NFL rushing touchdown leader (1950: 11 rushing TDs)

2 All-Pro seasons

2 Pro Bowls

I always wanted to go to Notre Dame. I never thought I was good enough, but I had a tryout, and they offered me a scholarship. I was a little surprised but really happy.

The first day of practice at Notre Dame, the freshman coach said, "Linemen over here and backs over here."

I wanted to be damn sure I didn't get mixed up. I was in the front row of the backs when Coach Frank Leahy turned to us and said, "You, you, you, and you."

I was one of the "*Yous*" and played safety.

Leahy stopped practice three times and said, "Who made that tackle?"

They had to ask me my name the first time.

The next day, they said, "Lujack, where are you?" I raised my hand, and they said, "Down there." That's how I started playing defense at Notre Dame.

The previous year Notre Dame had a single-wing team

and was undefeated. My freshman year, 1942, was the first T formation offense Notre Dame ever had.

Whenever the varsity was playing a single-wing team the following Saturday, I would be the single-wing tailback on offense, scrimmaging against them. If we were playing a T formation team, I was the T formation quarterback. I had never played T formation quarterback before. Our high school team was Jock Sutherland's kind of Pittsburgh team, single-wing.

I won four monograms [letters] my sophomore year. I made first team in basketball and baseball. In between innings in baseball, I won the high jump and javelin.

In football I played defense full time and was the second-team quarterback behind Angelo Bertelli. When Bertelli left halfway through the season to go into the service, I took over as the No. 1 quarterback at eighteen years old. I didn't think about my age; I knew I could play and was ready.

We were national champions that year but lost the only game I lost in college. It was the last game of the season, against Great Lakes [a naval training center]. We scored on them to go ahead with about a minute left. They scored on a long pass in the last thirty seconds, after we had tackled them in the backfield two or three times.

We thought maybe we could win that one after we went ahead, but Great Lakes had pro players and knew how to score. The second to last game was Iowa Pre-Flight, and some great pro players were on that team too. They were eligible to play college ball because they were in the service.

After the season I volunteered for the navy and was in for two weeks short of three years. Coach Leahy also joined the service and didn't coach. He didn't know where I was, and I didn't know where he was.

It was pretty much assumed that I would remain the No. 1 quarterback when I returned, although we had good players under me. George Ratterman, who went into pro ball, was the second-team quarterback. Frank Tripucka, a darned good player, was the third-team quarterback. I played both offense and defense when I came back.

I was the thirteenth winner of the Heisman Trophy in 1947. Jay Berwanger, a great player out of the University of Chicago, won the first one in 1935.

Winning the Heisman was kind of a surprise. We were playing the last game in California against Southern Cal. After the ball game was over, they said, "You won the Heisman Trophy, and you have to go to New York."

I said, "How do you get to New York?"

"You got to fly."

I never flew before in my life.

When I ended up in New York, they had my oldest brother and my dad there as guests of the Heisman people, as a surprise. That was terrific.

In those days you could be drafted on what the normal four years would have been. I entered Notre Dame in '42, so my graduation year would have been in '46. The Chicago Bears drafted me in the first round of the 1946 NFL draft, following my junior year, but I didn't even think about for going my senior year at Notre Dame.

There wasn't much negotiating with Bears owner George Halas. In those days if you didn't sign up, you couldn't go with any other team. He pretty much said, "You better sign a contract or you don't play."

I signed a four-year contract for $17,000, $18,500, $20,000, and $20,000. That was supposed to have been a high deal. Looking back on it, I still think it was cheap. [Laughs.] It seemed to me like the stands were always filled up.

George was not very close to the players. A lot of times we didn't like him because we didn't think we were paid enough. We'd have meetings all day long and even at night. We had quarterback meetings on our only days off. But I'm not too sure that all of the coaches weren't as demanding, and keep in mind that he was an owner.

The first pro game that I played was against Green Bay. I was playing defense, and the guy I had to guard came down and broke out to the side. The pass didn't go to him. Going back to the huddle, he said, "You All-American son-of-a-bitch, you're going to have a long day guarding me!" I never had anybody talk to me like that on a football field before.

He didn't catch any passes that day, and I intercepted three. The interceptions tied a Bears record, and I wound up with eight through the twelve-game schedule, to lead the league. I made first-team All-Pro as a defensive back.

That first year up, Bobby Layne was the quarterback, I was the quarterback, and Sid Luckman was the quarterback. They got rid of Layne, thinking I was going to take over, which I did. George Blanda was drafted my second year.

Bobby and I were great pals when we were on the team together. We'd always stay after practice and throw passes to each other. He was a good friend, and I was really sorry to see him go. After he performed so well in the pro leagues, I was glad he did leave.

My third year, I made All-Pro on offense as a quarterback.

I still hold the Bears record of 468 yards passing in one game. I threw for 6 touchdowns in that game, and we beat the Cardinals 52-21, despite being the underdogs.

I was surprised my yardage total was that high. You don't keep track of stats in your head; you just want to win. It was a league record at the time [1949], but it only held for one year and one game, when Norm Van Brocklin beat it [554 yards in 1951, still a record].

The Cardinals had a great team. They had Paul Christman at quarterback, Pat Harder at fullback, and Elmer Angsman and Charley Trippi at halfback.

We had a strong rivalry against the Cardinals. When I say rivalry, I don't mean against individuals but teams against teams because they were both Chicago teams. Off the field we were friends. Christman and I lived in Park Ridge, Illinois, and played together on a drugstore baseball and soft-ball team.

If we averaged 15 passes a game, that was throwing it a lot. Now they average 30. Plus they've got great receivers now, developing in high school and college, coming into the pros ready to play. Back in our days offensive ends had to also be good blockers because we ran the ball more. When you only throw 15 passes a game, you better have decent blockers.

In 1950 I set a record by scoring 11 rushing touchdowns in a twelve-game season. I think my average per gain was around 7 yards. When you fade back and throw and the receivers don't find an opening, you better run with it because somebody's gonna kill you. You take off, see an opening, and go. Sometimes they knock you flat on your you-know-what.

We played all our home games at Wrigley Field. The end zone was really close to the brick wall. A lot of times our guys ran into the wall. You knew it was there, but you still tried to make the catch and banged into the wall.

When it was cold, it was *cold*. It would be zero degrees. It was so cold one time that we had our cleats sharpened to make them pointed. You weren't supposed to do that because that could hurt other people's faces. That didn't help, so I think we only did it that one game.

They used to give you shots where it deadens the pain. Heck, we took shots for everything. You'd get shots before the game because you knew you were going to need them. I had shoulder separations, and I took shots for that. Both shoulders are still separated from football. They're not dropped down a foot, just maybe a half inch, but you can feel it.

My four-year contract was up after the 1951 season. I had the chance to become the quarterback coach at Notre Dame under Leahy's last two years, 1952 and 1953. I felt that was a good way to repay Notre Dame and Leahy for giving me a scholarship. Plus, when you have knee and shoulder problems, you give retirement some thought. I felt that was enough after 1951 and retired.

I became an automobile dealer in 1954, and I was in that for about twenty-five or thirty years. I retired from that about twenty years ago.

A week from tomorrow my wife and I will have been married for sixty-five years. I play golf about five days a week. I stay in reasonably good shape. I have no ailments that I know about, other than that this tightens up and that tightens up. I don't have any of what you'd call sicknesses; I've been very lucky about that.

I loved going to Notre Dame and seeing games now. I enjoyed the game of football as much as I've enjoyed anything that I've ever been in.

# 7

## George Taliaferro

Running back, wide receiver, quarterback, defensive back,
  punter, returner
Indiana University
Drafted, 1949 (Chicago Bears, 13th round)
Los Angeles Dons (AAFC), 1949
New York Yanks, 1950–51
Dallas Texans, 1952
Baltimore Colts, 1953–54
Philadelphia Eagles, 1955
3 Pro Bowls
1949 AAFC Rookie of the Year
First African American drafted by an NFL team

[The Yanks/Texans/Colts were one franchise.]

I was born in 1927. I had three brothers and a sister; I was second in the group. My dad wasn't able to find work during the Great Depression before getting involved in the steel mills in Gary, Indiana. I was a pretty good athlete and wanted to be a boxer. When my mother said I couldn't box, the only other avenue was to play football. My dad made a plea for me. He said, "If you're not going to let him box, let him play that game called football"—about which my mother and father knew absolutely nothing.

When I was twelve years of age, my dad asked me—he didn't tell me—to dig up a little plot of land so that he could have a garden next to our home. He said, "I'd like it if you could do it tomorrow and have it done by the time I return home from work."

I said, "I'll do it."

No more than ten minutes after I got out of bed at eight o'clock in the morning, with the intent of digging that lot up, six guys in the neighborhood coerced me into going to the swimming pool at the local park, promising to help dig the plot of land.

I got into the water, and it was cold as ice. It was a 90-degree day and I just enjoyed myself until I found myself asleep on the warm concrete. I awakened and asked the lifeguard what the time was. It was 4:10, and my dad would be home at about 4:15.

When my dad walked in the house, I walked in right behind him. He walked through the house to look at the area I was to have shoveled. He used his index finger in his right hand and beckoned me to where he was standing. In the calmest voice he said, "A man is no better, no worse, than his word." My dad never uttered another word about that incident to me, but those were the words by which I ruled my existence.

During the time I grew up, the Indiana High School Athletic Association did not allow the all African American high schools to participate in sports against the other high schools. I didn't play against the white high schools in football, basketball, and track until my senior year in 1944.

I learned everything I possibly could in all three sports. I played my heart out because that's what I wanted to do, but there were no statistics kept about what I was doing.

Fate had it that we played an exhibition game against Roosevelt High School in East Chicago, perennially the high school football champion in the state of Indiana. We had played our last game on November 7, 1944. East Chicago Roosevelt's coach asked my coach if he would reissue our uniforms to play a game on the fourteenth, to help East Chicago Roosevelt stay fit for the championship game on the twenty-first. We played, and my high school, Roosevelt High School in Gary, beat East Chicago Roosevelt.

That's how I got a scholarship to Indiana University.

The University of Chicago had dropped out of the Big 10 Conference after the 1939 season, and the Big 10 had become the Western Conference with nine teams. Michigan State was not a member of the Big 10 Conference until 1949, when it became the Big 10 Conference once again. My freshman year, we won what was the Western Conference.

One of my Indiana teammates, Ted Kluzewski, became an incredible pro baseball player, but he could have played pro football equally as well. In those years we played both offense and defense. Kluzewski was a tight end on offense and a defensive end on defense.

Then there was Pete Pihos. Pete Pihos at the age of eleven or twelve saw his father, a policeman in Chicago, murdered. He left Indiana University in 1948 and went to the Philadelphia Eagles, where he was an All-Pro for the twelve years that he played. When he died in 2011, a sports writer called to inform me and asked me to make some comments about him. I said, "In my opinion Pete Pihos is the best football player to ever play at Indiana University."

My freshman year, I played football from August until November, took my final examinations in December, and was going home for semester break. I was offered a free ride to Gary with a man whose daughter had attended high school with me. As we got ready to pull away from the curb, I looked in the rear view mirror and saw the postman. I asked the man if he didn't mind waiting so that I could see if I had any mail. I was looking forward to getting a letter from the Pepsi Cola Bottling Company to go to the Waldorf-Astoria in New York as one of the top sixty-five football players in college. Instead I got a letter that said, "Greetings: Report to Indianapolis, Fort Benjamin Harrison, at eight o'clock on February 4, 1946."

It was a draft notice.

My parents and I had been told by a member of the draft board in Gary that if I stayed in the state of Indiana for school, the chances of my going into service would be almost nil if I made good grades. I made good grades and played good football, but I played too well against the University of Michigan. Their coach was a very powerful person in the Midwest and had my draft rights transferred to Chicago.

When I got to Camp Lee in Petersburg, Virginia, three Michigan players whom I played against were there. They told me that their coach told them that Taliaferro was going into the service and wouldn't be playing at Indiana in 1946. It came true.

I have a love/hate relationship with Michigan. They thought I was good enough that they didn't want to play against me, and the coach had me drafted. That's the hate part. The love part was that while I was in service, I met the young woman to whom I am married today. We have been married sixty-one years. I couldn't be but so happy that Michigan had pulled off the coup to get me inducted into the service.

I had made second-team All-American my freshman year. I spent 1946 in the service. I returned to Indiana in time to play football in '47 and made third-team All-American. My junior year, 1948, I made first-team All-American.

I was eligible to play professionally and chose not to return my senior year. I am the only player in the history of Indiana University to be a three-time All-American and to make an All-American team each year I played.

In 1949 the National Football League and the All-American Football Conference were into hiding players. I signed a contract with the Los Angeles Dons of the AAFC before the National Football League draft. I then became the first African American to be drafted to play in the National Football League, by the team that I absolutely adored—the Chicago Bears.

From the age of eight, I told everybody that I was going to be a great football player and that I was going to play for the Chicago Bears. There were no African American football players in the National Football League when I was growing up; that was the dream of an eight-year-old kid. I kept that dream alive by being the very best that I could be and dedicating my life to playing football at the highest level possible.

When the Bears drafted me, I thought it was the most incredible thing that could happen, but I never talked to the Chicago Bears about playing for them. I never told anybody I would do something that I didn't do after the garden plot incident at age twelve.

I had given my word to the Los Angeles Dons.

I was the Rookie of the Year for the All-American Football Conference in 1949. We played very good football, much better than the sportswriters wanted to believe. The Cleveland Browns, the New York Yankees, the Chicago Hornets, the San Francisco 49ers, and the Baltimore Colts were all in the All-American Football Conference. The Browns won the championship of the All-American Football Conference the four consecutive years that it played football: 1946, '47, '48, and '49.

The conference folded at the end of 1949. Four teams from that conference were given the opportunity to participate in the National Football League: the Colts, Yanks, Browns, and 49ers.

The Cleveland Browns then won the NFL Championship in 1950 for their fifth consecutive professional football championship. That's how good we played football in the AAFC.

The players from AAFC teams not invited by the National Football League were put in a player pool and drafted the same way the college kids are drafted today. I was the second person picked in that draft.

I played for the New York Yanks in 1950 and 1951. In 1951 I made the Pro Bowl for the first time. The Pro Bowls were always held in Los Angeles and were much, much different than they are today. We actually played the game of football at the highest level.

Playing for the Dallas Texans in 1952 was horrendous because of the discrimination. My wife and the wife of Buddy Young, the only other African American on the team, could only sit in the end zone at the Cotton Bowl to watch us play. They could not sit on the 50-yard line, where the other wives sat. Buddy and I complained to management, and then my wife and Mrs. Young said, "We're African Americans, and we will sit where all African Americans sit."

Let me make discrimination more graphic for you: I stood in the end zone at the stadium in Norfolk, Virginia, in 1953, when I was a member of the Baltimore Colts. George Preston Marshall, the owner of the Washington Redskins, was standing maybe ten feet behind me. I was the last Colt to be introduced on the offense. George Preston Marshall shouted, "N——s should never be allowed to do anything but push wheelbarrows!"

I scored multiple touchdowns that game. My performance on the field was my salvation. That was the thing that absolutely helped to motivate me to be the very best athlete that I could be—and the best human being.

Marshall was the last NFL owner to integrate his team. In 1961 Secretary of the Interior Stewart Udall chaired the committee over land use in the United States. He refused to allow the Washington Redskins to use the new stadium that had been built in Washington DC using public funds unless there wasn't to be any discrimination. George Preston Marshall felt that he could override Udall, and it's my understanding that President Kennedy was the person who made Udall's decision official.

The Redskins fielded their first African American players in 1962.

Professional football integrated in 1946, the year before Jackie Robinson played major league baseball. Marion Motley and Bill Willis integrated the Cleveland Browns of the All-American Football Conference. Kenny Washington and

Woody Strode integrated the National Football League that same year with the Los Angeles Rams.

My getting into pro football was not a tenth as difficult or traumatic as Jackie Robinson [getting into baseball] because Jackie was alone. There were no other African Americans playing baseball—Jackie was by himself.

I had a very close relationship with Jackie Robinson. What the average person does not know is that Jackie had a temper quicker than a rattlesnake. He didn't mind, and he could fight.

Marion Motley and Bill Willis told me about one of the greatest compliments I've ever been paid. I was playing with the New York Yanks, and the Browns came to play us in New York. Marion and Bill told me, "You really must be some kind of a football player because you are the one player that Paul Brown gives special emphasis to and puts up special defenses to stop."

There was no way we were going to beat the Browns. Paul Brown brought guys into a system that was second to none. He was that good and that far ahead at that time.

I met Paul Brown at the Superdome in New Orleans in the mid-'80s. I recognized him, walked right up to him, and said, "Coach Brown, my name is George Taliaferro. I wanted to make your acquaintance."

He said, "The guy from Indiana."

That told me that Marion and Bill were not just pulling my leg. He knew what I could do.

I was the only player in the history of the National Football League to play seven positions: punter, passer, running back, defensive cornerback, wide receiver, punt returner, and kickoff returner, and I did it both ways. I promised my mother and father that I would be the best conditioned athlete to play in football as long as I played, and I lived up to it.

I retired at the age of twenty-eight, used up from taking so many hits. I was physically and mentally prepared to take it, but over the seven-year period that I played, it took its toll.

I always said that if I were ever traded, I would not play the next year. I was traded to the Philadelphia Eagles in 1955. I played the '55 season and kept my word.

George Halas, the Bears owner, contacted me after I retired. He said, "Son, I'd still like to have you play for me."

I said, "Mr. Halas, I am nowhere near the football player that I used to be, and I'm not going to play anymore. But I thank you, thank you, thank you. I'm going on with the rest of my life."

Today I am the chairman emeritus of the board of directors of COTA—Children's Organ Transplant Association. I have raised over $66 million in twenty-three years for any child who needs a transplanted organ, bone marrow, or tissue to receive a second chance at life. I know of 1,800 children we've helped. One was a little twin girl in Indianapolis. We have replaced every organ in her body over a four-year period. She's now five years of age and the most incredible little girl you've seen in your life.

You know how they say, "That's just one story in New York?" Well, that's just one story in my life. Here's another: Don Shula was a teammate of mine on the Colts. He was as knowledgeable as anybody about the game of football and the people who play it. All of us—Gino Marchetti, Art Donovan, Buddy Young—we all said, "He may not be able to play the game, but given an opportunity, he's going to be a great coach."

When he became the head coach at Miami, I was living in Baltimore and a member of the NFL Alumni Association. We had a meeting in Baltimore the night before the Dolphins played the Colts, and I asked Shula what he thought his greatest asset was. That was the question—no more, no less. He went on to expound eloquently about understanding the game of football and the people who play it.

I looked him dead in the eye and said, "Don, the greatest asset you have is that you're white because if you were African American, you would never have the opportunity to do what you're doing."

After Shula had been with the Dolphins for several years, I was assistant to the president at Indiana University. Shula called me to ask if we had any defensive backs that I would recommend. My youngest daughter was dating a young man who was a defensive back, and I said, "Don, the only problem is you will have to teach him how to locate the football."

Don drafted him in the tenth round. They found out during his physical examination that he had arthritis in his left knee. Don called me and said, "I'm going to keep him on our practice squad and have our trainers work with him." He only had 80 percent use of his knee, and they couldn't alter that condition. After a year they let him go. Unfortunately he never had an opportunity to play pro football.

You've just got to be in the right place at the right time and have someone with some influence make a recommendation. They will give you an opportunity where other players don't have that inroad. You have to be skilled, but you also have to be extremely lucky. I was both. My time had arrived when I played football against East Chicago Roosevelt in high school and was recommended by one of the best high school coaches in the state. That's all it was because none of the statistics that I'd achieved ever appeared in print.

None of this would have been worth a nickel had I not overcome all of the barriers—every single one—that were put in my path to deter me from succeeding. That was my motivation. I said, "I'm going to prove that I'm as good, if not better, than anybody who plays the game of football."

# SECOND QUARTER

*Players Whose Careers Began in the 1950s*

The 1950s proved rocky for the NFL's legal team. In 1953 in *United States v. National Football League*, federal judge Allan Grim ruled NFL bylaws prohibiting teams from licensing individual broadcasting rights violated the Sherman Antitrust Act. The case related only to television rights and stopped short of questioning whether the league itself constituted a trust.[1] The decision would, however, force the NFL to return to Judge Grim's courtroom in 1961 to validate a contract with CBS.[2]

In 1957 Bill Radovich, a former All-Pro, claimed he'd been blacklisted after signing an AAFC contract. He sued the NFL for damages and argued the league had violated antitrust laws. The Supreme Court surprised the NFL, concluding that the two rulings exempting Major League Baseball from the Sherman and Clayton Acts (*Federal Baseball Club v. National League* [1922] and *Toolson v. New York Yankees* [1951]) didn't cover pro football. The majority opinion rendered by Justice Tom C. Clark noted that Congress had introduced four pieces of legislation in 1951 to extend baseball's exemption to other sports, but none were passed. Furthermore, he referenced two 1955 Supreme Court rulings that refused to include professional boxing and theatrical attractions under *Federal*'s and *Toolson*'s protective umbrellas. Justice Clark went so far as to opine that *Federal*'s ruling held "dubious validity" in the first place.[3]

Congress raised an eyebrow, and Tennessee senator Estes Kefauver suggested a study of the antitrust status of professional sports by his anti-monopoly subcommittee.[4] NFL commissioner Bert Bell made several trips to Washington, defending the league's practices before Congress. Bell gained sympathy with many Congressional members but met ferocious disapproval from New York representative Emmanuel Celler.[5] Representative Celler, the House Antitrust Committee chair, saw no difference between pro sports leagues and other businesses subject to antitrust laws.

In June 1958 the House passed legislation to grant full antitrust immunity to pro sports leagues. Representative Celler (who had authored a restrictive amendment to the Clayton Antitrust Act with Senator Kefauver in 1950) convinced Senator Kefauver's subcommittee that adopting the legislation without limitations would bear horrendous consequences for both professional athletes and the general public.[6] Senator Kefauver's subcommittee rejected the bill entirely, terminating the bill before it reached the Senate floor.[7]

Before *Radovich* NFL owners had ignored player proposals for improved benefits and had refused acknowledgment of the NFL Players Association (NFLPA). The decision and resulting Congressional microscope led Bell to recognize the NFLPA at a House subcommittee hearing without consulting other owners.[8] It also fortified the players' bargaining position, allowing them to win a minimum wage and much desired pension fund.

Weaving on-field magic between off-field disputes, the NFL's adolescent years of the 1950s swelled the current that became today's tidal wave. The 1958 NFL Championship Game between the Colts and Giants remains one of the most famous contests in sports history and represents a flashpoint in the league's popularity.

The number of NFL icons who began their careers in the 1950s exceeds the number of superstars from all previous decades combined. Bart Starr, Johnny Unitas, Frank Gifford, Sonny Jurgensen, and Paul Hornung are a sampling of household names that would permanently establish the NFL in America's heart.

## Pro Football in the 1950s Timeline

1950    Korean War begins, sending over two hundred NFL players to war, including fourteen who fought in World War II. Following December 1949 agreement, four AAFC teams begin NFL play: the Cleveland Browns, San Francisco 49ers, Baltimore Colts, and New York Yanks. Colts fold after one season. Yanks eventually move to Dallas before becoming today's Colts franchise.

1951    NFL Championship televised nationally for the first time.

1953    Judge Allan Grim rules NFL bylaws violate portions of the Sherman Antitrust Act.[9]

1956    Former Heisman winner Vic Janowicz suffers partial paralysis in auto accident. Redskins exclude him from payroll, citing a non-football injury.[10] NFLPA is founded with members of all teams except Chicago Bears.

1957    NFL owners vote down measure to recognize NFLPA.[11] Supreme Court rules that Major League Baseball's antitrust exemption doesn't apply to the NFL in *Radovich v. National Football League*.[12] NFL players negotiate a $5,000 minimum salary afterward. Median income for U.S. male professional and technical workers: $5,601.[13]

1958    Millions watch the NFL Championship Game on television, an overtime contest between the Colts and Giants that popularizes pro football like never before. NFL eliminates the draft's "bonus pick" after Congress warns system borders on a lottery.[14] National Hockey League (NHL) players threaten antitrust lawsuit, win $7,000 minimum salary and increased pension benefits as a result.[15] Median income for U.S. males with four years of college: $6,710.[16]

1959  Pension system for NFL players established, though specifics murky. Players claim Bert Bell orally agreed to include players retroactively, including AAFC veterans. Players attempting to collect retroactive benefits in the 1970s are denied, lacking written record of agreement.[17] Packers announce $72,612 profit in 1958, thanks to $75,000 television contract.[18] Vince Lombardi named head coach of the Green Bay Packers.

## Notes

1. United States v. National Football League, 116. F. Supp. 319 (1953), Leagle.

2. National Football League, 196 F. Supp. 445 (1961), Leagle.

3. Radovich v. National Football League, 352 U.S. 445 (1957), Justia. com, U.S. Supreme Court Center.

4. John A. Goldsmith, "Estes Eyes Probe as Court Refuses Pro Grid Immunity," Deseret News and Salt Lake Telegram, February 26, 1957.

5. "NFL Chief in Washington: Bert Bell Pleads Case before Congress Group," St. Petersburg Times, March 21, 1957.

6. "Celler Attacks Lobby, Raps Baseball's Feudal Lords," Lewiston Morning Tribune, July 25, 1958.

7. "New Sports Bill in House," Washington Observer, January 16, 1959.

8. "Bell Endorses Players' Union," Leader-Post, August 2, 1957.

9. National Football League, 116 F. Supp. 319 (1953), Leagle.

10. Gary Gillette, exec. ed., The ESPN Pro Football Encyclopedia, 1st ed. (New York: Sterling Publishing, 2006), 1068.

11. "NFL Rejects 14-Team Loop, Player Association Denied Recognition," Toledo Blade, February 3, 1957.

12. Radovich.

13. Bureau of the Census, Historical Statistics of the United States: Colonial Times to 1970, Bicentennial Edition, part 1 (Washington DC: Bureau of the Census, U. S. Department of Commerce, 1975), G 374.

14. "NFL Eliminates Bonus Pick, Bell's Method Voted Down," Milwaukee Sentinel, January 30, 1958.

15. "NHL Sets Minimum Scale, Ups Playoff $$$," Milwaukee Sentinel, February 6, 1958.

16. Claudia Goldin, contributor, *Historical Statistics of the United States: Earliest Times to the Present*, vol. 2, part B, "Work and Welfare" (New York: Cambridge University Press, 2006).

17. Soar v. National Football League Players' Ass'n, 550 F.2d 1287 (1st Cir. 1977), Casetext.

18. "Packers '58 Profit: $72,612," *Milwaukee Sentinel*, January 20, 1959.

# 8

## Yale Lary

Defensive back, punter, returner

Texas A&M University

Drafted, 1952 (Detroit Lions, 3rd round)

Detroit Lions, 1952, 1953, 1956–1964

3-time NFL champion (Detroit Lions, 1952, 1953, 1957)

NFL punting leader (1959, 1961, 1963)

9 All-Pro seasons

9 Pro Bowls

1950s NFL All-Decade Team

Pro Football Hall of Fame inductee (1979)

I signed a contract for $6,500 my first year. That's what they offered me, and that's what I signed for. A lot of teams were struggling, and maybe they couldn't afford any more. Today they make $6,500 walking out of the dressing room.

I was married, had children, and couldn't live on just an NFL salary, that's for sure. I did what I had to do. I sold shoes for my dad's shoe store. Later in my career I rode a truck for Falstaff beer, called on joints, and took orders for beer. I was always doing something to make money.

We beat Cleveland in the 1952 NFL Championship Game. We didn't get championship rings; we got a letter jacket and $1,200. We beat them again in 1953, 17-16, scoring the winning touchdown in the last two or three minutes.

I went into the service in '54 and '55, missing two years in Detroit. I got my commission from Texas A&M and went into the service as a second lieutenant. I got promoted to first lieutenant and commanded a company during the Korean War. I returned to Detroit in '56.

In 1957 Bobby Layne broke his ankle in the second to last game of the season, and Tobin Rote came in. We played at San Francisco in a playoff game and were in the locker room at halftime, trailing 24-7. It was like a high school locker room, and we could hear the 49ers laughing and joking at halftime. They didn't end up laughing and joking after the game. Tobin Rote had a fabulous day, and so did Tom "The Bomb" Tracy. [The Lions won, 31-27.]

Tobin Rote had the most fabulous day he's ever had in his life in the championship game against the Browns. We won 59-14.

I'll never forget: I was covering Ray Renfro, and we were ahead by a lot. We were real good friends in Fort Worth. Ray came down the field and ran across. I was covering him, and they threw it to somebody else. He said, "You know, Yale, this is the longest f*ing ball game I've ever played in my life." [Laughs.]

And it was for a long time. That's the worst they've ever been beaten, I believe. Win some, lose some, I guess.

It wasn't my primary goal to win the punting championship; my goal was to play defensive back. I started punting in junior high and continued through high school and college. Punting was my extracurricular, and I really loved it. I punted in the cold weather, hot weather, rainy weather, and with the ground frozen with ice. Nowadays maybe one in a hundred might punt in bad weather. I would have loved to have punted in these domes.

I played in nine Pro Bowls. They're different than now, when defensive linemen just stand up and look and watch the ball game. They don't want to get hurt, and I don't blame them, but we weren't like that when I played. I retired after the Pro Bowl in '65 [following the 1964 season].

I had a broken nose five times. I got ruptured vertebras,

and they had to put a brace on my knee for three games. I'm lucky I didn't get hurt permanently. Now I have rheumatoid arthritis, my joints are messed up, and my knees are hurting. I think that's probably due to a lot of hard workouts, hits, and a lot of body contact.

In the early 1950s everybody in the league gave $25 to hire a lawyer to try to find us some kind of retirement plan. George Halas told his players if they gave $25, he was going to cut every one of them. He was the only owner who wouldn't go along with our attempt to formulate a retirement of some sort.

I'm glad for what I'm getting; it's better than nothing. The NFL makes a lot of money, and the head of the players union says they're going to take care of the old guys, and they don't do it. They gave us a $1,000 increase after ten years without giving anything. I'm not playing Pollyanna, but I think we're being ignored.

I hope there's a few out there that remember me and the era that we played in, which was really the foundation for the game today. Y. A. Tittle, Bobby Layne, Doak Walker. I played with and against some fabulous ballplayers.

Bobby Layne said he never lost a game; he just ran out of time. They still have that Detroit Curse from when they traded Bobby Layne to Pittsburgh. He said they'd never win again. They haven't won a championship since 1957.

I still have that letter jacket for winning the 1952 championship. I got it in mothballs, and it's in mint condition. Maybe I could sell it and get some money. [Laughs.]

I had a fabulous career and met so many wonderful people; I wouldn't take anything for it.

# 9

## Frank Gifford

Halfback, wide receiver, defensive back
University of Southern California
Drafted, 1952 (New York Giants, 1st round)
New York Giants, 1952–1960, 1962–1964
NFL champion (New York Giants, 1956)
NFL Most Valuable Player (1956)
6 All-Pro seasons
7 Pro Bowls
Co-host of Monday Night Football, 1971–1997
1950s NFL All-Decade Team
Pro Football Hall of Fame inductee (1977)

My father worked in the oil fields in the San Joaquin Valley. Most people in that part of the region were migrants from Oklahoma who came out for the oil boom during the Depression. Like the rest of my family, I was going to go in the oil fields.

I went to Bakersfield High School, and the attendance officer was a guy named Homer Beattie. He was also the football coach. He talked me into going out for football, and I did pretty well.

I was majoring in woodshop and flunking. I couldn't have cared less. Coach Beattie told me if I had a good senior year academically, he probably could get me a scholarship to USC, where he had gone to school.

I got almost straight A's my senior year but still had to go to junior college. I made Junior College All-American and got recruited by *everybody*. I said, "No, I'm going to SC."

At USC I got interested in studying. I'd never bothered to do that. [*Laughs.*] There were some really amazing things that happened long before I lived.

My first contract as a No. 1 draft pick was $8,000 for the year—not a minute—and a $250 bonus for signing. [*Laughs.*] I tell Giants players that story today, and they crack up.

After my first year with the Giants, I moved back to L.A. in the off-season and studied acting. I started doing a lot of stunt work and got a Screen Actors Guild card. I did want to play pro football, but I was really interested in acting. Ultimately that led me to a broadcasting career.

Don Maynard was a rookie with us in 1958. He became a great friend and one of the greatest players of all time. He came from Texas, and what was amusing about him was that he was afraid to get in the subway. We played in Yankee Stadium and lived in a place called the White Hall Hotel in Manhattan. Maynard wouldn't get on the subway until I came down and showed him how to get on and off. There were just too many people when he looked around. [*Laughs.*]

My teammate, Tom Landry, No. 49—he was the best. He created the 4-3 defense, which they still use today. A lot of people don't realize that—he was the guy that *invented* the 4-3 defense.

Our defense included Andy Robustelli, Dick Modzelewski, Rosey Grier, Sam Huff, Harland Savare, Emlen Tunnell, and Jimmy Patton. Those are legendary guys; they really are.

Now my son just graduated from USC. My daughter's studying acting in L.A. now, and she's going to start taking classes at USC too.

It's been quite a journey but a lot of USC.

# 10

## Johnny Lattner

Halfback, defensive back, punter, returner

University of Notre Dame

Heisman Trophy winner (1953)

Maxwell Award winner (1952, 1953)

Drafted, 1953 (Pittsburgh Steelers, 1st round)

Pittsburgh Steelers, 1954

1 Pro Bowl

I had about seventy or eighty scholarship offers. I chose Notre Dame because of the tradition, the academic challenge, and the proximity to my hometown, Chicago. Our stadium's capacity was about fifty-nine thousand. Out of those fifty-nine thousand, I bet you 35,000–40,000 of those people were from Chicago. I was actually playing in front of my home crowd.

My coach, Frank Leahy, had played in the '20s and early '30s for Knute Rockne. Leahy got hurt and went up to a hospital in Minnesota. Rockne was in the hospital at the same time, and they spent about two weeks together in the hospital. Leahy drew out what Rock knew about coaching and went on to be a very successful coach. I think Leahy started coaching at Michigan A&M, which eventually became Michigan State. He didn't go into that rah-rah stuff; he was very fundamentally sound.

When I showed up at Notre Dame as a freshman in 1950, they were undefeated four years in a row: '46, '47, '48, and '49. Freshmen weren't eligible to play because in those days they wanted to make sure you got your studies in order and got used to college life without the pressure of a varsity football schedule.

My dad died my freshman year. Our quarterback, Johnny Mazur, visited him in the hospital and promised my dad that if there was an opportunity, he would give me the ball so I would score.

I played most of our first game my sophomore year on defense. We were winning pretty big over Indiana, and Leahy put me in on offense during the fourth quarter. We were on the 5- or 6-yard line, and Mazur called my play off tackle. There was a big hole, and I walked in for a touchdown, in honor of my father.

I started playing both ways in the third or fourth game of the season. Our regular right halfback got hurt, so I played. In those days they could platoon you in and out; you didn't have to stay in for a whole quarter until my senior year, when the NCAA wanted to cut down on recruiting and scholarships. They wanted to give small colleges an opportunity to not have as many scholarships and still play varsity football.

I won the Maxwell Award my junior year, 1952, and finished fifth in the Heisman voting. Billy Vessels won the Heisman as a senior, and Paul Giel, a great halfback from Minnesota, came in third. I didn't have thoughts of winning the Heisman because Paul was also a junior.

My senior season, we played Georgia Tech at home on October 24. They were undefeated thirty-two games in a row, and we were undefeated for the season.

Right before the half, Georgia Tech scored a touchdown to tie the score. We went in at halftime, waiting for Coach Leahy to appear. Leahy was in the back, and all of a sudden Father Hessburg, Father Joyce, and the trainers went back there. Leahy had had some kind of attack. Donny Penza came back crying, saying, "Coach is dying."

He didn't die, and we outscored Georgia Tech 3 touchdowns to 1 in the second half. Leahy coached us the rest of the year.

That year you had to play both ways. I got a lot of publicity because I had played both offense and defense most of my career at Notre Dame. I was on the cover of *Time* magazine before the Pennsylvania game.

That Friday they had a blizzard, and we couldn't fly into Philadelphia. We had to get on a train, ride it the whole night, and got into Philadelphia around nine or ten Saturday morning. We went to St. Patrick's Church for church and got on the field ten minutes late. We were penalized 15 yards for delay of game. Pennsylvania scored the first touchdown, and we scored the second and third. We beat them by 10 points.

We went undefeated that season and only tied one game, at Iowa. That was kind of controversial. Iowa scored with about two and a half minutes left in the first half. We worked it all the way to the 14-yard line with about six seconds left on the clock but no timeouts. Frank Varrichione from Natick, Massachusetts, fainted. He really was faking an injury. He went down and didn't move. We didn't have nose guards [facemasks] in those days, and his nose was in the dirt. The officials had to stop the time as two reserve tackles came in and dragged Frank off the field.

The rules were that as soon as the injured player left, time would start again. While they carried him off, a substitute tackle came in. Ralph Guglielmi then threw a touchdown pass to Dan Shannon. We kicked the extra point and were tied at halftime.

Ironically late in the second half, we were again down by 7, with no timeouts. With less than two and a half minutes left, we worked the ball to about the same position that we did in the first half. Frank fainted again, stopping the clock. Frank wasn't supposed to faint—the left tackle was supposed to faint. The reserve tackle came in, we called the same play we called in the first half, and Dan Shannon caught it for a touchdown. We kicked the extra point and tied Iowa, 14-14.

The *South Bend Tribune*'s headlines that night were "The Fainting Irish Tie Iowa 14-14."

Nothing that perfect could ever work on the spur of the moment. We practiced that play. Leahy was a perfectionist, and we were prepared. The clock stopped, and the reserve tackle was on the field before Varrichione left it. As soon as Varrichione was dragged off, we snapped the ball without a second wasted.

That tie indirectly was the cause of our not winning the national championship. It was our only flub. Maryland was 10-0-0 and won the national championship. They then lost to Oklahoma in the Orange Bowl. We had already beaten Oklahoma.

At the time, you're just happy to be a winner. You don't really think of the national championship as the end of the world, but the older you get, you think, "Oh gee, we could have been the national champs." It does hurt a bit because we were the only undefeated team that year.

When the Heisman was being voted on, our athletic director, Moose Krause, said, "Go home and we'll let you know." I went home, did a little work, and got a call from Moose. He said, "You won the Heisman Trophy."

I hopped over to Moose's office. Leahy was there, and some pictures were taken. Moose said, "About four of us are going to New York in a week. You can come with your girlfriend."

I said, "Well, I'm not dating my girlfriend." Eventually I married the girl, but we weren't dating at the time.

I took my mother. She had never flown and never been to New York. We flew into New York and got to the Downtown Athletic Club. That was probably one of the first times a female member of the Heisman entourage stayed at the Downtown Athletic Club. Before that women couldn't stay overnight.

She enjoyed the heck out of it. The day before the big program two members of the club took my mother and myself out and wined us and dined us. We ended up at the Copacabana about two o'clock in the morning. At four in the morning one of the guys from the athletic club sat down next to my mother and said, "Mrs. Lattner, tomorrow's going to be a rough day."

My mother said, "You know, instead of a martini, I'll have a Miller High Life."

That was the night of her life.

I was the nineteenth Heisman winner. I received the award right at the gym, at the Downtown Athletic Club. There were nine hundred people in the gym, and the fire department said, "No way. On the thirteenth floor, if there was a fire, everybody would die." The year 1953 was the last time they had any award in the gym at the Downtown Athletic Club.

The Heisman was a great award. The feeling gets bigger and bigger as you get older. I go to the presentation every year and enjoy the heck out of it.

I also won the Maxwell Award again in 1953. I always felt sorry about that. When I won it my junior year, I told the story about my dad dying and how he never saw me play. I think the reason I won it my senior year was because they wanted to hear the second half of the story. [Laughs.] It was a nice honor, and I enjoyed it. Tim Tebow and I are the only players to win the award twice.

The Steelers drafted me, and I found out through the papers. I was drafted in the first round, the seventh-overall pick.

Coach Leahy's friend helped negotiate my contract. I got a $10,000 salary and a $3,500 bonus. A lot of schoolteachers didn't make that much money in those days. That was a lot of money for me too. My dad never made that much.

I played a lot in 1954. I scored 7 touchdowns, caught some passes, was on the kickoff team, the punt return team, and played some defense.

I also played in the All-Pro Game out in California. It wasn't even televised, but it was an honor. Otto Graham was our quarterback, and I caught a couple of his passes. Otto grew up in Illinois and played at Northwestern. I remembered him playing there when I was a little kid, and he was one of my boyhood heroes.

I had joined the air force ROTC while at Notre Dame, during the Korean War. If you went to college and your grades were bad, your selective service board would make you eligible for the draft. If you were in the ROTC program, they left you alone. Leahy made sure everybody that was on scholarship was in the ROTC program.

I was stationed at Bolling Air Force Base as a second lieutenant, and I played football. We had one of the best air force football teams before the Air Force Academy was built. We beat everybody. We used to scrimmage the Redskins and even gave them a good battle. We had about seven All-Americans on the team, including quarterback Bernie Faloney and Chet Hanulak, both from Maryland, and Ernie Warlick, who played with the Buffalo Bills.

I was running a punt back against Fort Jackson at Fort Jackson. I was going all the way but got tackled from behind. My knee swelled up, and from there on it kept swelling. Finally, in a game near the end of the season, it went out on me.

I went to the doctor, and he said, "One of your cruciate ligaments is torn. I can't do anything about it. I could bring the ligament down and tie them, but your knee would be stiff. I can clean your cartilage out, and you'll be able to run again."

He cleaned my cartilage out, and as soon as my knee got better, I started running on it. I could run full speed, but when I went back with the Steelers and all the hitting and cutting, my knee kept swelling, and I retired. When you play with the big boys and you're injured, you could get hurt really bad.

With today's medicine, I probably could have played longer. I would have had the knee operated on right away. They can do a lot more today.

You're not going to play football forever. I had a taste of pro football, I played college football, and I played high school football. I played the whole gamut, and I enjoyed myself immensely. It came to an end quickly, but that's part of the game.

Players should prepare themselves and always have the idea of what they will do when they quit or get hurt. That's why it's so important to get something out of the college education. You can do as well in the business world as you did as an athlete.

I got married in 1958. I coached at a Catholic high school in Kenosha, Wisconsin, for one year and two years at the University of Denver. Denver gave up football, and I gave up coaching. I came back to my hometown of Chicago and opened a restaurant.

After five years the restaurant had a bad fire, and my Heisman Trophy burned. I sent the clippings of what the trophy looked like to the Downtown Athletic Club, and they made me a new one. It cost me $900.

I now use the trophy for charities. If a charity wants to use it to auction it off for a week or whatever, they can have it if it's available. I raised a lot of money on the charity side using that philosophy. I don't see the trophy too often. [*Laughs.*] It's always out! But it's better to have it raising money for charities than sitting on a mantle collecting dust.

Football was a great part of my life, and life is kind of short. Enjoy what you got, be thankful for what you've done, and don't do anything to embarrass yourself or your family.

That's my advice.

# 11

## Cotton Davidson

Quarterback, punter

Baylor University

Drafted, 1954 (Baltimore Colts, 1st round)

Baltimore Colts, 1954, 1957

Dallas Texans, 1960–1962

Oakland Raiders, 1962–1968

2 Pro Bowls

At a very young age, my name was Francis. To me it was a girl's name, and I hated it. My hair was very white. Someone said something about "Cotton Top," and the name Cotton took on. I was tickled to death.

Gatesville, Texas, where I grew up, was a very small town. There was no TV, and if you had a radio, there was so much static that you couldn't understand it. We didn't even have phone service besides a little community crank phone. You could call somebody, but everybody could hear it. It wasn't very secretive.

I committed to playing college ball at Rice, but I hadn't traveled too far out of the county yet and didn't know if I would be happy there.

The pastor at my church played guard for Baylor and talked me into looking at Baylor. I think it worked out better because I was able to come home some, and my parents were able to see our games.

My junior year, we were in the 1952 Orange Bowl [Georgia Tech 17, Baylor 14].

We opened my senior season at Cal with a victory. The

West Coast papers gave us a good write up, and we got a high ranking. The next week, we went all the way across the United States to Miami, played down there, and won.

We were ranked third in the nation before playing Texas [on November 7, 1953]. The Texas coaches had said they didn't think it'd be good if we spent the night before the game in Austin because their fans were out of hand. The fans came by our hotel almost hourly, blowing horns, trying to keep us awake.

We played very well, but Texas beat us 20-21. It was a blocked extra point. That knocked us out of that third rating, and we didn't go to a bowl game that year.

Had we gone to a bowl game, I probably wouldn't have gotten to play in the East-West Shrine Game. Scouts at that game told me they were interested. I had no thought of playing professional football.

My head coach at Baylor, George Sauer, called me to his office and said that Weeb Ewbank, the head coach of the Baltimore Colts, had called. I was their No. 1 draft choice.

Weeb and I met at the student union building. Weeb said, "What do you think it's going to cost to get you?"

I said, "Coach, I have no idea. I don't know whether $5 or $50 is a contract. I need to talk to Coach Sauer."

I went across the street and talked to Sauer. The team from Calgary, Canada, had called and said they wanted to sign me if I wasn't happy with Baltimore's offer. Coach Sauer told me, "I think you'd be better off playing in the states since you live here." I told him what Weeb had offered, and Sauer said, "That's probably not too bad."

I signed and that was it. It wasn't a lengthy decision. [*Laughs.*] I'm embarrassed to even say what I signed for. It was a small amount—I'll just say that—and I was the No. 1 draft choice. When I got up there, I found out very few of the Baltimore Colts were making more money than I was, even the veterans.

My knowledge of professional football was nil. I had never

seen a game until I played in one. It was mind boggling. I had a good college coach, but we never had a lot of meetings discussing what we might do against a certain ball club in a certain situation. With Weeb I learned football that I'd never even heard of. He went into detail on defensive alignments and sets, the weakness of a defense, and how to attack it. I had to study more there than I did in chemistry.

What hurt me was I was there for a week and then had to go to Chicago and play in the College All-Star Game. I missed a full week. I was just beginning to pick things up, and then I was gone. It was hard to catch up. I didn't play a lot in the first several games of the season. I just wasn't ready.

Back then the officials didn't have a lot of rules to make calls on because so much was okay to do. [*Laughs.*]

Buddy Young was a running back we had. He was a great kid and had been in the league for several years. We were playing the Chicago Bears, and they had a defensive end that played real aggressive. Buddy said, "Cotton, when you throw the ball, don't stand there and watch it. Move around because this guy will come up and knock the fool out of you in the back of the head. And they won't call it."

That's when I realized part of the game was that you better take care of yourself.

Fred Enke and Gary Kerkorian were the two quarterbacks with me my rookie year. Enke, an older quarterback, was retiring. Kerkorian was in his third year, but he was going to go to law school. I was the only quarterback coming back that next year. I thought, "I'm at least going to have a chance."

Instead I got my draft notice and had to go into military service. That left Baltimore with no quarterbacks, so they drafted George Shaw. Then they picked up Johnny Unitas. When I came back from service in '57, Unitas had already established himself as a top-of-the-line quarterback.

When I went to Baltimore in 1954, I wore No. 19. That was my college number. When Unitas came in, he picked it up. I came back in '57 and said something about it. He said, "Well, you can have it back. It was yours before it was mine."

I said, "No, that's not a big deal."

He kept 19 and made it a very popular number [*Laughs.*] I wound up wearing 18.

Unitas and I roomed together during the '57 season. He was one super person, and we really had a good relationship. He was as good a person as he was a player. I backed him up and punted for Baltimore.

Before the '58 season I knew I wasn't going to play and made a big mistake. I asked Weeb to let me out if I could find somebody that wanted me. I talked to Canada and we worked a deal. That was the biggest mistake I've ever made in my life because the Colts won the championship. I could have been there punting and backing up Unitas.

I did get to play quarterback in Canada, but I got my shoulder hurt midseason. I couldn't play and came home.

John Bridgers, a defensive line coach at Baltimore, got the head coaching job at Baylor. He called and asked if I'd be interested in putting the Baltimore offense in. I was on his staff for the '59 season.

Lamar Hunt and Hank Stram contacted me about playing [for the AFL's Dallas Texans], and Hunt came down and talked to me.

Hunt and Stram were two great people. A whole lot of us owe a lot to Lamar Hunt for developing the American Football League. I don't think it would ever have gotten off the ground if it hadn't been for him and the way he worked at it. Hunt went ahead in a way that people could afford it and in a way that he was going to commit his life to making it work. He was very personable and very I guess you'd say down to earth. He's not like a lot of owners you see that are on a different pedestal.

Hank Stram had a good football mind. He had been an assistant at a couple of colleges but never a head coach until he got the job in Dallas. He actually coached Lamar Hunt at SMU, when Lamar played football there. I don't know if Lamar played much, but I think that's where he first met Hank.

I was the first quarterback for the Dallas Texans (now the Kansas City Chiefs). We weren't picked real high in 1960, but we won 8 ball games [8-6 record]. Back then the AFL didn't have the top stadiums to play in, and they didn't have security like places do now.

We played at Boston in I guess you'd say a big high school stadium. We were down with about fifteen seconds to go, and a field goal would not win it. I threw a long pass to Chris Burford. He caught it and fell on the 1-yard line.

Everybody thought the game was over and came out on the field. The field was covered with people, and the officials ruled that we still had one second left. They backed everybody off the field as much as they could, but fans were packed all around the end zone. Their toes were almost on the out-of-bounds line.

We had time for one more play, having to score a touchdown to win. I had Burford on my left, and we ran him on a quick slant. I dropped back, looked to the right for a count, then turned and threw back to Burford. A fan came out, ran right in front of Burford, knocked the ball down, and ran out of the end zone.

The officials never did call anything.

I went to Hank on the sideline and told him, "Hank, we need to protest because a fan came out and knocked that ball down." I don't think he saw what went on. We never did get a protest going and lost the ball game.

I told John Madden about it when I was at Oakland. Later on he was doing the commentary on a game, and they showed the film clip. He said, "Son of a gun. Cotton told me about that, but I thought he was lying." [*Laughs.*]

In '61, I played in the AFL All-Star Game. In fact I was MVP of that ball game, throwing 4 touchdowns. Everybody has a good day every once in a while, you know. [*Laughs.*]

I thought everything was in good shape, but the Texans picked up Lenny Dawson in the off-season. Hank Stram had coached him at Purdue. We had a pretty decent exhibition season, and as far as what he did and what I did, it was pretty similar. They just decided to go with Lenny.

Oakland was struggling and really needed players. I think they'd won two ball games in two years. Dallas traded me there.

Hank called and I said, "I'm not going to California."

That was eight o'clock in the morning. Five o'clock that afternoon, I was on a plane going to Oakland. [*Laughs.*] We came up with a contract that I felt I had to have if I went out there.

That first year wasn't rough—it was *terrible*. [*Laughs.*] Our talent just wasn't as good as other people's. At quarterback when you have a line that's not as strong as the defense's, you're going to take a beating.

I shouldn't have been out on the field a lot of the time. I had my sternum separated and my shoulder hurt twice but continued to play.

We only won one game, the last game of the year. I was so beat up and upset that I told everybody, "I'm through with football and I'll see ya sometime." I left Oakland thinking I'd never play football again.

Al Davis called and said he got the coaching job. Al coached on the All-Star team with Sid Gillman when I was MVP.

I said, "Al, I'm through with football."

He said, "We'll make it a different program."

I wound up telling him I'd come back.

At least 50 percent of the players were new. They weren't drafted kids; he picked up guys he heard were cut or unhappy.

Al Davis sat down with Tom Flores and me. He said, "You two guys can take us, and we can win with you. We'll just go week by week. If a guy has a good game, he'll start the next game."

We played back and forth at quarterback. Tom and I roomed together and were happy with the situation. We were 10-4 Davis's first year, going from 1-13 to 10-4.

This is what Al Davis did great, for myself and for the whole team: he prepared you and didn't take anything for granted. He covered *everything*. Blitzes can determine a game if you can't handle them. Al wanted to make sure you had the tool to handle any blitz they threw at you. When you have that going and you make it work a couple of times, all of a sudden your confidence level goes to the top. I became more confident than ever that I could handle any situation on a football field. He'd given me that gift. That's why I considered him a great coach.

Oakland had never beaten San Diego, and in 1963 we were down 17 points with eleven minutes to go. We scored 31 points in the last eleven minutes of the game to beat them. We had a big punt return and that fired us up. The ball bounced our way, we made good things happen, and the defense shut them down. I ran for a touchdown and threw 2 touchdown passes.

That year we beat everybody in the AFL's Western Division—San Diego, Kansas City, and Denver—twice. We lost some games to Eastern Division teams, and that kept us from winning the division championship. I went to the All-Star Game again and threw the winning pass to an Oakland receiver [Art Powell, with forty-three seconds left].

Everything worked out good until I got my shoulder torn up in training camp of '67. I was throwing to my left; my own player came in from the right side and caught my arm when I started forward, tearing the muscles loose in the front part of my shoulder. I had to have surgery and missed that entire season.

They traded Flores to Buffalo for Daryle Lamonica. I came back the next year, was in pretty good shape, but my arm wasn't quite as strong as before. I never did play much after that.

1. Cotton Davidson led the Raiders to a 31-point fourth-quarter rally against the Chargers in 1963.

I went with the Raiders to the Super Bowl but didn't play. It was in Florida in the Orange Bowl. That was Lombardi's last game, and Green Bay really had a good day and beat us pretty badly.

I stayed on, and they got George Blanda. He was backing up and kicking. I was on the squad, but a lot of times I wasn't active. I was in the press box on the phones to Lamonica. If I had it to do over, I'd have probably retired and not gone through that.

The next year I did some scouting for Oakland. Grant Teaff got the Baylor job and wanted me to come down. I took the job and spent twenty-two years coaching quarterbacks, receivers, and the passing game. We won the conference twice and went to eight bowl games.

I guess like most careers there were good and bad times. I felt good at Baltimore but got behind when I went to the College All-Star Game. I was coming back the next year and got drafted into the army. Those are setbacks, and I would have loved to have had the opportunity to skip them and see if I could have produced.

The AFL started and I had two good years with Dallas, and then I got traded to Oakland. I felt that was a setback, but it turned out to be a good thing.

I was with Unitas, Dawson, and Lamonica. I competed with them, and it was fun. They were great guys, very good friends, and I'm proud for them and for what I was able to do with them.

I came to Baylor in 1949 and left in 1992. That's how long I was in the game as a student/player, professional, and coach. It was a great life, I met a lot of great people, and I made friends with a lot of good players and people. I'm still in contact with a lot of them.

It may not be for everybody, but it was a good life for us. I want to thank the good Lord for giving me and my family this life. I don't think it could've turned out much better.

# 12

## Bob Skoronski

Offensive tackle

Indiana University

Drafted, 1956 (Green Bay Packers, 5th round)

Green Bay Packers, 1956, 1959–1971

5-time NFL and Super Bowl champion (1961, 1962, 1965, Super
  Bowls 1 and 2)

1 Pro Bowl

I went to a high school about twenty-five miles from my home.
I spent a lot of time trying to get home after school, either
walking or hitchhiking. I had no time for sports.

As a junior in high school and never having played a bit
of varsity football, I went to wait for my friend, who was a
starter on the football team. Our school was a Catholic high
school, and I kicked a ball back and forth to this priest while
I waited. I was booming them; you couldn't believe it! One of
the coaches ran over and said, "The head coach would like
you to report to the locker room tomorrow and get a uniform."

When I got my uniform, they said, "There's no positions
open. Make him a center because nobody wants to be one
of those."

I liked the blocking part and the tackling part. I wasn't
exactly a farm kid, but I was from the country. We played
football without pads as kids and enjoyed it.

I was recruited by several colleges. I had chances at places
like Notre Dame and North Carolina, pretty good football
teams then.

My older brother, Frank, got tired of working in a mill and

wanted to go to college. Frank was an athlete, but he wasn't going to play at the college level. I told the people recruiting me that I'd love to see my brother go to the same school. My father wanted that actually more than anything.

I decided on Indiana, mainly because it was the only school that was interested in taking both my brother and myself. We went to Indiana with scholarships, although my brother ended up working his way through school because he played little football to begin with.

I learned a couple of important things playing college ball. Number one: let your play do your talking for you. You're never going to talk someone out of something on a football field. You're going to make it right by getting the right kind of blocks and the right kind of tackles.

The second thing was don't ever give up. It's a tough game, there's a lot of tough guys in it, and you just got to be that way. Not every kid is cut out for that, but I enjoyed it. It was a way of expression for me from a poor family and small community.

I heard from a lot of pro teams. They sent out questionnaires to get your 40 speed, your weight, how much you could bench press, those kinds of things. I had a feeling I would probably be drafted, but I didn't know by whom or what round. I got drafted by Green Bay in the fifth round. I actually considered going to Canada because the money was better, and at that point that interested me.

I had never in my life been to Green Bay. I can't tell you my first impressions were great. That town was thirty-two thousand people. I believe the stadium only held 18,000–20,000 people. It was an all-wood structure. You could shake it at one end, and it would shake all the way around!

Bart Starr was picked in the seventeenth round of the draft that I was drafted in. Forrest Gregg was also in it (second round).

You don't forget when you meet Bart Starr. He's the perfect gentleman and a kind, thoughtful guy. He's a hard worker—*the hardest worker.* He's all the things that people said about him.

We always felt Green Bay was a great place for players to be, especially when you were winning. It wasn't a good place to be when you were losing. Everybody knew who you were, and you couldn't hide anywhere.

When they first saw me play, they kidded me about having to get better to help. But it worked out. I loved the people and I loved the area. I ended up getting married there, raising a family there, and having a business there.

I took an ROTC commission while I was in college and had to fulfill that obligation after my rookie season. I had to go into the service for three years, but after twenty-three months they released me because I had a seasonal job playing football. They let me out in time to start the 1959 season.

I came back to a new coach and new stadium. When I first saw Lambeau Field, I was surprised. It looked kind of big to me.

Because the Packers hadn't won many games, they were drafting off the top. They accumulated a good group of players. We were going to be better. All we needed was a coach like Vince Lombardi. Lombardi taught us the spirit and the will to win in everything. He wanted his guys to be complete men in every way and be the best they could be at what they did, not just as football players. He was emphatic on that and had lots of reminders for us in terms of slogans. You learned something from all of them. I think I got about fifteen pages of them.

"Fatigue makes cowards of us all." That's an interesting statement because it does. When you're tired, you're not playing hard.

"Anything is yours if you want it bad enough." We players would give each other the business during games. Looking at each other would be enough or looking at him on the sidelines. [*Laughs.*] You'd be reminded of those slogans.

Lombardi had a great slant on the game. He had a very perceptive mind about it, a great imagination about the things that you could do, and a great teaching style. Boy, he could teach.

I don't know how many days we spent on learning the sweep, trying to perfect it. We stayed on that one play for a long time. It was amazing; I never saw that done in football before.

We went through every possible circumstance that could occur on the field—if you had an odd-man front, an even-man front, a four- or six-man line. We learned that you could run the sweep into probably forty or fifty different defenses.

Running it until we were blue in the face and then knowing every situation made the sweep successful. The defense may change things on the line of scrimmage and things happen fast, but no matter where people were, we knew how to run the play from practice.

Success leads to confidence. We had a decent amount of success, and guys became very confident in the game plans and the people.

After losing the 1960 NFL Championship, Lombardi told us the same thing he told everybody else: that we weren't ever going to lose another playoff game. Actually he told us that we weren't going to let them out of the stadium until we beat them. [*Laughs.*]

We beat the Giants for the NFL Championship in 1961 and '62, and the Cowboys in 1966 and '67. Both were extremely good football teams that, like us, were pretty much in their prime. I had great respect for the guys I played against on both of those teams. They were as good as any players playing. Of course, I think a player ought to always think he's playing against the best player that ever played. If you don't, you may get beat.

Coach Lombardi made the difference. We had a chance to understand ourselves, what it took to win, how important it was to win, and how valuable it was.

We had good players, yes. Were they better than other teams? Maybe not in all cases, but Coach Lombardi could get the best out of a guy. He knew how to feed egos when they had to be fed, and he knew when a guy deserved a kick in the butt verbally. He could time that stuff extremely well. Anybody who does that, it doesn't make any difference if it's football or business or your family, that's an important thing.

In the 1967 NFL Championship (Ice Bowl), we dealt with the weather like it wasn't even there. The game of football, as we were told by our boss, was made to be played in any kind of condition. It wasn't played necessarily on a dry field, a wet field, or a no-grass field. It's played wherever it's played, so don't be worried about the weather. Everybody contends with it, both you and your enemy.

On the last drive we decided to take advantage of some things that we observed during the game. People were reacting certain ways and based on those reactions, we thought there were some things we could probably do. Fortunately it worked.

On the last touchdown, I just tried to keep my guy in his position so he couldn't get across the inside to stop whoever had the ball. I didn't know Bart was going to keep the ball. He decided that because of the slippery handling, it was best not to take a chance on a handoff. [Bart Starr scored the winning touchdown with seconds left in the Packers' 21-17 victory.]

I didn't see Bart go over the goal line. We were not the kind of team who was looking at where the ball was going. Everybody was trying to do their block to the best of their ability.

Lombardi kind of referred to retiring in speeches during the week before Super Bowl 2. We beat Oakland 33-14 for our third consecutive championship.

Winning three straight was immensely more difficult than winning two straight. A lot of people want to stop records and prevent a team from being the first to do something. We would too. That's the game.

I think in our own way each of us had a farewell moment

with Lombardi. I played one more year. I think my body may have told me to retire.

Life after football has been very fulfilling. Almost all of the guys got into some kind of business, and many of them did very well, making the complete man kind of thing: success in football and in business.

# 13

## Bart Starr

Quarterback
Drafted, 1956 (Green Bay Packers, 17th round)
Green Bay Packers, 1956–1971
NFL completion percentage leader (1962, 1966, 1968, 1969)
NFL Most Valuable Player (1966)
5-time NFL and Super Bowl champion (1961, 1962, 1965, Super
    Bowls 1 and 2)
Super Bowl Most Valuable Player (Super Bowls 1 and 2)
4 All-Pro seasons
4 Pro Bowls
1960s NFL All-Decade Team
Pro Football Hall of Fame inductee (1977)

I began football in the ninth grade. That year the Montgomery, Alabama, school system created a junior high school league and put teams together from three or four schools.

My high school coach was a wonderful teacher and prepared us well. All of us who were relatively talented in high school were offered scholarships. I was honored to have the choice of deciding between the University of Kentucky, where Bear Bryant was beginning his career, and the University of Alabama.

Although I wanted to go to Kentucky and play for Coach Bryant, I wanted to continue being able to see a young lady I started dating my junior year in high school and who has now been my wife for fifty-nine years.

I made the great decision to stay in Alabama so I could chase her and have a date from time to time while she attended

Auburn on the other side of the state. [*Laughs*.] My decision was based more on that relationship than football because I would have gone in a heartbeat to play for Coach Bryant.

I had two very strong first years at Alabama. I played a considerable amount of time and lettered as a freshman [throwing a touchdown in the Orange Bowl].

As a sophomore, I played a great deal and played very, very well. We played in the Cotton Bowl against Rice. One of our players, Tommy Lewis, came off the bench in the middle of a play and tackled our opponent, running back Dicky Moegle, as Moegle ran down the sidelines. The officials awarded Moegle a touchdown.

I was a defensive back on that play, removed some distance from our player coming off the bench, toward the center of the field as opposed to being on the sidelines. I had a direct shot look at it. [*Laughs*.] I couldn't believe what I was seeing.

It was very, very surprising that one of our players did that. But the flip side is knowing what a competitor and energized guy he could be at times. I guess deep down inside it may not have surprised us at all. [*Laughs*.]

As a junior, I was injured. As a senior, we had a coaching change, and the coach went with the younger players, sophomores who were going to be there longer than the seniors. I didn't play much as a senior and didn't have a lot to show for my junior and senior years.

I was hoping I would be drafted, but I didn't necessarily expect to be drafted. Scouts hadn't seen me play as much as they would have under different circumstances.

When football season was over, I'd go over and watch basketball practice every time I could. I'm a huge basketball fan, and I was blessed to have developed a nice friendship with Johnny Dee, the basketball coach at the University of Alabama.

Dee ironically was a close friend of the director of player personnel for the Green Bay Packers. The knowledge and information that he was able to convey to me regarding this friend of his was extremely helpful. Coach Johnny Dee put in the good word and really helped me get to the Packers because I didn't have much of a resume.

The greatest challenge in going to Green Bay was making the team. Going up there as a very low round draft choice, your chances aren't going to be great.

I worked and trained harder than I'd ever done at any time in my life between the end of my senior year in college and first going to Green Bay. I wanted to be in the greatest condition and best shape that I could be, practicing as much as possible so that I could perform as though I'd been in their system for some time.

Playing quarterback, you need to be a leader. To me being a leader means you have to be very committed and focused on what's demanded and expected of you and also focused on how you are to help lead that team by following through on those causes while continuing to improve *your* capabilities.

I need not tell you that with the salaries we were paid in those days, having off-season employment really helped. I had a good friend in the automobile business, and I got a job selling automobiles at his dealership in Birmingham. I did that for three years. I also was blessed to work with the Ford Motor Company and Mike Ditka. Mike and I worked together for two or three years in the off-season, participating in promotional activities like appearing at celebrations or dealership openings. We had a great relationship. He and I didn't talk that much about football, but it would be brought up by others in the gatherings.

Coach Lombardi began each year stressing the desire to excel. He was never interested in being just good. The first thing you want to do is eliminate the just good level. We were taught that from the first meeting of the year. He wasn't interested in being just good, he wanted to be *Excellent*! I think that's a great lesson for anyone because there is a big difference.

As we moved forward and worked our way up toward a championship game, you came to fully appreciate and magnify the words that Coach Lombardi stressed over and over. Words like *commitment, preparation*, seeking to *excel*.

The key to success in any game of championship caliber, such as the 1967 NFL Championship (Ice Bowl), is the study, preparation, and planning that goes into getting ready to play that game.

We spent a *lot* of time studying the Cowboys, their defenses, what they were doing and accomplishing, and we structured our objectives to play as well as we could against that. It was really a lot of fun in preparation but also a great challenge because the Cowboys were an outstanding team. We had been very fortunate throughout the year to have a great season, and we were very honored and proud to be in that championship game.

The night before was extremely cold, and it hardly warmed up at all the day of the game. As a result, the ground was as hard as this desk that I have my hand on. *It was that hard.* As the game progressed, the footing became poorer. We really had to be careful of what we were trying to execute and how we were going about doing it.

You plan for what you'll want to do in certain down and distance situations and at certain time elements in the game. We came down to the last few minutes, but the field had become very unstable. That was a big factor in our play calling on that final, game-winning drive.

You had to be very aware that the ground didn't enter into the play you called, causing the back to slip. Those kinds of things can really hurt you in circumstances like that. We tried a couple of end runs, and that's a good example of what we could not do.

We got down to the goal line at the south end of the field. The ground was very, very slick there. I went to the sidelines and told Coach Lombardi about the ground and that the running back was slipping and sliding. I told him that I was standing upright underneath the center, and I could shuffle my feet and then lunge into the end zone.

You'll have to excuse my language, but Coach Lombardi's response was, "Well, then run it. Let's get the hell out of here." [*Laughs.*] I'm laughing going to the huddle like I'm laughing with you right now. That really cracked me up.

We called a wedge play, with our right guard and center doubling, wedging on the defensive left tackle of the Cowboys. Dallas had a charge we called a "submarine technique"; they charged so low you couldn't block them; all you could do was fall on them. Everyone except that defensive tackle—no disrespect to him; he was just so tall, he couldn't get down that low.

We knew the play would work. We'd seen it. We ran it a couple of times earlier in the game, and it gained a minimum of two yards.

Normally when we called that blocking technique, I'd turn and give the ball to the fullback running to my right side. I mentioned to him that I was not going to give it to him; I was going to keep the ball. I kept it, and we were able to score the winning touchdown. [The Packers' victory gave them a berth in Super Bowl 2.]

Coach Lombardi was always very appropriate in how he chose to say things. After the Ice Bowl, he was extremely pleased and expressed that very well. He had a great way of expressing himself to you in different sets of circumstances. He saluted us, congratulated us, and commented on the great efforts by the entire team for what they had done in a tough game and tough conditions.

I've been richly blessed with the career that we've had, the life beyond it, and the things we've learned from it.

My wife and I were privileged to get to know a couple in Appleton, Wisconsin, working with some people affiliated with the Rawhide Boys Ranch. We would visit and just become more and more interested in seeing how we could help and assist the young men. Their backgrounds are rather shaky and unsteady. They need the help and assistance they have not been receiving at home.

I was also blessed to have gone to a wonderful university, the University of Alabama. I want to stress that, even though it was difficult for me in those last two years. My situation there changed dramatically, and I just had to do the best I could.

Those things can happen to people, and I think it's a strong whistleblower for those out there who read or hear those kinds of stories to note that if that happens to them, there are opportunities and ways to rebound and come back from something. We need to do that and be very, very strong and tough when we have to be.

# 14

## Paul Hornung

Running back, kicker, quarterback

Notre Dame

Heisman Trophy Winner (1956)

Drafted, 1957 (Green Bay Packers, first-overall pick)

Green Bay Packers 1957–1962, 1964–1966

4-time NFL and Super Bowl champion (1961, 1962, 1965, Super
Bowl 1)

NFL points leader (1959, 1960, 1961)

176 points scored in 1960 (single-season record for forty-six
years)

NFL touchdown leader (1960, 15 TDs; tied with Sonny Randle)

NFL Most Valuable Player (1961)

3 All-Pro seasons

2 Pro Bowls

1960s NFL All-Decade Team

Pro Football Hall of Fame inductee (1986)

When I was in about the seventh or eighth grade, there was a
kid who played in my hometown of Louisville, Kentucky—a
great athlete named Bunky Gruner. I'd always go out and
watch Bunky because I admired him. He went to Manual
High School, ranked No. 1 in the state of Kentucky. Here I
go out and watch them play this high school team from Birmingham, Alabama, ranked No. 1 in the state of Alabama.
Bart Starr was their quarterback.

They beat our team from Louisville 49-0, and Bart threw
6 touchdown passes. I always told Bart, "I remember Bart

Starr. That's the first time I ever saw you play, and you threw 6 passes against the number one team in the state of Kentucky." He's a beautiful man. He's never let anybody down. He's real boring because he's perfect. He's the perfect man.

I played football in grade school during sixth, seventh, and eighth grades in the Catholic Football League in Louisville. Then I played in high school of course. We got a great school program in Louisville still to this day. It's a very serious league for those kids.

When I signed on with Notre Dame, I didn't know Coach Leahy was retiring. I don't know if I would have gone there knowing that because I really wanted to go to Kentucky. I wanted to go with Bear Bryant.

Freshmen were eligible at Kentucky, but they weren't eligible at Notre Dame. I had to wait to be a sophomore before I played. I could have played right away at Kentucky—with Bear Bryant. That ain't bad, is it?

Bryant always told me, "If you'd have come to Kentucky, I'd have never left."

I said, "Coach, you're talking to *me*. I know about money now. Don't tell me that. The moment they offered you all that money, you were on the first horse out of town." [*Laughs.*]

Bear Bryant was the best college coach of all-time.

I played every down in college. I led Notre Dame in rushing, passing, punt returns, and kickoff returns. I kicked off and punted. On defense I was second in tackles and first in interceptions.

Tom Harmon, who'd been an All-American at the University of Michigan, had a radio and TV show. He called me after my senior season and said, "Congratulations."

I said, "For what?"

He said, "Haven't you heard anything today about an award?"

I said, "No."

He said, "Well, you just won the Heisman Trophy."

I said, "Aw, come on."

He said, "You just won the Heisman Trophy!"

I really was surprised. You know, 2-8? I'm still the only player in the history of the Heisman that's ever won it on a losing team.

First pick of the draft in those days was a bonus pick. Each team put their name in a hat, and you drew them out. Fourteen teams; here comes the bonus pick. After that the draft starts in predetermined order: 1, 2, 3, 4. Next year, the thirteen remaining teams were eligible for the bonus pick. Pick a team out—they got the first [bonus] pick. I was the first pick of the 1957 draft.

We used to play the Cowboys in Dallas every year in the Salesmanship Game—that was their big preseason game. Of course they had Bob Lilly on defense.

We had a false trap play where the left guard pulled to the right, and Bart would hand the ball to Jimmy Taylor over left guard. That was supposed to pull Lilly to his left, have him step out of the hole, and Jimmy would go right up the gut . . . but Lilly never followed the guard, and he'd kick the crap out of Taylor.

In the huddle I'd say, "Bart, call the false trap for Jimmy. He loves that play."

He'd call the false trap and Jimmy would say, "No, no, no! Don't call that play!"[*Laughs.*]

Coach Lombardi was a disciplinarian, and he did it right. His way was the only way, and everybody abided by it. He kicked everybody's butt and made them believe. He was a great motivator.

He'd say, "Do you want to make more money?" That motivates everyone.

There haven't ever been ten football players in the front of the draft as good as our draft. I was the number one pick, then Jim Brown was drafted, and then the best lineman of *all time*, Jim Parker. There's no better player than Jim Parker was—the best was all he was.

Len Dawson, John Brodie, and I were three quarterbacks, all three No. 1 picks and all three all-stars. Then you add John Arnett and Ron Kramer, who made All–Big 10 basketball three years in a row, jumped track, and played baseball.

[Four of the first eight picks—Hornung, Brown, Parker, and Dawson—earned Hall of Fame honors. Arnett, Brodie, and Kramer were each named All-Pro and perennial Pro Bowl players.]

# 15

## Sonny Jurgensen

Quarterback

Duke University

Drafted, 1957 (Philadelphia Eagles, 4th round)

Philadelphia Eagles, 1957–1963

Washington Redskins, 1964–1974

NFL champion (1960)

NFL passing yardage leader (1961, 1962, 1966, 1967, 1969)

NFL touchdown pass leader (1961: 32 TDs)

2 All-Pro seasons

5 Pro Bowls

1960s NFL All-Decade Team

Pro Football Hall of Fame inductee (1983)

In college I played offense and defense. My head coach at Duke, Bill Murray, recommended me to the Eagles as a defensive back. I only threw the ball fifty-three times my senior year.

The Eagles offensive coordinator, Charlie Gower, came down and worked me out. Duke's backfield coach, Hall of Famer Ace Parker, said, "You should look at Sonny throwing the ball. We didn't take advantage of his skills, but you'd be missing the boat if you didn't."

The era I played in, the 1950s, '60s, and '70s, was a great era to play in because it was a player's game. We controlled the game on the field as they did in the' 30s and '40s. In the '30s and '40s you couldn't even talk to anybody on the sidelines. I talked with Sammy Baugh about controlling the game many times and didn't realize there once was a penalty if you talked to anybody off the field.

In the huddle you'd try to get everybody in the right frame of mind. You used psychology and motivated people. On third down you'd ask the tackle if he could make the block and the running back if he could get you a first down. You knew who wanted the ball, who didn't want the ball, and who wanted to make the block.

It's a coach's game now. They choreograph everything.

I've talked with [current] coaches about this, and they've said, "It's more sophisticated. We have everybody up in the box and on the sidelines with radio controls and microphones. They can evaluate the play as it's being run."

I said, "That makes a lot of sense. I'll tell you what I'll do: I'll call the play in the huddle, signal it to you, and you can do all the evaluating you want."

I remember in 1969, under Vince Lombardi, reporters asking him before our first game, "Are you going to call plays for Sonny?"

Lombardi said, "If I haven't been able to convey to him what I want him to call in the game tomorrow, you should fire me as the coach right now."

It's not play calling that wins games. It's execution. You could call the worst play in the world, but if you convince the people that it was the right play and execute it, then it was the right play.

In 1957, my rookie year, I started four games and won three of them. The first game I played in, I called all the plays at the line of scrimmage against the Cleveland Browns and won.

I made $9,000 my first year. They wouldn't go to mini-camp for that now. Our training camp was seven weeks. Now they go two weeks. You didn't know if you were going to make the team or just be pushed by the wayside. You had to apply yourself and be fortunate enough to be with a team that needed you.

We played a preseason game against the Baltimore Colts and their huge defensive line with Gino Marchetti, Art Donovan, Big Daddy Lipscomb, and Don Joyce. Instead of looking where the defenders were before the snap, getting a pre-read, finding where to go with the ball—all I could see was those four monsters.

I went back to throw the ball and took off running around end. Marchetti or Donovan hit me on the sideline and said, "Let me tell you, you little frickin' green rookie: if you ever cross that line of scrimmage again, we'll kill you!"

In eighteen years, I never went back over there.

The Eagles had some real veterans like Chuck Bednarik, the great linebacker. The best advice he ever gave me was after a home game we played against the Redskins my rookie year. We were coming off the field at Shibe Park after winning the game, and Bednarik said, "Put your helmet on, kid!"

I put my helmet on, and people were throwing full beer cans at you. I was a rookie that just had a winning game. I said, "Geez Louise, what are they going to do when I lose?"

In 1961 we were playing the Dallas Cowboys at home, and I was introduced at Franklin Field [where the Eagles began playing home games in 1958]. I ran out on the field, and fifty-five thousand people booed.

The first play of the game, I threw a pass, and it was intercepted. In today's game a coach would have you run a draw play to get back in the game. As a quarterback calling your own plays, you couldn't start sitting on the ball and get afraid. You had to be aggressive.

I got back on the field, threw the ball on first down, and was intercepted. I'd been booed when introduced, my first pass was intercepted, and my second pass was intercepted. I'd been booed three straight times.

People started coming out of the stands and throwing things at the bench. The trainers got into a fight behind the bench because people were throwing stuff at us.

I could have just sat on the ball, but that's not trying to win. Before the third quarter was up, I'd thrown 5 touchdown

98                                    SECOND QUARTER

passes. I think about fifteen people clapped out of fifty-five thousand. [The Eagles beat the Cowboys 35-13 in week 11 of the 1961 season, propelled by Sonny's 351 yards passing.]

In the *Philadelphia Inquirer*, I said, "Let them boo. It motivated me." You had to take it that way.

Norm Van Brocklin came in '58. We only won 2 games that year. We also had a new coach, Buck Shaw, but I learned under Van Brocklin. He was a great tutor because I didn't have much experience dropping back to throw the ball in college. We went 7-5 in '59 and won the championship in 1960. I played a little, not much.

Van Brocklin taught me timing and looking defenders off. I used to stand right behind the huddle, watch what play he'd call, and watch him throw a ball. I'd get in and do the same thing, but it wouldn't work. I go, "What the hell is he doing that I'm not? I called the same play." Again, it wasn't play calling; it was execution.

I learned in a hurry. Van Brocklin left, and in '61 I threw 32 touchdown passes and for 3,700 yards.

Everybody says, "You had a quick release."

Well, let me tell you something: if you're not blocking people, you get rid of the ball in a hurry.

We played the Giants one day, and our tackle couldn't block Andy Robustelli. He hit me seven straight times. Andy was such a nice man; instead of blindsiding me, he'd say, "Look out, Sonny!" I'd turn, and then he'd hit me.

A lot of hits put your lights out. You got concussions. They didn't have to try to tackle you. It was open season back there.

I remember Ray Nitschke hit me one night, and all I was seeing was stars going off. In the huddle I ran a draw play, ran off the field, and took smelling salts to go out there for the next play. A coach calling a play, does he know you're banged up or your lights are out? He's calling a pass play that you're maybe going to make a mistake on.

When facemasks started coming in, I ended up playing with one bar for most of my career; then I may have gone to two bars. It was there for protection, for your mouth and nose. It's changed into a cage on the helmet. Unfortunately it's turned into a weapon, and the cage becoming a weapon has facilitated concussions.

How do people tackle in rugby? They tackle with their shoulders. How did we used to tackle in the old days? People tackled with their shoulders. What do they tell kids now? "Stick that cage right in the middle of his chest to hit him."

It's not a protection thing now. They use it as a weapon—and very effectively, I might add. What do you get? If you're tackling, you move your head up, stick it in somebody's chest, and you're getting neck injuries and concussions. Take those cages off, and people will have to start tackling with their shoulders again.

In 1969 Vince Lombardi became coach of the Redskins. I finally had a coach that knew what it took to win. I talked to Bart Starr, Paul Hornung, and Max McGee. They said, "You're going to love this guy." They were right; I did.

I remember the first day at practice. I threw the ball a couple of times, and Lombardi said, "You're throwing the ball too quickly."

I said, "Coach, I have to get rid of it quickly because I'll get hit. We don't have the best offensive line here."

He said, "Don't worry about it. We'll give you the best protection you've ever had."

We had a big year offensively. After the season was over, he sat with the other coaches, congratulating me. He said, "You completed 65 percent of your passes, had a hell of a year, and worked hard. Next year you're going to complete 70 percent of your passes."

I said, "Wow."

"You didn't even know the system well this year, and you completed that many passes."

I said, "Yeah, but look how many times I got sacked. You said I was going to have the best protection I ever had."

Lombardi said, "You knew the personnel better than I did." He laughed and walked out of the room.

I just wish I could have had him for a longer period of time. He had a system of throwing a ball where you never had to force the ball into coverage. You read the coverage and reacted to the coverage on pre-snap, as the ball was snapped, and after the snap. You always were going with the numbers.

Starr had told me, "You have such intense preparation each week that the games are fun."

I said, "What do you mean, fun?"

"They're fun because you're ridding yourself of all this preparation you've been through."

You had a notebook that you filled up each week. We had plays on the left hash mark from the minus 40 (your own 40) on first, second, and third down; on the 50; on the plus 40 (the opponent's 40). The hash marks were wider in those days, and you'd have the same thing on the right hash mark, but there would be a different group of plays on each down. Lombardi conveyed to me what he wanted me to do in all the given situations.

We had plays for what we'd do up to third-and-twelve. One game, I was sacked on second down, and it was third-and-eighteen. I got up thinking about what to call. I looked to Lombardi for some help. He turned his back and walked away.

When I got off the field, I said, "Geez, I'm out there looking for a little help. I had a play for third-and-twelve, but I didn't have one for third-and-eighteen."

He said, "Neither did I. Don't be looking for me."

He had a great sense of humor. Yes, he was tough. That's why he was successful. He was a great communicator and was able to convey what he wanted done.

Practices were an hour and a half, but if they weren't going right, he'd say, "Everybody in" and would send everybody off the field. He did it up at training camp up in Carlisle. We didn't know whether to get undressed and go back to the dorm or what. They said, "Just sit here in your uniforms and wait for him."

Lombardi finally came in and said, "We're trying to get ready for the season. We have to have good practices. We were not having a good practice today. We can stay here as long as you want to, but we *will* have a good practice today. Everybody back out there."

We started the whole practice over. That's leadership.

I learned what it took to win from him. He was a great coach, and I would have loved to have played for him for a longer period of time. There's no question we would have won, and he said the same thing.

Lombardi died in '70, and Bill Austin took over. George Allen took over in '71. George Allen had been the defensive coordinator with the Bears and stressed defense. There's nothing wrong with that, but Lombardi was just the opposite. It was difficult because I had just played for the best guy in the world for me personally. I was getting a guy who wanted to win games 14-10. It was a tough time.

In '72 at Yankee Stadium on our first third down of the game I took three steps, threw the ball, and completed the pass. I thought the official had kicked me, and I asked him why. He said, "I didn't kick you, Sonny."

They were in an under defense, and I knew the defensive end couldn't have got there in three steps. I took a step and I found out why. My Achilles exploded, and that was my year.

I don't know what they do for Achilles now, but they had to take mine apart. They took my plantaris tendon and tied it into it, which takes your calf away. You have no calf on your left side, but hey, you had to get it done if you wanted to ever play again.

It was a very long rehab, but it was my left leg. I wasn't pushing off on it. It was difficult, but look, when you start playing that game, from year to year your body continues to wear down.

I remember a young guard saying to me, "Boy, I'd love to play this game one time 100 percent."

I said, "Well, it ain't going to happen." [*Laughs*.]

I had twenty-eight operations. I have screws in both shoulders. It hurts to walk. It's better than the alternative; I'm on the right side of the grass.

We controlled the game, we called our own plays, and it was a game. In '61 I was making $14,000, when I threw 32 touchdown passes. Television has increased the salaries. It's a very popular game, it's well sold, and they do a good job of marketing. There were twelve teams in the league when I came in, and we got thirty-two now. It's big business.

It's very interesting to me that of the nine head coaches I had in eighteen years, the best coach was the one that simplified the game. You hear about today's seven-hundred-page playbooks and things like that. They're making it complicated.

But it's still blocking and tackling. The guy who simplified the game more than any coach that I played for was Vince Lombardi. Did he win more than anybody else? Yeah.

You know who did the same in basketball? Red Auerbach. He had six plays and won 11 out of 13 championships.

# 16

## Jim Taylor

Running back

Louisiana State University

Drafted, 1958 (Green Bay Packers, 2nd round)

Green Bay Packers, 1958–1966

New Orleans Saints, 1967

4-time NFL and Super Bowl champion (Green Bay Packers, 1961, 1962, 1965, Super Bowl 1)

NFL Rushing Leader (1962: 1,474 yards)

NFL Touchdown Leader (1961: 16 TDs; 1962: 19 TDs)

NFL Most Valuable Player (1962)

6 All-Pro seasons

5 Pro Bowls

1960s NFL All-Decade Team

Pro Football Hall of Fame inductee (1976)

I don't know why I didn't follow in the footsteps of my two brothers. I got an older brother that's a very successful attorney and developer and a younger brother that's a CPA. I ended up being the jock and finding some type of ball to entertain me. [*Laughs*.]

I was more of a basketball player in my early years. I lettered on the Baton Rouge High basketball team as a freshman and played some American Legion baseball. Really, football was my secondary sport.

Baton Rouge was my hometown, so I attended LSU. We played both ways back then. I had better games at linebacker than I did running the ball.

I got my degree at LSU in teaching and coaching, and I've

basically never used it. This is my profession, what I was put on this earth for: to be in the entertainment business, to be a fullback.

I was the fifteenth player picked in the whole country. My first contract was $9,500. That was the going rate when we played twelve games and six exhibition games.

We won one ball game my first year, the worst season in Packer history. We were in the outhouse; then we moved to the penthouse in a year or two, when we got into the championship games.

I wanted the football because I'm going to make you some yardage. I'm going to hit people, and we're going to win.

I deliver the punishment; I don't receive it. Picture this: I got the ball, going down the sideline, and a guy or two is coming on me. When it's time to make contact, I'm going to initiate the contact and thrust my strength into his strength. I'm going to initiate the contact because our team may not need but twelve inches, eighteen inches, or thirty-six inches. I'm going to drop down and get that yardage instead of receiving the blow. If I initiate the contact, I can get you this here, stay inbounds, bring the chains out, and—whoop!—first down. We keep going with the ball.

See, there's a mentality. It ain't just cut and dried. There's a lot more to playing this game. You have to be mentally tough as well as physically tough. It's high intensity and very complex. It's very difficult for average fans to comprehend that. I don't know of many writers that can put it into words.

Let me give you an example: You got seventy plays per game, and each one takes five seconds, some maybe three or four. The ball's set, Bart's getting ready to hike it—one thousand one, one thousand two, one thousand three, one thousand four—play's over with. Everybody's going back to the huddle or off the field.

Lombardi gets you excited, and during those few seconds you're exploding and just annihilating your opponents. It's a real condensed kind of explosion.

This is some of Lombardi's philosophy in his coaching: getting his players ready to explode, be excited, block people, and be aggressive within that four- or five-second interval. It's a game of contact played on those five-second intervals. Guess what those five-second intervals come to? About twelve minutes out of the three hours that you're out there.

Therefore, the game itself is only about twelve minutes of running time. You're only exploding and making contact for twelve minutes out of the three hours you're out there. You got to be so fit to explode and do these things, how can players get tired and not execute and not perform?

It's an intense game, and I loved it. You got to love contact and want to compete. I don't know if people can really understand that to the depth that it happens.

Here [points to head] and here [points to heart]! We're going to find out what you're made of and how bad you want it. This is why these people go to the Pro Football Hall of Fame, and these people are also-rans.

In your preparation you have to get ready for the different defenses that you're facing. You know probably what they're going to do. Once you get that, it's another complicated situation where each individual player has to be on that same page. The more you do these things, the more you do them right.

It's physical, and you can—boom!—get a concussion and be out for the rest of your life. You're exposed to some violent situations and conditions, and you just have to be the one that delivers and does the best job with the aggressiveness.

We've had a good number go to the Pro Football Hall of Fame: five [now six] on defense, five on offense, plus Vince Lombardi.

You have to look back and say everybody did their part, and everybody made a contribution to all these things that are so complicated on offense and defense. You look back and feel good about being successful in our field of entertainment and my career in the professional football business.

# 17

## Don Maynard

Wide receiver, returner, halfback, defensive back

Rice, Texas Western College (UTEP)

Drafted, 1957 (New York Giants, 9th round)

New York Giants, 1958

New York Titans/Jets, 1960–1972

St. Louis Cardinals, 1973

5 All-Pro seasons

4 Pro Bowls

Super Bowl champion (New York Jets, Super Bowl 3)

NFL all-time career leader, yards per catch (18.7; minimum 600
   receptions)

Retired as all-time leader: receptions (633), receiving yards
   (11,834), 100-yard games (50)

AFL All-Time Team

Pro Football Hall of Fame inductee (1980)

I played football as a freshman at Three Way High School,
located about three miles outside of Maple, Texas. I lived
about 13.5 miles from the school, but the bus route took me
45 miles to get there and back.

I played backup quarterback in six-man football. I might
have gotten into a ball game once or twice. I moved around
to other schools, playing as a defensive back and a halfback
on offense. You went both ways because they only had about
twenty guys go out for football.

I won the state championship in the high and low hurdles,
so I had track offers everywhere in the country. I chose Rice

to study petroleum engineering. After a couple of weeks I quit football because I didn't like the way things were going for me.

I went home five times that first semester. Five hundred and eighty-five miles on a Greyhound bus when they didn't have freeways took a long time getting home and a long time getting back. My brother kept after me about staying in school and said if I didn't like Rice, I could transfer.

A buddy of mine went to Texas Western College in El Paso. He worked it out with the football coach, plus I had a chance to go there in the first place. I got out there and roomed with my buddy, a backup quarterback.

I was a redshirt, so I had spring training for four weeks; then in the fall I had twelve weeks' training and the next spring four more weeks. I learned how to play football on the redshirt team. When I got eligible, I stepped into the starting lineup, playing both ways. Playing safety on defense was my claim to fame.

I played alongside Jessie Whittenton, who played nine years in the NFL and was an All-Pro with the Green Bay Packers. We never had one pass caught behind us. I later was voted All-Time Rocky Mountain team as a safety, along with the first defensive back ever drafted as the first-overall pick in pro ball, Gary Glick, from Colorado A&M [now Colorado State].

Although my claim to fame in college was defense, I was behind only Jim Swink of TCU in averaging 7.5 yards every time I carried the ball in college. I led the nation one year or tied for it, catching 11 passes, and 10 were for touchdowns. I averaged 32.5 yards per catch, and that's probably still in the record book.

The three years I played we did pretty good, and we won the Border Conference in 1956.

You drafted a player after four years from the time he entered college. Because I was a redshirt, my class was '57. The Giants drafted me, and then I played another year in college football.

I was just playing college ball and going to college. When other things happen, well, they happen, you know. After I finished my last year of school, I worked all summer doing plumbing work and some other things. I decided, "Well, I might as well go up there and try out." I went to Salem, Oregon, to the Giants training camp at Willamette. I said, "I got nothing to lose."

When I got to camp, there was a great guy from Texas who played at SMU named Kyle Rote. He told me if I studied hard and didn't miss any plays, there was a spot for me. A position was open for a kickoff and a punt return guy, a fifth defensive back, a running halfback position, and flanker and split end behind him. Rote said, "Just learn the plays, don't miss any, and you can make the ball club."

They just went from thirty-three ballplayers to a team roster of thirty-five. That worked out great in my favor, and as a result I was kept by the Giants as a backup running back behind Frank Gifford and a flanker behind him on the right side. I was also split end behind Kyle Rote on the left side, the fifth defensive back, and the number one kickoff and punt return guy. Besides Gifford, I was probably the most all-around ball player they had.

I probably learned more in the first couple weeks of pro ball than I knew in three years of college. I learned different coverages and how they related to doing a zone coverage or man-to-man.

We were the first team to ever beat the Cleveland Browns twice in one regular season, and then we tied Cleveland for first place in the Eastern Division. We beat them again in a playoff game for the outright Eastern Division title. We went into the ball game against the Baltimore Colts for the 1958 World Championship.

You had all the great running backs for Baltimore; a great receiver, Raymond Berry; and Johnny Unitas, one of the best quarterbacks to ever play. We knew we had our work cut out for us.

At the time you just played the game. We just played our coverage, whether it's man-to-man or what we called one-free or zone coverage. It didn't matter if we were playing the Colts or the Browns or anyone else. I was on defense, playing safety, and they were either going to run left, right, or up the middle. That's it. You got yourself set for that type of situation.

The championship wound up being tied at the end of regulation, and it was the first overtime game ever played. It made history in more ways than one, and as everybody always says, it was "the Greatest Game Ever Played." That's what they titled it; I guess that's what it became and still is. [The Colts beat the Giants 23-17, with millions watching on television.]

When the American Football League was founded in 1960, Harry Wismer owned the New York Titans, who later became the Jets. He got Sammy Baugh as head coach. I played against Sammy Baugh's Hardin-Simmons teams for three years in college, and he took me to the Blue-Gray game.

I gave Baugh a call. I said, "Hey, Sammy, I'd like to play for you."

I wound up being the first New York Titan ever signed to a contract. I told my wife, "Well, back to New York."

Since I'd already lived there with the Giants, we lived in the same hotel. The Titans played in the Polo Grounds—just across the river from Yankee Stadium, as they say up there. I only had two or three blocks to travel to Yankee Stadium when I played with the Giants. Now I got on a subway and made one stop across the river to play in the Giants stadium—the New York *baseball* Giants.

Yankee Stadium was a baseball field, and so was the Polo Grounds. The field was shaped like a horseshoe. When we got there, they had to do a lot of grass work and dirt leveling. We played there probably four years.

The first year Shea Stadium was built, they worked a contract out and we played at Shea. Comparing the Polo Grounds with Shea is like comparing an old car or an old person to a brand new car or a twenty-year-old person dressed up, you know. It was nice to play under brand new conditions.

I'd kept up with Joe Namath in college. When Alabama played Texas in the 1965 Orange Bowl, he had an outstanding day. When the organization drafted him, I thought it was great because I'd already played with over twenty-five professional quarterbacks in my career.

Because of his knee problems, Joe had them operated on prior to coming to camp. We knew when he dropped back to pass, he was going to pass. He wouldn't be running the ball like Fran Tarkenton.

Joe was a great listener. I told him I'd help him be a better quarterback and he was going to help me be a great receiver because we were going to talk on every play ahead of time in workouts. With George Sauer, Bake Turner, and Pete Lammons, we only had one busted play in nine years. After twenty-five quarterbacks, I was glad someone came along that listened to what I wanted to do.

I don't care what the defense does. If they don't adjust to the way we run our patterns, we're going to beat you. I taught Namath something that no coach, even in today's game, has ever taught a quarterback to do: read the defender! To hell with the pass pattern; just read the defender. Whatever he does, do the opposite.

It's like if he's going to walk through the doorway, you don't walk straight into the guy. He kind of goes to the left, you go to the right, and you both get through the doorway. Or like driving a car down the highway; if that car comes across that center stripe, you better get further over. [*Laughs.*]

It's real simple. Let's say you're going to run a hook pass; you run down ten yards and hook. If the linebacker is moving back underneath you and you hook, you either fly to the right or to the left. Kind of like a fish hook. You just don't stand there behind the defender and get covered.

Whichever way you move, Joe throws the ball the opposite way. The linebacker dropping back into the hook area can't get it. In fact I can throw the ball with my left hand and he can't get it.

When you work on your passing game twenty, thirty minutes every day in workouts, you get things down where it's real smooth. It's like if you're going to eat eggs. You put your fork in your eggs, bring it up, open your mouth, and put them in. It's that simple, but sometimes coaches make it real hard.

You see a lot of guys today reaching out when they don't need to reach out. About that time if the defensive back hits you, well, he's knocked the ball loose. I always jumped back into the ball or came back to the ball. That way you got both hands and your entire chest. With that surface area it's like having four or five hands. They ain't going to knock the ball loose, that's for sure.

We played the Raiders in the AFL Championship a few weeks after losing a lead to them late in the "Heidi Bowl" game. It's like what everybody always says: any game you've played has nothing to do with the one you're playing today. You got to go out there and do your job in your position as a player.

The Raiders were ahead in the second half. Earlier in the game I told Joe I had a long pass when he needed it. In the third quarter, going into the closed end of Shea Stadium, we were on about our 30-yard line. Joe threw the ball, the wind caught it, and I was running straight down the field.

We always had the terminology of catching it over your left shoulder at about ten o'clock. The wind was blowing so hard that when Joe threw the ball, the wind caught Joe's pass and took it around to eleven, twelve, one, and two o'clock. I went all the way around and caught it at two o'clock, going out of bounds on the 6 yard-line. It was about a 59-yard pass.

On a play like that you just keep your eye on the ball. I know the wind's blowing, but it was just like adjusting to anything. Like if you're mowing your front yard, you just run the lawnmower down to where the grass ain't cut. You don't need to go over where it's already been cut.

That play set up the winning touchdown. In the huddle Joe called a pass pattern to me, but when we went to the line of scrimmage, he checked off because they changed their defense. Joe turned and Sauer was covered, Lammons was covered, and Mathis was covered. I did a delayed route—one of those deals that you set up by working twenty or thirty minutes every day for years—and came back open. Joe drilled the ball to me, and I caught it for a touchdown.

You do the same thing over and over, and it makes it real simple. I can still call 60, 61, 62, 63, 64, and 65—all pass routes. When Joe checks off at the line of scrimmage to 62, you know what to do.

Forty years later I still know exactly what I'm supposed to do on a 62 route. The out end does a fish hook. The tight end does the inside release, whether it's zone or man coverage, and runs a post. I go down and do 10, 12, square in. If Joe sees it, he hits it in what we call the first lane; if the linebacker went real wide to the outside, then he hits me on the second lane. It's real simple. Some coaches make football hard.

We had the number one defense in the league in 1967, our Super Bowl year '68, and even in '69. Our passing game was as good as that of anyone that will ever play football. We had a great special teams group, including the No. 1 field goal kicker in the league [Jim Turner].

The newspapers said we were 16-point underdogs before Super Bowl 3. We wasn't scared of nobody. It was the media that made up all that garbage.

Half of us don't even read the papers. I could care less because nothing they say matters. You just go out and play the other team. Even though the Colts had won something like fifteen straight ball games, we just went out there and played.

Guys back then played hurt. That's just part of football. Today you got a guy who breaks his fingernail and has to take a day off. Jack Youngblood played for the Rams in the NFC Championship and Super Bowl 14 with a broken leg.

You just go out there and play. Sometimes nobody knows about it or much about it, anyway. I got hurt and didn't tell anybody dozens of times.

"Sunday everybody gets well" has always been a comment for the old guys that played football. You may hurt all week, but Sunday everybody gets well. Some people naturally don't if they broke something, but that's just part of life.

The guys of the past were good, classy ball players. You might have one or two in the entire league that ever got in trouble. I'm not pointing the finger at anyone, but it's a shame that some of those guys do what they do nowadays.

Then you got the showboat acts. A guy jumps up after making a tackle; everybody sees him doing his Hoorah Dance, but they don't show the five tackles he missed that game.

Back then you always had to work in the off-season. The first five years I was a master plumber. The next seven I taught school, and then I did my own propane conversions and auto air conditioning for vehicles [Don converted engines to alternative fuels and installed air conditioning years before automakers.]

You had to save all you could, and it's been a struggle for myself and a lot of other guys. It's really a shame that a lot of the old guys have a pension that is only $200 a month. They had a deal a while back, and only one guy in the entire NFL was willing to donate a game check to the dire need fund that Mike Ditka's put together called Gridiron Greats.

A year after I retired, I told people, "I'll tell you whether football was worth it."

My buddies were all head coaches, principals, and superintendents of schools and probably retired on $50,000–$75,000 a year. I got an NFL pension that's about $428 a month [pre-2011 Collective Bargaining Agreement]. When I got through with football, I was seventeen years behind all my buddies.

# THIRD QUARTER

*Players Whose Careers Began in the 1960s*

Pro football's popularity, aided greatly by television, multiplied in the 1960s. NFL attendance topped 3 million in 1962, 4 million in 1966, and 6 million in 1969. In 1966 over 2 million paying customers passed through AFL gates, a number the NFL took thirty years to achieve.

In 1961 the NFL returned to Judge Allan Grim's courtroom, bringing along its shiny new $9 million contract with CBS. The league hoped its new method of negotiating broadcasting rights jointly would fall within the legal boundaries of antitrust laws. Judge Grim nullified the contract on the grounds that CBS, rather than individual teams, would determine what games would be televised in each market.[1]

Congress soon trumped Judge Grim by passing the Sports Broadcasting Act. Signed into law by President Kennedy, the act awarded an antitrust exemption to professional sports leagues with regard to television contracts. The NFL and CBS drafted a new contract equally distributing over $300,000 to each NFL franchise.[2]

Meanwhile, the AFL and NFL hotly competed to sign draft choices. Many players, especially Joe Namath and Green Bay's Donny Anderson, benefited enormously. Beyond offering higher pay, teams attempted to protect draft interests by pulling underhanded stunts and hiding players.

As higher salaries cramped profit margins, the two leagues

agreed to merge in 1966. To exempt the new league's television contracts from the Sherman Antitrust Act, Congress passed an amendment to the Sports Broadcasting Act of 1961. The bill met resistance in the House of Representatives, where Representative Emanuel Celler again fought to ensure that the new league's antitrust exemptions were limited in scope.[3]

Public Law 89-800, a 1966 tax bill allowing accelerated depreciation on real estate, contained an unrelated provision amending the Sports Broadcasting Act of 1961. The section expanded the antitrust exemption to joint agreements involving two or more professional football leagues.[4]

The merger didn't take full effect until after the 1969 season, possibly due to the AFL's television contract. The leagues established a championship game that Lamar Hunt would name the Super Bowl and wasted no time in holding a combined draft.

The merger smoked out the competitive negotiating power draft choices used to earn higher wages. Management successfully regained its "Sign or you don't play" stranglehold on the American pro football labor market.

Johnny Lujack, the 1947 Heisman Trophy winner who quarterbacked Notre Dame to three national championships, signed a rookie contract topping out at $20,000 per year. Twenty years later many starting players still made thousands less.

### Pro Football in the 1960s Timeline

1960    Pete Rozelle, named NFL commissioner, signs three-year contract worth $50,000 per year.[5] NFL headquarters moves to New York City. Dallas Cowboys founded; Tom Landry becomes head coach. AFL begins play, creating job opportunities for hundreds of players. AFL minimum salary: $6,500. Average salary for American male professional and technical workers: $6,343.[6]

1961    Median salary for U.S. males with four years of college: $7,586.[7] Judge Grim again finds NFL TV contract in violation of antitrust laws.[8] Within ninety days Congress grants NFL partial antitrust exemption.[9] AFL attendance reaches 1 million.[10] NFL sells championship game rights to NBC at rate of $615,000 for each of the next two seasons.[11]

1962    Washington Redskins add African American players for the first time, becoming the last team to integrate. CBS pays $9.3 million to broadcast NFL games in 1962 and '63, although Carroll Rosenbloom complains his Colts will lose money on the deal.[12] NFL regular season attendance tops 4 million.[13]

1963    Pro Football Hall of Fame announces inaugural class of members, including Sammy Baugh, George Halas, Don Hutson, Curly Lambeau, and Bronko Nagurski. NBC pays $926,000 for rights to AFL Championship.[14]

1964    CBS renews television pact with NFL for $14 million per season; pays additional $3.6 million to televise next two NFL title games.[15] AFL signs $36 million contract with NBC.[16] Congress passes Civil Rights Act.

1965    Bidding wars between leagues continue. Joe Namath and Donny Anderson sign deals worth $427,000 and $600,000 respectively. NFL's New York Giants hire kicker Pete Gogolak away from AFL's Buffalo Bills. AFL counters by signing NFL stars Roman Gabriel, John Brodie, and Mike Ditka to substantial contracts.[17]

1966    NFL and AFL agree to merge; Gabriel, Brodie, and Ditka contracts voided afterward. Congress excludes new league from antitrust legislation regarding television rights.[18] NFL raises goalposts 20 feet above the crossbar. NFL attendance breaks 5 million mark; AFL, 2 million.[19]

1967    First Super Bowl held in January. NFL and AFL hold first combined draft. On December 31, the Green Bay Packers defeat the Dallas Cowboys in subzero temperatures in NFL Championship Game, often referred to as "the Ice Bowl." Packers later win Super Bowl 2 for third consecutive championship.

1968  NFLPA finally recognized as a collective bargaining group in twelfth year of existence.[20] Training camp delayed before NFL's first Collective Bargaining Agreement (CBA) reached. Minimum NFL salary: $9,000 for rookies, $10,000 for veterans.[21] Median income for U.S. males with four years of college: $10,866.[22] New pension plan takes six years of pro ball for player to qualify. Six-year veterans granted $7,800 per year at age sixty-five; ten-year veterans, $12,000.[23]

1969  NFL attendance reaches 6 million.[24]

## Notes

1. United States v. National Football League, 196 F. Supp. 445 (1961), Leagle.

2. "Will Operate in Red, Colts Claim: Owner Says New TV Contract Will Cause Team 'to Take a Beating' Next Fall," *Milwaukee Journal*, January 11, 1962.

3. "Celler Refuses Request to Ignore Merger Plans," *Spartanburg Herald*, September 9, 1966.

4. "An Act to Suspend the Investment Credit and the Allowance of Accelerated Depreciation in the Case of Certain Real Property" (PL 89-800, November 8, 1966); http://uscode.house.gov/statutes /1966/1966-089-0800.pdf; accessed September 12, 2013.

5. "Rozelle of Rams, Surprise Choice, Picked as Commissioner of NFL," *Milwaukee Journal*, January 27, 1960.

6. Bureau of the Census *Historical Statistics of the United States: Colonial Times to 1970*, Bicentennial Edition, part 1 (Washington DC: Bureau of the Census, U. S. Department of Commerce, 1975), G 374.

7. Claudia Goldin, contributor, *Historical Statistics of the United States, Earliest Times to the Present*, vol. 2, part B, "Work and Welfare" (New York: Cambridge University Press, 2006).

8. *National Football League*, 196 F. Supp. 445 (1961), Leagle.

9. WTWV, Inc., v. National Football League and Miami Dolphins, Ltd., 678 F.2d 142, U. S. Court of Appeals, 11th Circuit (1982), Open-Jurist.

10. NFL Communications Department and Seymour Siwoff, *2012 NFL Record and Fact Book* (New York: Time Inc. Home Entertainment, 2012), 534.

11. NBC Sports Communication Department, "The History of the NFL on NBC," Super Bowl 46 Media Guide; http://press.nbcsports.com/docs/history-of-the-nfl-on-nbc.html.

12. "Will Operate in Red, Colts Claim."

13. NFL Communications Department and Siwoff, *2012 NFL Record and Fact Book*.

14. NBC Sports Communication Department, "The History of the NFL on NBC."

15. "NFL Gold Rush Nets Another $3.6 Million," *Milwaukee Journal*, April 18, 1964.

16. NBC Sports Communication Department. "The History of the NFL on NBC."

17. Edwin Shrake, "The Fabulous Brodie Caper," *Sports Illustrated*, August 29, 1966.

18. "House Approves Pro Grid Merger," *Milwaukee Sentinel*, October 21, 1966.

19. NFL Communications Department and Siwoff, *2012 NFL Record and Fact Book*.

20. Tex Maule, "Pro at the Conference Table," *Sports Illustrated*, October 14, 1968.

21. "History." NFL Players Association official website, https://www.nflplayers.com/about-us/History/; accessed September 12, 2013.

22. Goldin, *Historical Statistics of the United States*.

23. Alfred Wright., "Owners and Players Fumble on in Philly," *Sports Illustrated*, August 3, 1970.

24. NFL Communications Department and Siwoff, *2012 NFL Record and Fact Book*.

# 18

## Carroll Dale

Wide receiver

Virginia Tech University

Drafted, 1960 (Los Angeles Rams, 8th round)

Los Angeles Rams, 1960–1964

Green Bay Packers, 1965–1972

Minnesota Vikings, 1973

3-time NFL and Super Bowl champion (Green Bay Packers, 1965;
   Super Bowls 1 and 2)

3 Pro Bowls

I grew up in the hills of southwest Virginia. The little townships had their population peaks from the late 1930s through the early '50s, when coal mines were hiring. We have several towns close together in the hills, little boom towns. They developed high school rivalries, and the closer you are, the more of a rivalry it becomes. I don't know if there's ever been a graduating class over two hundred in any of the schools; the majority would be less than one hundred.

My dad was a coal miner, lugging in low coal by hand with a shovel. No one in my family had ever played football, but in junior high I'd see the football team walking from their dressing room in the gymnasium to the practice field. I got to go to one game as a seventh grader.

As kids do, you play make believe. I started playing make believe football in the seventh grade. I didn't have a football, but I had Carnation condensed milk cans with both ends in them so you could throw them with a spiral. I'd throw, run, and catch—being both the quarterback and the receiver.

Eighth-grade football was the earliest organized football you could get involved in. I went out for the JV team in eighth grade and was an offensive tackle. The next year, I played JV and maybe dressed with the varsity in home games. As a sophomore, I became a receiver. My junior year we won our district championship and tied for it my senior year.

With my dad being a coal miner, I wouldn't have any other opportunity to go to college. If I could get a football scholarship, I at least could give it a shot.

At that time they did not have a National Letter of Intent, but the Southeastern Conference had a letter of intent. The first day of signing was December 7, and I played a basketball game on December 6. After the game I went out to eat with coaches from the University of Kentucky, Tennessee, and Georgia Tech—all three of them. I don't know who paid. [*Laughs.*] I might have paid my own. We sat and talked until midnight.

Tennessee was the closest to my hometown, about 150 miles away. At the time it was a three- or four-hour drive because we didn't have interstates. I signed at Tennessee, and they started talking about making me an All-American before I ever got there.

After signing, I visited Virginia Tech. Coach Frank Mosley said, "Son, we'll offer you an opportunity to get an education and an opportunity for you to play all the football you want to play." The message was that it was up to me. "We'll offer *you* the opportunity." At Tennessee the selling was, "*We're* going to make you an All-American."

Knoxville, Tennessee, was a pretty good-sized city even back then. The University of Tennessee was co-educational, and there were a lot more distractions or temptations, whatever you want to call them. We had some students from the area go to Tennessee and get into some trouble socially and academically.

Virginia Tech had two hundred females on campus with an enrollment of five thousand. The town of Blacksburg would remind you of one of those little towns I just described to you. It was a fit for me. I chose Virginia Tech.

Coach Mosley did not believe in freshmen playing on the varsity, but during training camp a receiver who might have been All-Southern Conference had a career-ending ankle break. Another experienced senior end had to pass one class in summer school. That gentleman went on to become a medical doctor, but he flunked the course to be eligible to play. Virginia Tech didn't have a lot of depth, so they brought me up from the freshman team as a backup before the season opened.

We played the opening game against East Carolina, and the left end in front of me sprained his ankle. The next game we're playing Tulane in the old Sugar Bowl stadium, and here I am starting right out of high school.

That was back during the time of the limited substitution rule. Limited substitution meant that if you came out during a quarter, you could not reenter. You played offense, defense, and special teams. I started my second game and played mostly sixty minutes in the next 38 games—pretty much my whole college career.

The limited substitution rule was done for parity so that the big schools with a lot of money wouldn't have a big advantage. They took it out in the early '60s. That enabled the schools with the most money to use the platoon system, and they've advanced that over the years to having people only play on 3rd and long and punt returns.

Playing sixty minutes definitely helped when it came to mental toughness. Back in our day the coaches had us going without fluids, especially during practice, which was part of working on your mental toughness. It would be very unusual to get any water, even at Green Bay. There were ice buckets around, and Coach Lombardi would turn his head at practice so you could get some ice to work on your cottonmouth. In college I remember sucking to try to get fluid out of my T-shirt under my pads.

That's one way the game's changed big time: the hydration factor. It's amazing that we didn't have more deaths in football brought about by head prostration and dehydration.

My first professional year was 1960. Just prior to that they had changed the rule against clotheslining, when a linebacker sticks his forearm up, bringing it around to hit the runner in his Adam's apple. It's just like running into a clothesline in the yard.

The rule change resulted from the 1959 College All-Star Game between the Baltimore Colts and the College All-Stars. A Colts linebacker clotheslined a running back named Don Brown, and Brown swallowed his tongue. If it hadn't been for the oral screw that opened his mouth, he would have choked to death because when you swallow your tongue, your jaws lock.

I believe a year or so before I turned pro it was still legal to grab the facemask. Another rule they had prior to my being involved in professional football was that the ball carrier had to be stopped and held down for a few counts, almost like college wrestling. Runners could crawl—even if they went down by contact—and move forward until the referees blew him down. If you look at old film, it's interesting to see that.

I was drafted by the L.A. Rams. A coach came by and told me that I was lucky to have the opportunity and whatever they offered me—with a big $500 bonus on top of that. My salary topped out at $8,000. That was the only offer, and I didn't ask for more. I love to play so much that if I'd had the money, I'd have paid them just for the opportunity to play.

It was in 1960 that the American Football League started, and I was also drafted by the team that became the Oakland Raiders [Minnesota's AFL franchise]. They never made contact.

The Rams had just made big changes in their organization because Pete Rozelle had just left for the NFL office as commissioner. Elroy "Crazy Legs" Hirsch was the general manager, and Bob Waterfield was the head coach. They had three owners who evidently fought among themselves.

The Rams had won the NFL Championship in 1951. At that time Crazy Legs Hirsch was a receiver, and Bob Waterfield was at quarterback. Instead of a championship ring those guys got a black watch. The title of the new staff was "The Return of the Black Watch." Hamp Pool, the head coach of that championship team, was our offensive coordinator. Don Paul, our linebacker coach, and Tom Fears, our receivers coach, played those positions on the '51 Rams.

They traded for guys like Gene Brito, who had been All-Pro with the Redskins. He was a defensive end and had a pose he'd take, standing straight up with his legs crossed waiting for the offense to come out. We had Les Richter, whom they had traded eleven people for. Ollie Matson was thirty-three years old and another guy they traded a high number of players for [9]. We had Bill Wade and Frank Ryan as quarterbacks. They traded Wade to the Bears and Ryan to Cleveland. Both of them won championships—Wade in '63 and Ryan in '64.

Deacon Jones and I were teammates. Deacon was a sprinter in college and would race anybody on the team, 50 yards for $5. I don't remember anybody ever beating him. Even Elroy Hirsch raced him one time, and I know he beat Elroy. Elroy was forty years old, but that's still pretty young in his day and time. I never raced Deacon because I didn't gamble, and a good reason not to gamble was if you didn't have $5.

I think they had plans to keep three wide outs. When I got there, they had Red Phillips, Jim Phillips, and Del Schofner. As we approached the regular season, Schofner pulled a hamstring.

I made the team and ended up starting the first game simply because Schofner got hurt. I caught five passes against the St. Louis Cardinals, and one of them was a one-handed, 53-yard touchdown.

Breaks and opportunities are really a big part of it. When you have opportunity and then have success, it gets attention.

Tom Fears decided after my rookie year—after Schofner pulled a hamstring and went through a spell of not being able to catch—to let Schofner go and keep me. Schofner went on to the New York Giants and made All-Pro, playing with Y. A. Tittle and in three straight championship games.

Bob Waterfield coached for about a year and a half and quit midseason. Tom Fears went to Green Bay. We had losing seasons all five years I was with the Rams.

In the spring of 1965 I was working during the off-season as a sporting goods salesman in a small town 150 miles from where I grew up. The coach from one of the high schools called early one morning and said, "Have you seen the Roanoke paper?"

I said, "No."

"Your picture's in it."

"For what?"

"You've been traded to Green Bay."

I said, "You're kidding."

That was the first I heard of it.

That's one of those things that you're jumping up and down about in my case. If you had picked a team that you would want to go to, it would have been Green Bay. They'd been world champions in '61 and '62 and just barely missed out on being in the championship game in '63 and '64. Plus it's a small city, so here comes that fit again. As a country boy, for me to go from L.A. to the smallest city in the league was perfect.

It was a situation where Max McGee was thirty-four, and at that time when you hit that age, they felt like your legs were gone. The Packers worked out a deal, trading a draft choice and linebacker Dan Currie for me. I loaded up for training camp, taking my whole family. I figured, "Hey, if you don't make it, you've had a vacation," because there's a possibility that you won't make the team.

To give you a little indication of the kind of people that were there, when we got to Green Bay, we didn't have a place to live, and we didn't have the technology where you can see what's for rent on the Internet and close the deal before you arrive. My wife and two kids moved in with Cherry Starr, Bart Starr's wife. They stayed there for two weeks with Cherry while we were in training camp. That was a very nice gesture.

I came in and got the Packers straightened out, and they moved from second in their division to being world champions. [*Laughs.*] Except one thing evens that story out: the Rams started winning after I left.

We ended 1965 tied with the Baltimore Colts and had to play an extra playoff game. The script was that Unitas was out, their second-string quarterback Gary Cuozzo was also out, and they're using a running back [Tom Matte] as their quarterback.

We start the game and a pass goes through a receiver's hands, and Don Shinnick for the Colts intercepts the ball and is running it back. Starr goes to hit Shinnick on the 1-yard line, gets injured, and goes out. All of a sudden the superstar quarterbacks are not a factor. Zeke Bratkowski, my former teammate in L.A., comes in. That was a hard-hitting game, and I believe Zeke also had to be replaced at one point for a series because he got hit hard in the head. In this day he probably wouldn't have reentered because they would have said he had a concussion. He did come back and play, however, and performed very well.

We tied the game at the end of the fourth quarter on a disputed field goal.

We ended up beating the Colts 13-10 in the second-ever NFL game to go into overtime. We listened to the Colts cry the entire off-season and absolutely heard all of it. The next season, the goalposts were extended another ten feet, and they put an official right under the goalpost to make sure we didn't have any more disputed field goals.

It so happened we played the Baltimore Colts very early in the schedule the next year. They did not whimper and moan that they were the better team after that game because we quieted them down. I don't remember what the score was, but we had an unquestionable victory [24-3 in week 1 of the 1966 season].

We played Cleveland in the 1965 NFL Championship at Lambeau Field. It snowed six inches. It wasn't extremely cold, but we ended up having a muddy field. It was Jim Brown's last game in the NFL. The Browns were reigning champions at the time. It was a close game, and we were very fortunate to win, 23-12.

The next two years, we played the Dallas Cowboys in the NFL Championship. Dallas had the high-profile offensive team, and we were one of the top defenses. In both games we were up 14-0 early, and something happened to have it close back up.

In the first one in Dallas they were coming back at the end of the game. Inside the 5-yard line, almost sure to tie, they had a motion penalty. We stopped them on a run attempt or two. Then Don Meredith's doing a rollout pass, and our linebacker, Dave Robinson, puts a great deal of pressure on him. Meredith throws off his back foot, and Tom Brown intercepts it in the end zone. End of game.

The next year was the Ice Bowl with minus 15 on the thermometer and a 55-below wind-chill factor. We're up 14-0 and Bart fumbles, and they get a score. Willie Wood fumbled a punt, and they picked up 10 points off of those 2 turnovers. I don't know how many times Bart got sacked in that game, but in the second half, bless his heart, he was hit a *lot*.

The great play on Dallas's part was running Dan Reeves to the left on a sweep before he pulled up to throw. When you look at the film, you see our defensive backs putting it in reverse big time because they're all coming to stop the run. Lance Rentzel catches that pass for a touchdown to put them ahead, 17-14. Finally we get the ball with time running out and a chance to win.

The Cowboys said they weren't going to get beat deep. Bart was able to maneuver and throw to the running backs. Boyd Dowler caught an intermediate pass for 12 or 14 yards, hit his head on that hard ground, and went out. Everything else was either a run or a pass to one of the backs or the tight end underneath. The guys made the plays and got it down to the point where Bart could run that sneak. We were very fortunate to win, and as somebody said in the highlight films, "It was very close to being the Tom Landry Trophy rather than the Vince Lombardi Trophy."

Anytime you have close games, it always enhances the program. Regardless of who your favorite team is, it'll at least keep you awake. Somebody's going to win and somebody's going to lose, and you kind of identify both ways.

We were very fortunate to be able to win all three straight championships. The Dallas games were great games that could have gone either way. The 1965 playoff against the Colts, that one could have gone either way too. If the referee had made the opposite mistake and called that field goal no good, game over. It wouldn't have been a tie, it wouldn't have gone into overtime, and the Colts would have won.

The championship games paid bonus money that I think had something to do with attendance. They were somewhere between $7,000–$8,000 and close to $10,000, depending on where you played. For the first two Super Bowls the winners got $15,000 and the losers made $7,500. Even after we'd won championships, guys were still working in the off-season.

Winning the NFL Championship and the Super Bowl definitely changed the pressure in the off-season. That was a chance to double your salary. I can assure you that you didn't get big raises like you hear of now, when people play up as free agents.

Negotiations in Green Bay were with the general manager, and the general manager was Vince Lombardi. After hearing stories from other people, it seems a lot of owners were difficult to deal with too. They tried to keep everybody low, and if you made any extra money, it was done through some kind of bonus clause. Some teams gave bonuses based on individual achievement, on whether you led the team in receiving or rushing yardage.

Coach Lombardi would never do that because that's individual. Coach Lombardi would say, "The only bonuses I'll write in are team bonuses: win 10 games, win 11 games, win 12 games." You had to ask for it, and you might have all of those and possibly a championship bonus in your contract.

One year I was negotiating with Lombardi and signed a three-year deal. The only bargaining point I could come up with was that I was the team chapel leader. Knowing he was a religious man, I said, "Coach, I tithe 10 percent to my church in Virginia. If you'll send my church 10 percent of my salary, I'll sign." Lo and behold, he agreed to that. What appealed to him was that the increase didn't show up in my gross salary at all. The Packers were making a donation.

Minnesota picked me up on waivers after Dan Devine became coach of the Packers and cut me. Vikings coach Bud Grant said, "What's this in your contract about sending 10 percent to a church in Virginia?" I told him the story, and he said, "We're just going to add that 10 percent to your contract and let you worry about it."

That's one example of how football has changed a great deal, in not only the volume of money, but also the fact that agents didn't really exist in our time.

I heard this after I got to Green Bay because it happened before I got there. Jim Ringo, the Packers All-Pro center, walks into Coach Lombardi's office and says, "This is my agent." They chat a minute, and Coach Lombardi excuses himself and leaves the room to make a phone call. Lombardi comes back and says, "Unfortunately, you're talking to the wrong team. You need to talk to the Philadelphia Eagles."

I mentioned that I signed as a rookie for $8,000. Later in my career high-end draft choices were signing for between $12,000 and $14,000 with bonuses as high as $3,000–$5,000. Things really took off with the Joe Namath, Donny Anderson, and Jim Grabowski deals, within that two- or three-year period. Then the AFL-NFL merger took place, and the idea of outbidding somebody didn't exist.

We became eligible to draw our pension at age forty-five. The talk was, "Football players don't live that long, so you ought to draw it at forty-five, invest it, and make money." That was bad advice because at fifty-five it tripled about every ten years. It would be at least $1,200 or $1,300 a month if you waited to fifty-five. If you waited to sixty-five, it would have been in the $5,000–$7,000 range.

At one point a few years ago we got a 30 percent increase. So someone making $300 might have gotten a $100 increase, and if somebody were making $7,000, he got a $2,100 increase. Then they had a ten-year payout, but when you took that payout, it was over after ten years. Then you had nothing, and 30 percent of zero is zero. There are at least two cases I know of like that.

There's no need to sit around and say, "Oh man, I was born too early." Be thankful for the opportunity you had and the fact that you got that opportunity. If you happen to be one of the lucky ones to win a championship, you're very fortunate because a lot of great athletes played for long years and never had the opportunity to play in a playoff game.

It's a team sport, and it takes everybody, every minute on every play. Coach Lombardi said, "It takes a better team to repeat as a champion than it did to become one."

You have to be able to win when you're not ready to play. I can tell you from experience that no matter how good you are, you can't just roll your helmets on the field and expect the other team to roll over. You had to fight. One of Lombardi's favorite sayings was, "Football is a game of inches." All of his speeches probably made the difference where our players reached down and got one smidge extra to get the job done. Which leads to another one of his quotes: "Lying exhausted on the field of battle, victorious, is a great, great feeling."

# 19

## Austin "Goose" Gonsoulin

Defensive back, returner

Baylor University

Denver Broncos, 1960–1966

San Francisco 49ers, 1967

AFL interception leader (1960: 11)

5 All-Pro seasons

5 Pro Bowls

AFL All-Time Team

First member of the Denver Broncos

I didn't like the name "Goose" at first. It started at Baylor University. We had a coach named Hayden Fry, who went on after Baylor to other colleges. My senior year, I was running a punt back, and he hollered, "Come on, Goose!"

I thought, "I hope that doesn't stick," because a goslin is a small goose.

I go in the dressing room and everyone starts calling, "Hey, Goose!" When I went to Denver, they asked if I had a nickname and I said, "No." I was running a punt back again, and one of the coaches hollered, "Come on, Goose!" and it just stuck. I'm proud of it now.

In high school I played both offense and defense. People didn't throw the ball much back then. The guy named outstanding quarterback of the league threw only 1 pass, and I intercepted it. I led the district in pass receptions with 12 but made 13 interceptions. One of my high school coaches wrote in the paper, "Austin could skip college and go straight to pro."

My family was real poor. We didn't have a car, telephone,

or a TV. Dad was a hard-working guy, but he just didn't make any money.

I got offered scholarships to Texas, LSU, Baylor, and others. When I visited Baylor, most of those guys wore blue jeans. At Texas they were dressed up. Well, I didn't have any dress-up clothes. [*Laughs.*] I had one pair of Levi's, and that was it. I chose Baylor.

When I was a junior, there was a guy that played for Rice University, All-American Buddy Dial. Before the last game of the season our coach said, "Goose, you're going to cover Buddy Dial. When we're on offense, he's going to cover you. The game's going to rest a lot on your shoulders."

I thought, "Thanks a lot! This guy's an All-American." [*Laughs.*]

I outdid him in the game. I had 170 receiving yards, ran a punt back, and really had a good game. Pro scouts were there, and the New York Giants drafted me. I wasn't eligible because I was a junior. I thought if I was drafted as a junior, I was really going to be drafted as a senior.

My senior year at Baylor, John Bridgers was the coach. The team elected me captain, and Bridgers asked the team to vote again because he didn't want me as captain. They voted again and kept me in. When we ended the year, I talked to Bridgers about pro ball. He said, "You might have a chance. Would you want to play in any bowl games?"

There was a new all-star game in Phoenix, Arizona, called the Copper Bowl. I went out there and got named the outstanding back of the game.

I was drafted by the Dallas Texans. A guy from the Texans took me out to eat and said, "We're going to offer you a contract."

I said, "How much is that?"

He said, "$8,500."

I said. "$8,500. . . . Hmm. How much are you going to give me tonight?"

He said, "I'll give you $750."

I said, "Okay, good!"

The Texans traded me to Denver before we ever played for an All-American from TCU named Jack Spikes. I think it led back to that Copper Bowl because Dean Griffin was part of selecting that team before becoming the Broncos general manager.

When I got to training camp, they only had three coaches. I had more on my junior high team. [*Laughs.*] And they didn't have any money. I thought, "This franchise isn't going to make it."

They must have had 125 guys show up when I got there, and 500 must have gone through that camp. Everybody that would get cut in Canada or the NFL was given a tryout. We had so many people come through that it would have been good to get hurt and sit on the sidelines until they quit bringing people in.

We started the season against the Patriots. They were a 19-point favorite because we lost every exhibition game. It was the first regular-season AFL game ever played.

I intercepted the first pass ever thrown in the AFL. At the end of the game the Patriots were driving, and I intercepted another pass, stopping them from scoring. We won the game after they thought we were that big of an underdog.

The next week I intercepted 4 passes and 1 the game after that. I had 7 in 3 games.

We came in the dressing room, and guys interviewed me. I said, "What's the record?"

"14."

I said, "Gee, I'll beat that, no sweat." But I didn't. [*Laughs.*] It kills me because there were a bunch of tips that I'd be so close to picking off and not get.

I ended up leading the league in interceptions with 11. That's still a single-season record in Denver. Steve Foley finally beat my career record by 1 interception, but he played in 150 games and I played 108. I wish they'd put a little asterisk by that like they did with Roger Maris beating Babe Ruth. [*Laughs.*] I retired with the most interceptions for a safety in AFL history [46] and got 5 interceptions in Pro Bowl games.

It's a mental game between you and that quarterback. The quarterback looks for the linebackers and the safety. Is the safety in zone coverage, man coverage, or is he going to blitz? You do a lot of moving around and faking him out. You can't use the same tricks every time because he'll figure that out.

If a guy's running a post pattern, I act like I'm staying on the other side of the field, helping the other cornerback. The quarterback will look at his receiver and check me out. If I'm not in the right position, they'll go ahead and throw the ball. That's where I could make up the speed, come over, and intercept the ball.

Quarterbacks try to read everything they possibly can. We played a home game against the Bills in 1960. They had a guy named Elbert Dubenion who was super fast. They put him in as a slot back, running deep patterns, carrying two or three of us that way. Their quarterback read that and threw to other players coming across because nobody covered them. Buffalo jumped on top of us real quick.

It was 38-7 with five minutes left in the third quarter. It started snowing, and there was some wind. The snow came down sideways, and it was hard to see. We were used to it. We'd practiced in the snow because they wouldn't cover the practice field.

Our quarterback, Frank Tripucka, could really throw. He and Lionel Taylor, a real good receiver, just caught on fire. The game ended tied at 38.

A lot of teams came into Denver and ran out of gas. They'd be sucking on that oxygen mask trying to get some air. I'm sure that's what happened to Buffalo.

A doctor told me that your blood has to change over, and it took 2–3 weeks to adjust. I used to go up a month early and work out. I'd be all in shape, go up there, and be out of shape.

We didn't have a good team when we first started. We were trying to build something, but the money was short.

Our dressing room was hardly nothing. We had four showers for forty players. We had to take turns taking showers. Instead of this big locker that you can stand and dress in now, we had two-by-fours, chicken wire, and a nail to hang your pants on.

Our general manager, Dean Griffin, was so tight, you never knew what he was doing. We scored a touchdown in the first home game, kicked the extra point, and the ball went into the stands. Griffin left the sidelines, went up, and took the ball away from a fan. He was booed, but he got the ball.

There was no job security whatsoever. They would cut or trade you and leave you in New York. If you didn't make that team, you had to fly back, get all your junk in Denver, and go home. All on your own money.

The two buses after the game would be loading up, and they would tell a player to get on the other bus because he'd been traded.

I thought, "What kind of life is this?"

We made a big swing up east my first year. I said to myself, "I ain't going to get caught on the road." I brought this big ol' suitcase so I'd have enough clothes to wear if they traded me. Dean Griffin said, "I don't know who the hell owns that big suitcase, but I've been paying extra money for that! Somebody's going to owe me!" I kept quiet.

The owners had the upper hand. If they decided to cut you, they'd cut you, and you couldn't go anywhere. If you were trade bait, they would trade you, and you might go somewhere you didn't want to live.

I was playing in the Pro Bowl one year, and the owner of the Broncos, Cal Kunz, came up to me and said, "I'm going to fire our coach, Frank Filchock, and I'm going to have to hire another coach. Do you know anybody?"

I said, "I know somebody real well. His name's Jack Faulkner. He knows the Sid Gillman system, the best system in football right now."

Cal said, "Line it up, and we'll go out to dinner tonight."

We went out to dinner, and they hired him. Faulkner got Coach of the Year his first year.

I figured when I went back the next year, I would get me a good contract out of that deal. Faulkner didn't give it to me.

I said, "Jack, you know who got you this job? Me."

He said, "Yeah, I know that. As a matter of fact, we just drafted some real good defensive backs," giving me a hard time.

I said, "I'm going to play out my option."

Playing out your option meant you'd play for one year at 10 percent less on the contract you signed the year before. Whenever you got through, you were not obligated to come back with that team. The only way you could become a free agent was to take less money. At the start of the next year you could sign with any team you wanted.

It wasn't a bad idea, but what happened is that nobody would pick you up. It was like they had an agreement. If they had a good player, they could hold his salary down. You tried to negotiate, but if playing out your option is your only course, what do you do? They can keep you at that same salary, or you got to take a 10 percent cut. If you get hurt, you're out.

In the Pro Bowl games normally all the conversations went toward salary and contracts. I played in six Pro Bowls.

The AFL Pro Bowls were really neat. I loved that game because you were playing with the best. You didn't make a lot of money, but it was really good to play in them, and people would watch you on TV back home. Getting elected to the Pro Bowl was a special thing back then.

I played in another exhibition game against Oakland at

the Los Angeles Coliseum. After the game was over, this guy comes into our locker room and says, "Hey Goose. Good game."

"Thanks."

He handed me a piece of chalk and said, "What's the hardest play for you to cover?"

I thought, "Somebody's up to something." I drew an easy play to cover.

Our general manager walks in and says, "Al! What are you doing in our dressing room? Get out of here!"

That was the first time I met Al Davis.

Al would do anything. He used to wet down the field inside the 20-yard line when we'd play in Oakland. His team would have their long cleats on, and we'd have the little short ones. It'd be a sunny, dry day, and I'd think, "Gall dang, it's wet down here." We'd pick about it, and somebody would say, "Oh, the sprinkler system is messed up."

"Yeah, right. I know who turned that spigot."

Al did a lot for the league and tried extra hard to win. "Win, baby, win." That was the kind of guy he was.

Sometimes Al'd call me in the off-season and say, "I'm making a trade with Denver. What do you think of this guy?" Hewritt Dixon was one guy he asked about. We had him playing at tight end. I said, "He's good, but I'd play him at fullback because he's one of the hardest guys I've ever had to tackle." Dixon ended up making All-Pro at running back in Oakland.

The most popular play back then was the post pattern, where the guy runs down about 10 yards and angles toward the goalpost. They tried to tie up the free safety and then run the post. If they could get that done, they could throw a long ball and score. The only way to prevent that was you couldn't let them get away with a lot of easy catches across the middle.

Don Maynard and I are good friends. One time he came to Denver, and we went out to eat Mexican food. I was so glad he was eating that Mexican food because I was going to pop him good in the game. [*Laughs.*]

He came across the middle, and I saw the quarterback throwing to him. I always tackled high, about in the chest with the helmet, and leaned on their body so their legs bent over. I did that with Maynard.

He was laying on the ground gasping for air. We were in the huddle and could hear him. They called time out and Namath hollered, "Maynard, get your butt in the huddle! What's wrong with you?" Maynard slowly got up, walked to the huddle. and said, "[Cough] Goose hit me. [Wheeze] Goose hit me."

Someone said, "Do you want us to get him?"

Maynard said, "[Cough] NO! He'll get me again! [Wheeze.]"

I was a pretty good size for a safety and really lowered the boom on some of those guys.

We were playing the Oilers and Billy Cannon, a Heisman Trophy winner from LSU, caught a little swing pass. I came running up, trying to hit him low and flip him up in the air. Right at the last minute I ducked my head, and his knee hit the top of my helmet.

All they had in the helmet were little cloth straps, with a round piece of sponge on the very top. That blow was so severe that it broke the helmet straps, and I swallowed my tongue. When you swallow your tongue, your tongue flips back and covers your windpipe. Our trainer was supposed to have an oral screw to twist your mouth open so he could reach in with rubber-tipped scissors, grab the tongue, and flip it out.

Well, we didn't have any of that. Our poor little ol' Denver Broncos didn't have hardly any medical supplies. The Houston trainer came over, backed everybody off, and said, "I'm going to break his teeth out with my scissors so I can reach in there and get his tongue."

My roommate was a big ol' guy from Texas named Bud McFadin. He pressed real hard against my jaw, my jaw opened up, and they got my tongue out. I was out for a long time and woke up in the hospital fully dressed in my uniform. I said, "What in the world happened?" They told me that story about swallowing my tongue and that they didn't have to break my teeth out with the scissors. I thought, "I'm so glad they didn't do that!"

That year three of us swallowed our tongue for the Broncos. One was a middle linebacker named Wahoo McDaniel from Oklahoma. He became a pro wrestler after football. Then there was a Jerry Tarr. He was going to be an Olympic hurdler, and they talked him into playing for the Broncos. We had a reverse on the kickoff, where a guy would catch it, go to the sideline, and Tarr would come around. A defender came along, put his arm out, and hit Tarr right in the Adam's apple. Tarr was still conscious and came running to the sideline going, "EHR! EHR! EHR!" They threw him down on the ground and got his tongue out.

Going into the 1967 season, I was All-Pro, captain of the team, and went back to Denver to play. They had a new coach, Lou Saban. We'd usually stay in a hotel in town before training camp. We were at the hotel, and some guy called saying, "You've been released."

I said, "Released? What are you talking about?"

"You've been cut."

I wasn't sure. When somebody just calls you on the phone, you don't know if they're pulling your leg. I got into my car and started driving. I was listening to the radio, and a guy comes on and says, "Well, we lost ol' Goose today."

Just la-la-la-la.

I'm thinking, "I've got a wife at home, two kids, and no job." I had a job in Texas that summer, but I quit it to come back to Denver for football. Lou Saban never said one word to me. It really hurt to leave Denver after all those good years.

When I got home I thought, "Man, I can't believe my career's over. I still got a lot of years left to play."

The 49ers called, saying they still had my draft rights in the NFL and wanted me to try out. I got on a plane and flew out there. It was down to three guys making the team, with two roster spots left. I was one of the three guys.

Coach Jack Christiansen calls us over and says, "You guys are going to run a 50-yard dash. I'm going to put whoever loses on waivers."

I thought, "Whoa. Talk about putting the pressure on you."

I won so I didn't have to worry, but they sent the third guy packing.

I was the first guy to go from the AFL as a starting player to the NFL as a starter. My contract was a couple thousand more with the 49ers than with the Broncos. I think I was around $25,000 by then.

The 49ers had John Brodie, who would fire that ball. He was a drop back, split-T quarterback. Playing in the Pro Bowls I saw a lot of great quarterbacks, and Brodie was equal to, if not better than, the others.

We thought we were going to win everything. Things didn't happen right for us, and we were 7-7.

We played the Minnesota Vikings that year, and they threw a pass to the tight end. The other safety caught and turned him, trying to get him down. I came across the weight of those two guys, hitting the tight end across the chest, trying to knock the ball out. A shooting pain went down my arm. I ended up injuring my neck. I missed two or three games and came back as a starter. I was tackling and hitting those guys just like I always did.

When I went back to play the next season, the 49ers told me, "You can't play because you hurt your neck."

"Hurt my neck? I've played seven games since I hurt my neck!"

They sent me home, and that was the end of my career. I felt like I could have played more, but they didn't do anything to check me out. They just said I was hurt.

I tried to get a job, but I had no skills; I wasn't a carpenter or plumber. I'd played football all those years while other people learned that stuff. Football was my vocation.

I should have got into coaching. We had a special teams coach, Ray Malavasi. I showed him the defensive side of things, and then he became head coach of the Rams. I thought, "I'd sure like to go out there." But anyway, that passed me by.

I did okay on my own after I got out in the public and started doing things. I had a construction company that had a little over 1,000 employees at times, and I had 390 full-time people working for me. I was also on the board of three or four banks.

I missed football, though. I still miss football.

After all that happened in Denver, they did me great. When Pat Bowlen took ownership, he started inviting us back. We play golf together, and we know the guys playing now.

In 1984 they had the original Ring of Fame, and Bowlen selected me. I thought I was a forgotten guy. All of a sudden my name's going to up there in the Bronco Ring of Fame.

I said, "I hope they put Austin Gonsoulin."

They put "Goose."[*Laughs.*]

It was right on the 50-yard line, so every time we watched the game on TV, we could see my name, "Goose Gonsoulin." That was a *big* deal. It was a thrill.

After all those years the fans have been so great. Every time something comes up, they vote for me. They selected a twenty-five-year team, and I made it. They just had a fifty-year team, and I made the second team.

Back then we weren't playing for money. It was really for the love of the game, and that's what I love about being recognized today after all these years.

Nineteen sixty was a long time ago.

# 20

## Dick Frey

Defensive end, offensive guard

Texas A&M University

Undrafted

Dallas Texans, 1960

Houston Oilers, 1961

AFL champion (Houston Oilers, 1961)

I grew up in San Gabriel, California, before they had organized Little League and stuff like that. We were very involved
in our neighborhood playing football as kids. We organized
our own teams and played different neighborhoods. We didn't
have any coaches; we were kids organizing our own league.
My brother and I had a good buddy up the street who used
to play on those neighborhood teams, and sometimes his
dad would play with us.

I really looked forward to playing football in high school.
In California they took your age, weight, and height and
gave you certain points for each. If you didn't have many
points, you would be classified as a "C." If you were bigger,
you'd be a "B," or else you could be on the varsity. If you
were varsity size but weren't good enough, you might play
on the JV.

My high school career was very disappointing. Because I
was small, I was a C the first year and didn't play. The next
year I was still a C and was going to be a starter. The morning of the first game they double checked my heart because
I'd shown that I had a murmur. Then they told me I couldn't
play. That was my first two years of high school. The next

year I was a B, and I played one play. My high school career ended with me playing junior varsity football as a senior.

California had a good junior college system. I didn't get a chance to play in high school, but I decided to try playing in junior college. The first year, I was on the junior varsity at Pasadena Junior College. The next year, I was on the varsity, my first varsity experience. I played a lot but wasn't a starter.

I transferred to Texas A&M and was ineligible for one year. The first varsity game that I ever started in my life—at any level—was with Texas A&M in 1951. We went out to the state I grew up in and beat UCLA, 21-14. That was real exciting to be back home and starting my first varsity game of all time.

I lettered at A&M for three years. I was primarily a defensive lineman, playing tackle or defensive end. We didn't have a championship team, but it was fantastic.

I went into the air force and was stationed in Germany. Football was a big thing in the service. I don't know how many bases have teams now, but then it was a big morale thing not only for those playing, but also for the people on base going to the ball games. We had a base commander who really wanted to have a good football team, and we won the European Air Force Championship in 1953 and 1954.

When I got out, I coached high school football in Kaufman, Texas. When I was in high school, not many coaches thought weight training for football was good, thinking it made you muscle-bound. It was really coming in when I was coaching during the '50s. I wished I had been lifting when I was playing.

While coaching, I learned things about football that I wished I'd known when I was playing. I wanted another chance to play. When the American Football League organized and prepared to have a league in 1960, I thought, "I'm going to see if I can get myself ready."

I went into the Dallas Texans office to get a tryout. Well, they weren't very interested in a guy who hadn't played in six years. Normally they would sign you to a contract contingent on making the team, but they wouldn't even do that for me. I kept going back in there; I went four or five times. All I wanted was a tryout. One day I decided they were either going to kick me out or give me one. Finally they gave me one.

They had a tryout camp before their main training camp. There were thirty or forty people in that tryout camp. They sent nine or ten of us to the regular training camp, where they had maybe sixty-five players and kept thirty-five or forty. I was fortunate enough to make the team. They gave me a shot to play, and I appreciate it. It wasn't a championship season, but we had a good season.

I was really going to work to get better in the off-season, but in working out I messed up my knee and never let it fully heal. When the next season came along, it just wasn't going quite right. Coach Hank Stram called me in during the final cut and said, "Dick, it looks like that leg's not going to get well. We're going to have to let you go."

I went down to Houston for a sales job I worked in the off-season. The leg got okay after a couple weeks because I hadn't been working out. I talked to the coach of the Oilers, and he said, "We'll put you on the cab team." The Oilers went to Boston and played to a tie, leaving a 1-3-1 record. The coach got fired, but I stayed. [*Laughs.*]

The new coach was Wally Lemm. Since I could play defensive end or offensive guard, I think they thought they could keep me as a reserve at those positions and keep another quarterback or something like that. Just the chance to get picked up again was fantastic, and then we started to win. I was getting to play, though I wasn't a starter.

Our quarterback was George Blanda, and our running back was Billy Cannon, who I believe was the highest paid player in the league. I made a little more with the Oilers than my league minimum $6,500 contract with Dallas.

We went out to California and beat the Chargers in the AFL Championship Game. It was very exciting for me to go

2. Dick Frey is all smiles remembering the 1961 Houston Oilers championship.

with a championship professional team where I wasn't even able to play high school football. My buddy and his dad that I played neighborhood football with were both there for the championship game.

I forget exactly what our winner's share was, but it wasn't very much. [*Laughs.*] I wasn't making very much anyway, and it did not double my salary, but it was great to be a part of it, and we got rings. Mine got stolen when my house was robbed about ten years ago. I lost my college ring and my Oiler championship ring. The other day I was thinking it'd be interesting to go to a ring person and see if they could get the official okay to make a duplicate to pass on to my grandkids.

My first year as a pro, 1960, was a big year for me personally. I got to play a year of pro ball, and I also met my wife on a blind date in March. We married in June. Between then and the time that would have been my third season, she got pregnant twice, but both pregnancies ended in miscarriages.

I signed with the Oilers again for what would have been my third year, and she got pregnant again. I thought, "Son of a gun, with her losing two babies, I don't want to start football and then for some reason get cut and picked up by somebody else with her being pregnant." I didn't go back for that third year. I wasn't going to take a chance on getting cut because I wouldn't leave her pregnant to go someplace else. That ended my professional career, but I got a couple of good years and a couple of good memories in that.

My wife and I had a daughter. She's married now, has three kids, and was a missionary in Ethiopia for twenty years. We also had two boys. Both of them were good high school football players. One played quarterback at Wheaton College, a small Christian school in Illinois, and the other captained Army's football team.

I saw my B team coach, who had only played me in one play, at a high school reunion. He came up to me and said, "Boy, have I ever heard it about not playing you on the B team when you ended up playing professionally." I said, "Coach, on our last day of practice you got us all together and made the statement, 'Some of you haven't played as much as you think you should have, but if you keep trying and never give up, you'll make somebody's team someday.'" I told my coach that helped me all my life. It certainly helped me in my football career, but it's helped me in everything else. There's been a whole lot of things that I tried in life that I didn't succeed in at first. Whenever that happens, I think, "I'm on the B team, and coach says, 'If at first you don't succeed, keep trying.'"

I thanked him for that and then he thanked me for that. What that does is prepare you for life. I can quit or keep going. I just think, "Hey, this is just like hanging in there in football." Whether it's sports or some other area of life, things don't always go right, but you start over.

A couple of thoughts: Playing and succeeding in football is not the most important thing in life, but if it's your dream, hang in there. However, don't expect success in sports to be the most fulfilling thing in life.

I'm just going to throw this in, and you can use it as you want to: it's my understanding that a person's relationship with the Lord is the most important thing in life, and that does not invalidate their ability to play sports or do anything else.

If that's in the right order and your dream is to play football—or your dream is anything else—if at first you're not successful, hang in with your dream. To me that's one of the great advantages of competitive athletics. A lot of people that aren't sports enthusiasts don't realize that kids get a lot more from playing sports than the game itself.

Success doesn't come automatically to everybody, but some guys are successful right from the start. But you know something? The guys that were always first string from the time they put on a pair of pads, then went all the way through college, made All-American, and then turned pro without having to face some temporary setbacks—they weren't quite as ready for setbacks when they happened.

I lost my wife two years ago. That's the biggest setback of my life, but I had to trust the Lord when I got a setback in football, and I've had to trust the Lord when my wife died.

The setbacks in football set the stage for me to be able to hang in there, and it's helped me all my life.

[*Laughs.*] In a football game, when you get in in the fourth quarter, you know how many more minutes you have. When you get into the fourth quarter in life, you don't know how many minutes you have. At eighty-two years old, I know I'm in the fourth quarter. I don't know if I'm in the two-minute zone or just starting. Like in football, wherever you are, you keep going.

# 21

## Irv Cross

Defensive back

Northwestern

Drafted, 1961 (Philadelphia Eagles, 7th round)

Philadelphia Eagles, 1961–1965, 1969

Los Angeles Rams, 1966–1968

2 Pro Bowls

Co-host of *The* NFL *Today*, 1975–1989

I'm from Hammond, Indiana, not too far from Northwestern, in Evanston, Illinois. When I was getting ready to graduate from Hammond High School, almost every major school of note had some interest in me. Northwestern was high on our list because it's a private school with a strong academic reputation. That's what I was primarily concerned about. I didn't have any vision of being a pro football player. After meeting Head Coach Ara Parseghian, I was convinced Northwestern was the place I wanted to go. He made quite an impression on me with his desire to build a winning program and his concern about the kids coming in.

I got a first-class education. Working with that kind of pressure in the classroom was a good experience. I captained both the football and the track team and was elected to a couple of honorary societies. The thing I learned more than anything else was to work hard. When you work hard at what you're doing, you have a good chance of succeeding.

Pro football then wasn't as highly successful as it is now. Many people who played pro football did it as an afterthought. You played a couple of years, went to graduate school, and got a job someplace else. You used football as a stepping-stone to get to where you wanted to go.

I was ready to go to graduate school when the Philadelphia Eagles drafted me. They were defending world champions. I told them that if they felt like I wasn't going to make the club to cut me right away because I had to get back to school in the fall. They thought that was kind of odd, but that was my intention.

I wound up making the team. I had a $10,000 contract, which to me was all the money in the world. We always wanted to make as much money as we could, but playing and being part of the game meant a great deal to us. Playing was always the primary focus.

As an African American, I was treated differently in this country. That was the time we lived in. Before a division title game against the Giants, a guy sent a threatening letter to me. He called himself "the Eagle Eye" and said he was going to shoot me. We had things like that happen. As sad as it is, it was commonplace.

The guys who played ignored that. The feeling we had was let's do the best job we can, and hopefully it will open doors for others. I don't think kids today understand that we went through an awful lot of pressure.

This was the time when Martin Luther King was doing his marches, and a lot of ballplayers were involved either actively or quietly. You had to be because it was a movement that impacted the entire African American community, and there was no way you could say no. All of us were involved in some way with civil rights issues.

Dan Reeves and I went to Vietnam together as part of the USO program after meeting on the 1965 Pro Bowl team. It was a trip that you just don't ever forget. We spent seventeen days in Vietnam and visited several fire base sites and a lot of hospitals. Some of the guys wrote us and said how much they appreciated our being there and appreciated that we would take that risk. It didn't seem like much of a risk to us because we were only there for a short period of time.

In 1966, the Eagles decided to trade me, and there was nothing I could do about it. I went to the Los Angeles Rams. I knew Rams head coach George Allen from college, when he was on the Bears coaching staff. The Bears used to work out at Northwestern on bad weather days. Allen indicated that if he ever got a chance to get me as a player, he would. After he landed his first head coaching job with Los Angeles, he traded for me. That meant a great deal, and I appreciated that.

We had a real good defense, featuring the Fearsome Foursome of Deacon Jones, Lamar Lundy, Merlin Olsen, and Rosey Grier. Roger Brown came in later. It was an awesome front four, and I don't think anyone's ever had a better one.

The pass rush sets everything, even today. If the quarterback has five seconds to step up and throw, he can do that in his sleep. If he only has a couple of seconds with someone in his face, that's different.

We relied heavily on our front four. They always put pressure on quarterbacks, leaving them little time to throw. That allowed us to be particularly aggressive in the secondary because we didn't see multiple fakes from receivers very often. Guys broke out of their patterns right away to look for the ball. We knew that and could react even quicker, trying to get there before they did.

When I retired, I had a chance to join the coaching staff in Philadelphia. I ended up being a player/coach because I thought our secondary wasn't as sound as it could have been. I played that year and then finally retired before coaching another year.

I was invited to take a job with the Cowboys. Tex Schramm wanted to know if I'd be interested in working with him because they were building a new stadium in Irving, Texas. He was going to spend time with the stadium corporation and wanted me to help run the team as assistant to the president. I thought about that and said I didn't know if I wanted to do that.

Then Tom Landry called, came out to Philadelphia, and met with me for a long time about joining his coaching staff. Landry was a terrific man, a devout Christian with a great sense of fairness, and well-organized. That year he hired Mike Ditka and Dan Reeves. I would have been on that staff with them if I'd taken Tom's offer to work in the secondary for the Cowboys. I would have loved to work for Landry, but the opportunity with CBS came up.

I had been a stockbroker for a number of years while playing. I was the first black vice president of a major Wall Street firm. I advised banks, insurance companies, and mutual funds on running their equity portfolios.

I had a major decision to make because CBS gave me an opportunity to work as a game analyst for a couple of years. Then they said they wanted to start a new show called *The NFL Today* and wanted more of my time. I told my partners on Wall Street that I was leaving for a couple of years to do some television work and would come right back. Well, twenty-one years later.... [*Laughs.*]

I made many, many, many times more money as a broadcaster than as a player. The difference was night and day.

In those days you had to be a broadcaster before you joined a network. The network didn't bring a guy in just because he was a personality. Today I think personality almost overrides your ability to be a broadcaster. We were all broadcasters when we joined CBS. I had been on the air for a number of years in Philadelphia, both in radio and television. My show was the highest rated show in Philadelphia. That's why CBS invited me.

We had a lot of fun on *The NFL Today*. Everybody came in with the idea of trying to make the show as good as we could make it. Pumping our own egos wasn't important to us. We reported. You just didn't wing things and sing things off the top of your head. If Tom Landry did something and I reported it, it actually happened. I had it verified and had probably talked to the player directly involved. Today I hear, "I think this and I think that," but I don't see much reporting.

There were things I was aware of and didn't report because I thought they were personal and had nothing to do with the game. That's changed, and guys are now cautious about what they say around people.

Phyllis George didn't know an awful lot about football, but she added a lot of spark. Without her I don't know where we'd be today with female sportscasters. She came in at a time when women weren't on the air, particularly covering pro football, and did it magnificently. We always felt like she added a perspective we couldn't.

Brent Musburger and I had attended Northwestern at the same time. I didn't know him when I was there, but he covered the Northwestern sports teams—including the ones I was on. He went on to a radio show in Chicago and then went from WBBM-TV to *The NFL Today*. He's a great broadcaster, works hard, and is always well prepared.

From what I knew about Jimmy "the Greek" [Snyder], he was an honest person. If he gave you his word on a handshake deal, you could bet that was going to happen. He was a very loyal person that way. As a former player, I told him that we could talk about everything except football. We never really talked about what we thought about games. I felt a little uneasy, to be honest, having somebody on the show with a gambling background. The league always was pretty hard on that.

Jimmy once had a run-in with Phyllis George when Phyllis was dating John Y. Brown, whom she eventually married and who became governor of Kentucky. Because of that debate, Phyllis didn't want to be on the same set with Jimmy.

They set up a separate area for the Greek. You might remember him standing at a board with Brent, and they would check off various categories previewing games. It was in the studio but away from the set where Phyllis, Brent, and I would normally sit. As it turned out, it added a better dimension to the broadcast, and it wound up being a better show. [*Laughs.*]

Somebody asked the Greek a question about Afro-American athletes, and he said they were bred to be stronger by slave owners. I was later told that he saw that in a *Sports Illustrated* article, and that's what he was trying to recall. In any case he got a very bad reaction. I think the reaction was bad because it was in Washington DC, and it was the weekend of Martin Luther King's birthday. The comments hit the air, and he was pulled off.

It really hurt him. After he lost his position with CBS, he had a newspaper column that didn't go very well, and there were some other issues. I really felt sorry for the Greek. I would call him once in a while to see how he was doing, and he couldn't believe what had happened to him. His whole life was sports, and all of a sudden the rug was pulled out from under him. I always said that the Greek died of a broken heart. It's too late now, but I thought he wasn't given a fair chance to express what he really was saying. I understood it; he and I talked a great deal about it. The thing just seemed like a snowball going downhill, gaining its own momentum, and you couldn't stop it.

Life for me today is good. I've been blessed in so many ways you cannot absolutely believe it. All my life I've been a devout Christian, and sometimes I've been on the right side of that and sometimes not, but I've always tried to stay on the right side of it.

I get a pension from the NFL once a month. I've been talking to an awful lot of retired players about their situations, particularly in the area of concussions, and how they're being treated with that. It's a real problem. There are a lot of great guys struggling through no fault of their own, just because they got their heads smashed playing football.

Retirement issues didn't get resolved with the new Collective Bargaining Agreement [2011]. They didn't even come close. The thing that hurts more than anything else is that they signed this huge ten-year contract, and with a little bit of effort they could have resolved a lot of problems for retired players. I'm reading every day about guys making $100 million contracts, and some of the greatest guys I know gave everything they had to this game and are not benefiting from any of it. I just hope that there's a resolution, and that the active players today—or players ten or fifteen years from now—realize that one day they too will be retired players.

When we played, if you were good enough, you would be with one team your whole career. That was your home, your family. It was important to be a Minnesota Viking, a Philadelphia Eagle, or a Dallas Cowboy because you represented something—not only your family, community, or team, but also something beyond the sport itself.

To have people today look at those players and say, "We don't care about you," hurts. Without that effort, without the Johnny Unitases, the Jim Browns, the Don Merediths—without all the people who came through this league and gave what they had to it—it wouldn't be what it is today.

# 22

## Garland Boyette

Middle linebacker

Grambling State University

Undrafted

St. Louis Cardinals, 1962, 1963

Houston Oilers, 1966–1972

2 Pro Bowls

If I wanted to get an advanced education, I certainly had no money to pay my way. I needed an athletic scholarship. My nephew, Ernie Ladd, convinced me to check out Grambling. Of course once you talk with Coach Eddie Robinson, the deal is done.

Coach Robinson made every kid that walked on campus his kid. A lot of the kids didn't have father figures in the home, and he tried to fill that void. Before practice every day it was like a roundtable discussion. Everybody gathered round on one knee, and he was in the middle of it. He gave the rundown of everything that was against his philosophy.

"Boyette! [Coach Robinson would say]. I got a call from Dr. McNeill. You didn't go to his philosophy class today."

We had some veterans from the military who would smoke. "Lee! Did I see you walking around campus smoking today? That doesn't look good for athletes."

It went way, way beyond football. He worked the hell out of you on the field, but there were other issues this man addressed and not just with his own players.

A lot of kids at other schools were kids he just didn't have a slot for. He was always available and open to dialogue with other coaches' kids. It was a way of life with him.

My sophomore year we had the worst record in the history of the school [4-6 record]. The student body and alumni wanted to tar and feather us.

Grambling was probably one of the last schools in the country running the single-wing, where you had an unbalanced line and a wing back. The tailback in the formation was actually your quarterback and took a direct snap. Kind of like what they call the wildcat now.

After that losing season, a lot of us moaned and groaned about the single-wing. Coach Robinson got wind of it and met with most of us individually. He told us he was making big offensive changes in the spring. We then went 9-1. He merely balanced the line, made a quarterback out of the tailback, and ran the same damn plays. [*Laughs.*] It took us a whole season to figure that out.

He had speaking engagements all over the country. People wanted to know what he was doing. I understand that he'd give them this whole spiel. At the end he'd say, "Oh, by the way, we just evened the line, put the tailback under center, and ran the same plays." [*Laughs.*]

He would get into your head and never said anything profane besides "hell" and "damn." He always had an open ear. Some of us called it "ear hustling." I remember we lost a game, the only one we lost all season. He heard a couple of us talking about the loss and came by. He said, "If you'd just listen to me a little bit, you'd learn something. You know, football's pretty simple. If you don't let them score, son, hell, you can't lose."

If you don't let them score, no, you can't lose! It's *obvious.* [*Laughs.*] He walked off and went about his business, but we thought about it for thirty minutes.

Robinson would explain that football is just like war. In most cases if you outnumber your opponent at the point of attack, there's no reason why you should lose that battle. We had great athletes, but I think we were smarter than most

3. Garland Boyette enjoys discussing Coach Eddie Robinson.

of our opponents because of his philosophy and thought. He also would say, "Something's wrong if there's that big of a difference between college-aged kids. My eighteen- and nineteen-year-old kids should be as good as the next guy's eighteen- and nineteen-year-old kids."

He had his ways of keeping you in line. We had one linebacker that was always asking questions. The defensive coach would be up at the board, and this guy would ask, "Why do this and not that?" I guess the old man had heard enough. Coach Robinson went up to the chalkboard, called the linebacker up, and said, "Okay, put up the defense you think we should run."

The kid drew his defense—a blitz as I recall. He clobbered the offensive play.

Coach Rob said, "You do a very good job. You put your defense up, and now I'm going to put my offense up and attack it."

He drew his play up and scored a touchdown. He told the kid, "You know what happens up here? The last damn guy with the chalk wins the ball game." [*Laughs.*]

There's rarely a day that we don't say something about Coach Robinson. If ex-players get together, the conversation always starts and ends with something about Eddie.

I played on some pro teams that I don't believe could have beat that team we had in 1960. Willie Brown, a Hall of Fame defensive back, was our tight end. Ernie Ladd played tackle, and I played guard next to Ernie. Lane Howell, who played with the Eagles, played center. My two backups played in the NFL. Jerry Robinson, one of the greatest athletes to ever come along, was drafted by the Bears and the Chargers. Then you had Preston Powell and Jamie Caleb, who played with the Browns. Off that team I think seventeen guys wound up playing pro ball.

We didn't have the opportunity to go to other schools. The Big 10 and the Pacific Coast teams could only take in so many kids from their own regions; they couldn't handle every black kid from below the Mason-Dixon Line. We weren't eligible for bowl games or the national championship. Most of us measured ourselves when we got to camp and competed against guys from other schools.

Among ourselves we would actually laugh. "Wait a minute. This guy's a two-time All-American? He probably couldn't have made Grambling's team." At one point Grambling had more guys in the pro ranks than anybody. It was a tradition that we stayed ahead of the game in getting our kids into pro football.

Eddie had big contacts. Before the AFL came along, he was already sending kids to the NFL. He liked the old National Football League versus the upstart American Football League and preferred his kids to go NFL.

He would have pro players come back in the spring and assist. Willie Davis and Emlen Tunnell worked with us. Tunnell didn't go to Grambling, but he was a good friend of Eddie's and a teammate of Willie's. My sophomore year, Tunnell stood behind the defense, telling kids how they should handle things. One time he said, "Boyette, get over here!"

I came over to him and he said, "See what that guy's doing? I noticed you earlier, and you did this instead, which I liked." He talked four or five minutes before sending me back. He said—it scared me to death—he said, "I'm going to tell you this, and if you tell anybody else that I told you, I'm going to say you lied and I didn't know anything about it. You could play in the NFL right now." I liked to drop dead. He then said, "If you tell anybody else I told you, I'll deny it. You're about the third person I've ever told that to."

I grew up in a pro football environment. My brother was one of the Oakland Raiders' first signees, and my nephew Ernie and I grew up across the street from each other. I really didn't think too much about it. If it happened, it happened, but it never was one of my priorities.

I wasn't drafted. I got letters from just about every team in the league. It came down to dollars and cents. I think I turned Green Bay down because of a $500 difference in salary. The Cardinals sent me this letter that said to call this particular person if he wasn't at the airport to pick me up at a certain time. I flew into O'Hare Field for training in Lake Forest, just north of Chicago.

I got there and waited for the trainer. I was talking with three or four of the guys in the area they told us to go to. It built up to six or seven guys, and they were obviously veterans.

I asked one of those guys, "Where are all the rookies?"

He thought it was pretty funny and said, "Rookies reported here two weeks ago." [*Laughs.*]

Here I am a free agent, don't know what the hell I'm going into, and now I'm two weeks late to camp. But that's what the letter said.

The draft choices and veterans stayed in an air-conditioned dormitory. The rest of us, about twenty or thirty, lived across campus in a fraternity house without air conditioning. We named it the "Longshot House." I was the only one who made the team out of the Longshot House.

The big thing that most of us from small schools were up against is that we rarely played the same position that we played in college. I was a lineman in college. The Cardinals said they were going to play me at fullback and then at tight end. Out of the clear blue they said, "We're going to make a linebacker out of you."

I had never played a down at linebacker in my life. I had to learn how to play linebacker in a month's time during the preseason. It's hard because you had to compete with people who played all their lives at one position.

It was a blessing in disguise in a sense. A lot of the guys that played linebacker in college were uncomfortable when they had to get down in a three-point stance and rush. Whenever it came time for me to put my hand in the dirt, I felt right at home.

We had to grab the coaches' attention, and things to do were passed down to kids coming into the league.

In camp we had what we called a "blitz pick up." The linebacker lined up on one side of the ball, and the blocking back would line up on the other. The coach blew the whistle, and the running back would pick up the blitzing linebacker, one-on-one.

Every team has a superstar. All the running backs lined up behind each other, and all the linebackers would line up behind each other. If their star player was number three in the line and I was number five in the linebacker line, I'd move up to number three and beat the hell out of him.

One running back told me after practice, "Rookie, let me tell you something. You don't beat your teammates up like that. We're going to see if you make this ball club." [*Laughs.*]

I stopped doing what I was doing, but you had to get their attention. When the regular season came, I was a starter.

During that time you only had thirty-some players on a roster. You had to have a roommate, and if you were black, you were usually cut if you were the odd man out. In most cases they kept an even number of blacks on teams.

St. Louis was a bad scene. The climate wasn't right. Anybody who was with the Cardinals at that time could tell you about the meat man. This guy had connections to getting meat that he sold to the players. He refused to sell meat to the black guys. That type of thing.

There were a couple of very liberal white guys on the team, and it was a joke to them. [*Laughs*.]

"Hey Boyette, the meat man's coming tomorrow. You got your cooler?" They knew that if I'd approach the meat man, he'd say, "This guy placed an order two weeks ago, and I'm just delivering. I don't have any extra."

My first year, we played Green Bay in Miami. You knew growing up in the South that everything was segregated, but you didn't expect the NFL to be segregated. We're not talking the Stone Age here—it was 1962. We were on the plane heading to Miami. About thirty minutes out of Miami, the road manager passed out hotel room keys. Well, no black guys were getting any keys. He came back after giving out the hotel keys and gave each one of the black players a car key. Somebody got up and said, "You guys don't know about this, but we stay in one hotel, and the white guys stay in another."

"What?"

"When we get on the ground, they'll show you to your rental car. An escort will show you to the hotel where we're going to stay."

It was so funny, the defensive coordinator, Chuck Drulis, always made bed check. I called Chuck from the hotel and said, "Hey Chuck, what time are you going to make bed check over here?"

He said, "I'm not coming across that track! Just show up to the stadium on time tomorrow." [*Laughs.*]

This gets even funnier. This was the dawning of radicalism as far as the philosophy that young guys were thinking. We got together—Bill Triplett, Fate Echols, and a couple of the other young guys—and said, "If they pull this crap again, we're not going to participate. This is the end of this."

The car rental place must have lost a ton of money. Guys gave away batteries, spare tires, any accessory they could get out of the car. They left keys in the cars and said, "Hey man, you can have the car if you just want to drop me off at the airport." That was the last time we played under those conditions.

I was the first black man to play middle linebacker in the NFL. Many people think Willie Lanier was, but I played before he did.

I experienced racism from fans, players, and teammates. I got hate mail. As a matter of fact I still got a few letters stacked away somewhere. They'd make comments like, "Who do you think you are telling someone else what to do? Are you the head of the forum now? Some white man of substance should be playing there."

One black guy came to me and asked, "Do you think you're smart enough to play that position?"

I said, "They have you brainwashed also."

I made myself smart enough because I studied film. I studied the playbook inside and out. I could tell any of the other ten players on the field what he was supposed to do on any given play.

You have your game plan and learn the tendencies that you're going to be facing. By the time Sunday gets here, it's just a matter of refining what you already know. You might see a few wrinkles during the course of the game, but you'd be crazy to abandon what you do best.

That's what a lot of players forget. Teams do what they do best. I'm not going to rip my playbook apart and start doing something different than what I've done since training camp. The Packers are going to run that Green Bay sweep until the end.

You have a defensive coordinator calling the defense, but 90 percent of the time you're going to wind up changing it because of what the offense shows you. When they break the huddle, you know right away if you have a bad situation called from the sideline. The offense will show you something different, and you get the secondary, linebackers, and defensive line adjusted. You might not get the right play, but you'll know whether they run or throw the ball in that situation by the mere fact of down and distance. What do they do on a 3rd and 10? What do they do on a 3rd and 2?

In St. Louis I kind of got a reputation for being hard to deal with, and I probably was. I never got in anyone else's face, but I'm not going to be sitting here as a free agent with a No. 2 draft choice sitting on the bench, playing behind me, making three times my salary. Fix it, and fix it now. If you don't want to fix it, get me out of here.

I probably was in a scrap every other day with somebody. If I deemed you came after me wrong, I walked around with a chip on my shoulder. It was the only way I could survive.

I ended up one of the last cuts St. Louis made before the '64 season. I knew that teams would want me on the taxi squad, and I had contacts. I knew Bud Grant at Winnipeg and Jim Trimble at Montreal in the Canadian Football League. I got on the phone, and two hours later I was on a plane headed to Montreal. I doubled my salary when I went there. Plus it was 25 cents on the dollar more in Canada, so I more than doubled my salary. [*Laughs.*]

I got there one day and played a game the next. I hadn't had a chance to read the rules; I was trying to learn the playbook. We punted the ball to the opposing team. The returner took three steps and punted the ball back to us. I thought, "What the hell is this?" Our guy received the ball, took a few steps, and punted it back. I just stood there in one place and watched them exchange punts.

Coach Trimble yelled, "Boyette, you better run or you're going to get killed out there!"

The opposing team was trying to kick the ball through the end zone to score a "rouge," which is one point. We were punting it back trying to keep them out. Some of the best punters I've ever seen were in the CFL.

They didn't have a retirement plan in Canada. After playing two years up there and two years in the states, I would have only needed one more year to get a pension if I had stayed in the states. I said, "I'm going back."

There were some good stories in the Canadian papers about how I left the CFL. I went back up there having already signed my contract with the Oilers. I got to Montreal thinking, "I got to get out of here some kind of way. I hate to do this, but I'm going to create an atmosphere where they'll have to let me go."

On that first day I said, "I'm not going to go in until I sign a new contract."

They said, "Okay, sit down and we'll talk about it."

I was already making a decent salary for that time, so I told them to double it. I knew they weren't going to go for that.

They said, "Wait here. The owner lives in one of the western provinces."

They called him on the phone, came back, and said, "We're willing to meet you halfway."

I said, "All or nothing."

They called the owner again and said, "Okay, we're almost there. We're willing to give you what you want. Can you give us a break on some of it?"

I thought, "This is not working out."

I started cursing and screaming like a wild man. I hate to say it because it was so out of character for me. The secretary said, "What's going on in there?"

I said, "I'm tired of this! I'm not going to be caught up in this crap!"

A coach came in and said, "What's going on in here? We got secretaries around here. You can't be cursing and doing these things."

I said, "If you don't get the F away from me, I'll throw your ass off the second floor!" I grabbed him, and the secretary ran out of the office. I was bluffing like the dickens.

The coach said, "We're going to suspend you."

I said, "You do that."

I went back to the dormitory. After about an hour I heard this voice at the end of the hall: "Mr. Boyette, are you in your room?"

"Yes."

"Mr. Boyette, would you come out?"

I said, "Yeah, I'll come out. What do you want?"

"This is the Royal Mounted Police. You have to leave the country."

He quoted me some stature, Canadian law.

"When do I have to leave?"

"Right now!"

These two mounted police in their Smokey the Bear hats escort me down, and everybody's looking at me wondering what the hell's going on.

I got my things in the car and said, "I'll be heading back to Texas. I'll just cut across to Windsor and Detroit."

"No. You have to go to the shortest border, down to New York."

I said, "It doesn't make sense for me to go that way."

"I'll tell you what. You just leave the country and get the hell out of here as fast as you can, any way you can!"

That's how I bluffed my way out of Canada.

I did my thing for eight years with the Oilers and had a good time in Houston. I'm from Orange, Texas, originally, so it was just like being at home. I made two All-Star games with the Oilers and made life-long friends with Elvin Bethea,

4. Garland Boyette stands in the three-story home he designed and built himself.

Kenny Houston, and Zeke Moore. We had some decent teams, and we played on a couple of dogs too.

The atmosphere with the Oilers was a lot better than it was in St. Louis. I guess times had changed, and you had guys that were a lot more liberal. If the atmosphere had been here like it had been in St. Louis, I would have gotten out lickety-split.

Now they're realizing all those concussions we had are going to catch up with a lot of us. I don't know anybody who played middle linebacker that didn't get a lot of concussions. I'm yet to be in a position where I feel like it's really getting to me. I do forget things here and there, which I guess we all do when you get to be in your seventies.

Life's been good after football. I retired from Southwestern Bell quite a few years ago after a good career with them. Now I'm enjoying time with my wife and working in the yard. I have a couple of grandkids, and I enjoy them. I run down to the casino every now and then.

I think I had a good career. I made a lot of good friends along the way. I didn't get rich or anything, but I made a decent living. The big thing right now is that I'm enjoying life.

I think that's the fruits of what we all strive to say or do—being able to enjoy people and not walk around mad at the world. The world is what it is. If you contribute your little five-cent or ten-cent piece to it, I think we've all done well.

# 23

## Mick Tingelhoff

Center
University of Nebraska
Undrafted
Minnesota Vikings, 1962–1979
5 All-Pro seasons
6 Pro Bowls
240 consecutive games (third-most all time)

I grew up in Nebraska and went to the University of Nebraska. Right before the 1962 draft, a Viking coach came out. He said, "No one has you on their draft list. If we didn't draft you, would you sign with us as a free agent?"

I said, "Sure. I'll sign with whoever offers the most money."

I think I signed for $18,000. I drove to Minnesota from Nebraska for training camp on my own dime. That was 1962, and the Vikings started in 1961. I made the team and started at center right away.

We didn't have our own stadium back then. We played in the same stadium as the Twins. If you played in November and December, you had a chance to play in the snow. We played games that were below zero.

The most popular defense was the 4-3, with two tackles, two defensive ends, a middle linebacker, and two outside linebackers. There would be an over defense and an under defense, so there were about three defenses. If your tight end is on the right, you're strong right. In an over defense, everyone to the right would have a defensive guy over him in that situation. The defense would have more people on the left side in an under defense.

I played seventeen years and didn't miss a game. I was pretty lucky. No one's really hitting the center. They're trying to get away from you to get to the ball carrier.

I usually blocked the middle linebacker. There wasn't a lineman over me trying to hit me with his elbow. That's what they did: whack guys with their elbows. They could also head-slap you. They didn't do that to me much because they knew they'd get hit back.

The Chicago Bears weren't a very good ball club, but Dick Butkus was a very good middle linebacker. He would call me a few names. That was typical of what went on between the center and the middle linebacker. Officials would step in and tell us to knock it off. We'd wait for a while, and we'd start up again.

Before the game the officials always told everybody what you could and couldn't do. Any swear words, you're out of the game. They'd kick your ass out in a second if you said something. If you swore or said something to them, they'd say, "Say another word like that, and you're out of the game!"

If there was a fumble, the officials would be there right away and you couldn't jump on the guy because you'd get called. A lot happens in a fumble pile. [*Laughs.*] You do anything you can do to get the ball. *Anything.* You have to be careful because there's an official coming. You couldn't punch the guy because the official's there.

We didn't win any of our four Super Bowls. We beat the teams before and we beat them after, but that day we didn't. It was just a regular game for the players anyway. For the fans and television it wasn't, but for the players it's just a regular football game. They just got bigger and bigger every year. Super Bowl 11 was huge.

If you don't win the Super Bowl, you don't want to remember anything. I don't anyway. You gotta win.

I played 240 games, so that's a long time. You kind of know when you can't do the things that you used to do when you were young. You're always talking to the general manager and the coaches. I just said, "I've had enough," and retired.

I spent more time with my wife and kids. Life's been good to us. We still live here in Minneapolis, just about a mile from where we did when I was playing. A lot of teammates still live around here. Dave Osborne and Bill "Boom Boom" Brown live here. Milt Sunde, the guard that played next to me, also lives here. We get together once in a while and tell stories and all that BS that goes on among the players. [*Laughs.*] There's a lot of it when just the guys get together. When our wives are with us, we're pretty straight. My wife and I also get together with Stu Voigt and his wife every once and a while.

I get my retirement, and I don't even know how much it is, to tell you the truth. When we played, we always tried to save money and make investments. Most of the guys on our team would talk about it once in a while. Everybody knew they couldn't play forever. They tried to live a normal life, didn't blow money, and saved as much as they could. I worked as a stockbroker early in my career, so we're fine. It seems like all the old teammates are doing fine.

It was a good time. We didn't win the Super Bowls, but you had to play two games to get there, and we won those games. It would have been nice if we had won at least one Super Bowl, but we didn't, so what do you do? Enjoy it the best you can.

# 24

## Lee Roy Jordan

Middle linebacker

University of Alabama

Drafted, 1963 (Dallas Cowboys, 1st round)

Dallas Cowboys 1963–1976

Super Bowl champion (Dallas Cowboys, Super Bowl 6)

1 All-Pro season

5 Pro Bowls

My three older brothers played high school football in the little south Alabama town I grew up in. I naturally wanted to try whatever my brothers were doing.

I attended a small, Single-A school where you went into first grade on one end and you graduated out the other end at the twelfth grade. It was all in one building.

I got the opportunity to play before one of Bear Bryant's assistant coaches my junior year. I had a better game than the player they were scouting on the other team. He [the assistant coach] came over after the game and said they'd be back to watch me the next year. They came to every game my senior year in high school.

I didn't have a lot of college options, but back in those days, most people didn't have very many. It wasn't like they recruited you all across the nation like now. We didn't even know what airplanes were back in those days, so I wasn't flying here and there to visit campuses.

I had a chance to go to Southern Mississippi, and some other teams were interested, but once Coach Bryant offered me a scholarship to Alabama, I was hooked.

I still believe in his teachings today. He's got about ten items that he tells you to watch out for. If you have lazy people on your staff or as part of your team, get rid of them. People who won't look you in the eye and don't tell you the truth, people who don't have integrity, and people who don't work for the team and want all the credit for themselves—they're never going to be successful in a team concept. All businesses are a team concept.

I still look at those ten items every once in a while, just to refresh my memory and to make sure I'm still doing those things. I had them framed when I left Alabama and carried them in my offices. My office burned down seven or eight years ago, but I had another laminated sheet made up. I wasn't going to be without his words of wisdom.

There were two drafts back then. I was drafted in the first round by the Cowboys [NFL] and New England [Boston, AFL]. I just felt like playing with Coach Landry, and I wanted to play in the NFL. I also didn't think Boston's cold weather would be a very fun thing for a south Alabama kid.

The Cowboys started in '60, and by '65 we were very competitive. The first few years we were not a good team, but Coach Landry was adding the parts that were going to make up our run of being in the playoffs seventeen out of eighteen years and 5 Super Bowls.

In '66 we played Green Bay in the NFL Championship and should have beaten them. We played them again in the Ice Bowl in '67, and we also should have won that ball game. If it'd been on a normal field in normal conditions, we'd have won the ball game. No doubt in my mind. We also lost twice to Cleveland in the playoffs.

We came back in '70 in Super Bowl 5. We ended up giving it away to the Baltimore Colts, having four turnovers on offense. They kicked a field goal at the end of the game to win. The next year we came back, committed to winning the Super Bowl, and won. We finally got that jinx off our back.

The Cowboys and Redskins had only been playing three years when I got there. It hadn't been a rivalry then because we hadn't won anything. We weren't competing for their position in the NFC East.

When George Allen came to the Redskins, he made it very easy to be mad at the Redskins and compete against them hard. He made light of the Cowboys, but I think we got even with him on the tail end of that deal. We became so-called "America's Team," and they became the team that lost to the Cowboys on Thanksgiving Day every year. [*Laughs.*] But it was a tremendous rivalry, and it still is a strong rivalry.

As the defensive captain and middle linebacker, I thought utilizing all of our players was the most important part of my job. The coaches gave me the flexibility of being like a coach on the field. When I saw something from studying films, I'd recognize that we would have a better chance being in a different defense versus the one we had called. I audibled and put guys in position to make plays. I took pride in that and in knowing offensive sets. If the offense had any kind of tipoff, I would tell our linemen what was coming.

I would call whether it was a draw or screen because I recognized it before the snap. I would tell Bob Lilly, Jethro Pugh, and Larry Cole, and they knew how to play that instantly. It was a great feeling for me to be able to help other people play to their best and make plays for our team. They'd come back to the huddle and say, "How did you know that!?!"

I said, "I've been studying film! I learn those things. I look for them."

I studied quarterbacks, and during games I got to take some chances that turned into big plays a number of times. Ken Anderson up in Cincinnati—I guess I put myself in a position to play well against him because in one quarter I intercepted three passes and ran one of them back for a touchdown.

When I think of Tom Landry, I think of all the multiple formations in football now. Tom wasn't the inventor, but he was the one that took and put them into his offense every game. Every play was three wide receivers, men in motion, with an unbalanced line. He, Don Meredith, and Bob Hayes really brought change to the NFL. They forced teams to go from man- to-man coverage to zone coverage, trying to keep somebody back there deeper than Bob Hayes was going to be. Hayes could run about a nine-flat hundred-yard dash. The "World's Fastest Human" is what he was, and his Olympic record was not broken for many years.

I watched the Hail Mary pass from Roger Staubach to Drew Pearson, near the end of the 1975 divisional playoff at Minnesota, from the sideline. I was probably the first one out on the field, racing all the way to the end zone to help Drew and us celebrate the win. It was an unbelievable catch. Drew caught it between his forearm and his hip and then brought it into his hands. That was about as exciting as you can get in football. On the sidelines our jaws were hanging down thinking we were going to lose. Then we got the play that made us believe in winning games in the last two minutes. It made us believe in our quarterback and our offense a whole lot more.

Today I'm doing great. I'm fairly healthy, but I've had both knees replaced. I also need a shoulder replaced so I can't do weight exercises like I would like to do. But I've been very lucky to be healthy.

I stay active and walk a lot. I try to do an hour or an hour and fifteen minute walk at a time, four or five times a week. Mine is not a lollygag or slow-paced walk. Anybody walking with me, they're going to have to have a pretty good pace.

Our guys were so loyal to our team and worked so hard together. We had the best guys in the world as far as quality of people, and we also had the best players that you could ever hope to play with. People like Bob Lilly, Dave Edwards, Chuck Howley, and D. D. Lewis are super parts of the Dallas legacy for future Cowboy teams to try and perform up to that level.

# 25

## Tony Lorick

Fullback

Arizona State University

Drafted, 1964 (Baltimore Colts, 2nd round)

Baltimore Colts, 1964–1967

New Orleans Saints, 1968–1969

I'm from Los Angeles, California, born and raised. Right in front of my house, we'd play football, basketball, and baseball and run track in the streets. We went from the streets to recreational playgrounds and started playing organized sports and dancing. Anything they could teach you to keep you off the streets. They don't do that for kids today.

I'm exaggerating, but I got a thousand scholarship offers. I considered West Point until they said I had to take more chemistry, so they were out. The Naval Academy thought I needed more math, so that was gone. [*Laughs.*]

I didn't want to go to UCLA because they played a slow brand of football. USC was the powerhouse at that time, and a friend of mine was a coach over there. Did you ever hear of Al Davis, the owner of the Raiders? I knew him when I was in high school, and he was a coach at the University of Southern California. They recruited me, but I didn't want to go there. At SC, all the guys from my area were sitting on the bench, and I didn't want to be a part of that. I wanted to go to the University of Washington in Seattle. They treated a fullback right and let you run the football.

I went to the University of Washington, stayed two weeks, and it rained every day. I called Arizona State and asked,

"Does that scholarship offer still stand?" They said, "Yeah," and tried to offer me some other little funds, which, by the way, I'm still waiting for. [*Laughs.*]

I went to Arizona State and that was probably the best decision I could have made as far as college. I played for Frank Kush, a tough-minded guy.

Charley Taylor and I played in the same backfield. He was the halfback, and I was the fullback. Pro scouts weren't allowed to come on campus unless you started with Coach Kush, and he didn't want you to touch any of his players if they were still in school.

I had no idea that the Baltimore Colts were interested in me. Later on Kush told me, "They've been watching your games, watching you practice, seeing what kind of individual you are."

In 1963 they had people they called babysitters who would "babysit" you so you wouldn't sign with another team. The first time I got wind of the Colts was when their babysitter showed up.

I was drafted No. 1 by the Raiders and No. 2 by the Colts. I would have been Baltimore's first pick, but Al Davis circulated a rumor that I'd already signed with him. The Colts came back to see if I was available in the second round after I proved to them there wasn't a contract out there.

In those days they had all-star games you would play as a senior: the College All-Star game in Chicago, All-American Game in Buffalo, the East-West Shriners Game in San Francisco, the Senior Bowl in Alabama, and the Hula Bowl in Hawaii. Al Davis was coaching in the Senior Bowl, and I thought, "He's setting me up. He wants to get me to Alabama to try to change my mind about the Colts." I didn't go to the Senior Bowl.

I finally showed up at training camp after the other all-star games. I'd heard stories about the old-timers and what they did to rookies—you know, like make me dance in a hula skirt or something. It never happened. Maybe it was because I was so late to training camp.

I played my first game against the Pittsburgh Steelers in Canton, Ohio, in the Hall of Fame Game. It was the last preseason game before the season started. Head Coach Don Shula turned around and said, "Lorick! I want you to go in." As I'm running into the game, he says, "Don't mess up."

I went into the game and scored two touchdowns, 40 or 50 yards a piece.

We lost our first regular season game in 1964 to the Minnesota Vikings. I ran the ball one time and gained 11 yards. After that we won 11 games in a row and were considered one of the greatest teams ever assembled. After we got beaten 27-0 in the 1964 NFL Championship, you never heard that again. We played the Cleveland Browns, and their split end, Gary Collins, scored three touchdowns. Jim Brown had a good day. He didn't score a touchdown, but it was nice to see him run.

Shula wanted to call the first 6–12 plays, which was unheard of. We were great when Johnny Unitas called the plays. The first half dozen or more plays, Shula wanted to pass. We felt that we should have run the ball more. The wind was running at 10–15 miles an hour, and it felt like 10 below in the old Cleveland Stadium. Not doing what we normally did during the season, we got beat 27-0.

Most of the guys had jobs in the off-season. I sold beer for the National Brewing Company in Baltimore. We sold National Bold, National Premium, and a malt liquor that wasn't famous yet called Colt 45.

Guys were teachers or sales people. Even guys like John Mackey worked in the off-season, just like I did. Unitas might have been making about $100,000—a lot of money at that time—so he didn't need to work in the off-season. The rest of us were making $12,000 or $15,000; $15,000 wasn't bad money in 1964, but you had to work. I felt like I should be earning $50,000 or $60,000. That eventually happened, but it didn't happen in Baltimore.

In 1965 we had another great year and were tied with the Packers at the end of the season. They beat us in a playoff and went on to play in the championship game. The reason they beat us is the officials gave them a field goal that was never good. We were robbed, and that hurt. We were hoping Don Chandler would miss the field goal, and he missed it. Well, he didn't miss because the referees called it good. It seemed like it went high and over to the outside. We were clapping because it was no good. We would have won, and that would have been it. I'll never forget that. I thought, "Man, there's another $10,000 out of my pocket." Ten grand back in 1965 was a lot of money.

When calls like that go against you, you're demoralized. It really affects you, and it destroys you for that game. You get one shot, and that one shot kicked our butt. Our linebacker intercepted a pass, we had the ball, but we couldn't run the clock out. That game was a heartbreaker.

Halfback Tom Matte was our quarterback that year. Unitas hurt his knee, and then Gary Cuozzo played quarterback and separated his shoulder. We had to go into the playoffs with Matte as quarterback. It was different, that's all. I think Matte had played quarterback at Ohio State.

If you didn't make the championship game, you made the Runner-Up Bowl. We played our game in Florida against the Dallas Cowboys in January of 1966. We beat them 35-3, with Matte at quarterback. The best thing about it was we got to go to Miami Beach, Florida, for two weeks.

It was a great opportunity for me to play on a team that had Johnny Unitas, Lenny Moore, and Gino Marchetti.

The years I was there, Raymond Berry, Moore, and John Mackey would come back to the huddle and say, "I can do this, I can do that." I was shocked that Unitas listened to them. Everybody thinks Unitas made all the decisions, but that's not true. He had Mackey coming to him saying, "I can beat this guy on this route," and sure enough, he'd beat him for six.

Berry would come back to the huddle and say, "John, throw me a Z-out and I got him." Zip. Six points.

Unitas was an accurate son-of-a-gun. If Raymond would say, "I'll be right here," the ball was there. Precisely.

Unitas had great teammates. We called them bodyguards. We didn't want him to get hit because there went your play-offs and maybe a little extra cash. You had to protect him, and he was well protected with a great offensive line. Dick Sismanski was at center, Jim Parker and Bob Vogel at tackle, and John Mackey at tight end.

Jim Parker was considered, and I still consider him, the greatest lineman ever. He made All-Pro at offensive left tackle and left guard his whole career. He was 6-foot-5 or 6-foot-6, and his weigh-in was 285. Every time we had a weigh-in, he had to sweat some off, but he was 300 pounds when he played in the games.

You think you know things until you meet a guy who's been doing it all his life. I learned how to head butt legally from Parker. You stand up straight in front of your opponent and hit him straight in his numbers. When you hit him in the numbers, your head automatically is going to slide up into his chin. Boom!

Parker was a character. I called signals on the punt team and always called, "Red 22! Red 22!"

After a while Jim said, "How come you never ask me for my favorite color and say my number?"

I said, "What do you want me to say, Jim?"

"Purple!"

I called "Purple 77!" the rest of my career in Baltimore. [*Laughs.*]

Lenny Moore was one of great speed and a great guy who helped me get to know the system and people. He'd call me

"Tiger" and say, "Tiger, I don't like the blows. I can't take these blows."

"They never hit you, Lenny. You outrun everybody on that football field."

I'd laugh and just shake my head. He had some afterburners, but he always talked about how he didn't like to get hit. I didn't mind. I liked to bump into you and roughhouse it.

It's fun, the gratification you get out of beating up somebody. Some guys would like it. There was this kid playing for Minnesota, and every time he'd come across to block the punt, I'd stick him. Bam! Boom! Bam! Come across again, Bam! Boom! Bam!

He looked at me and said, "Damn, you are kicking my ass." He loved the fact I would bust his butt every time he came across.

To hear the press talk about it, I was hurt every year I played football. Every year there was some ache and pain—your knees hurt or your shoulders hurt. You didn't have time to sit on the sideline. You said, "Give me a shot; give me some ice; do something; I want to play."

You weren't respected if you didn't play. Everybody played hurt, whether it was a hand, elbows, neck, shoulders, or legs. We didn't cry; we just took shots and said, "Let's play."

I was icing my knees one time and looked over at a table in the dressing room. A teammate was lying back on the table. The doctor came over to me and said, "How you doing, Tony? I'll be with you in a minute."

The doctor pulled out a needle that was about 8–10 inches long. I said, "Oooh," thinking he was going to stick that needle in my knee. The doctor instead walked over to the other guy, who took that shot right in his groin. I looked at him and said, "Oh, boy." That scared me to death.

The doctor had to get up in there to his pelvic area because the ligaments had pulled off the bone. The guy went back in and played the whole game. Every time he took that shot, he played the whole game. He took it when he needed it, and sometimes that was every game.

Our owner, Carroll Rosenbloom, was a gambler. He bought the Colts franchise for $15,000 and sold it for $19 million. That first deal was just, "Give me $15,000 worth of season tickets and the team is yours."

He was always good to me. If I needed $5,000 or $10,000 when buying property, he'd give it to me. Every time we'd go out of town and play, he'd find the finest restaurants in town and take any of the guys on the team that wanted to go out to dinner. Of course everybody almost always took him up on it.

He had a lot of pretty women around him. We were taking off to go to Minnesota, and my roommate, Leonard Liles, was sitting next to me. Carroll Rosenbloom's wife, Georgia Frontiere, walked past us. Leonard was looking all gaga at her, and Carroll Rosenbloom walked by and said, "You can't afford that." We laughed at Leonard all season. Georgia Frontiere later owned the Los Angeles Rams.

John Mackey and a few others initiated the NFL Players Association. It was just getting off the ground in the '60s. He was our representative from the Colts, and I was his alternate. Eventually John moved up and was president of the Players Association.

I went to one Players Association meeting. It was me, John Mackey, Jim Marshall, and somebody else I can't remember. We were having a meeting in the Americana Hotel in New York City. On one side of the table were the players, and on the other side were the representatives of the owners. The one guy who stood out on the other side was Vince Lombardi. Everybody respected him.

Lombardi said, "We're not going to give you nothing! Nothing! Nothing!"

Jim Marshall stood up, lifted the table, and was going to turn the table over on Lombardi! John Mackey and I grabbed the table to stop him and said, "No, Jim! You can't do that!" There was no meeting after that.

I made the front cover of *Street and Smith's Pro Football Yearbook* in 1967. That year we were 11-1-2 after losing the last regular season game to the Rams. That left us tied with the Rams with the exact same records.

The Rams went to the playoffs though. The 49ers and Green Bay played a game that week, and if the 49ers beat Green Bay, we were a shoo-in for the playoffs. But Green Bay snuck in there again on us. We couldn't beat them on paper, couldn't beat them on the field, couldn't beat them with the referees. Green Bay was like a nemesis for us, and you gotta live with that.

I had some good runs with the Colts. Playing against Chicago, I ran on an off tackle play, spun around to where Dick Butkus was—and thrill of a lifetime—pushed off him and ran 60 yards. A little speedster came and caught me in the back, and I fell 3 yards. I just missed a touchdown.

My knees hit on the 3-yard line. If I'd been able to reach out and put the ball over the goal line, it would have been a touchdown. They didn't do that in my day. Where your knees went down was it. The officials walked up to you, got the ball from you, and moved it back. Look at old film and you'll see what they do. [Often players catch the ball and fall, keeping their knees parallel to the ball.]

In one game we were playing the Detroit Lions. The play was a 19-straight. I hit the line, came across the middle, and ran over the linebacker. I'm motoring down the sideline, and I see the end zone. All of a sudden the lights went out. I said, "Who hit me?" I looked up and saw Dick "Night Train" Lane. Well, he sure showed me "The Train."

In another game I was running the ball against Minnesota, running to my left on another 19-straight. The offensive line charged, struck a quick block, and I made my way. I got down to about the 3-yard line, and three or four Vikings were waiting for me. I thought, "I can't get away from these guys." I leaped into them, held the ball real tight, turned around, and started pushing with my back. Here comes Unitas. I pitched the ball to him, and he scored the touchdown. Tell me, who else can say, "Johnny Unitas scored on my pitchout?" [*Laughs.*]

I came off the football field, and Shula said, "Don't ever do that again."

I said, "That's six, isn't it?"

It's like he didn't want anybody to outthink him. I wasn't trying to be smart; this is a touchdown.

Shula wasn't a bad coach, but I think he felt it was his time to be a star. Eventually he became that star when he went to Miami. Baltimore had pretty good teams; he just didn't want to be a part of them. He wanted to be the headliner.

I don't think I ever impressed Shula. It seemed like he didn't get along with a lot of the people on the team. He didn't like Unitas *supposedly*; I knew he didn't like me.

Lenny Moore would say, "Tiger, they're not used to a brother from the West Coast."

I said, "Because I speak my mind? They better get used to it; we're a team. We signed a contract and get paid to win games." Maybe that's why Shula didn't like me. I was too outspoken.

Sometimes you'd see players come into training camp, a kid they might have been interested in two or three years prior to his being cut by another team. They'd bring him into training camp and bleed him of information on one of our opponents. Then a couple days later they'd say, "Sorry, we can't use you." Everyone knew they were good, but they'd cut them without giving them a shot.

I'd say, "That's not right; give that guy a shot."

I had a great year in '67, but the next year Shula didn't want me, and I had to go. I guess I was getting too old for him. I found out about being traded on the last day of training camp. I was married to a young lady who was sick, dying of cancer [she died a year later]. Owner Carroll Rosenbloom's son, Steve, said, "Carroll wants to talk to you."

I found out they traded me away to the New Orleans Saints.

I said, "Trade me away? I have a wife in the hospital dying of cancer and you want to trade me away? And I'm one of your leading ground gainers since I've been here?"

I played two years with the Saints. Tom Fears was our coach. I met Tom Fears in the 1950s, when he played for the Rams, and he signed an autograph for me. He also gave me Player of the Week certificates in high school. You'd be allowed to come by one of Tom Fears's taco stands and eat all you want.

He told me, "You're putting me in the poor house."

I said, "You keep giving me these Player of the Week things, I'm going to keep coming up here."

I never knew I'd end up playing for him. He was a nice, gentle guy. When I got to New Orleans, I said, "You don't know me now, but remember all those tacos you used to give me?"

He said, "I remember, Anthony." He called me Anthony; he didn't call me Tony.

The Saints had a bunch of old guys that had been traded from different teams. One was Doug Atkins, a defensive end from the Chicago Bears. He and Jim Parker would have famous fights on the football field. When you're playing a game, you're going so fast, the next thing you know you're running a third down and you failed, but that game film showing on that projector did not lie. They would stop at Jim Parker and Doug Atkins, and it was war. Doug Atkins was 6-foot-8, 280 pounds; Parker was 6-foot-5, 300 pounds, and they just collided. They fought, battled, snarled, and spit. Almost everything was legal then except for biting and scratching. They had some of the most epic battles in football. It was a pleasure watching them.

I didn't decide to leave football; they told me I was too old. They said they had to let me go and that no one was interested in me. I was twenty-eight years old.

I made a couple of phone calls and signed a two-year contract with the Patriots. They gave me a physical and said, "We gotta let you go. How long have you had this injury?"

I said, "I've been playing with this bad knee since I've played pro football. Six years."

I was still in shape. A guy from Canada called me. I told him I didn't want to play any more football. He told me to come up there and just sit around and watch. Well, I went up there, sat around, and watched. I almost learned how to speak French but wouldn't stay there long enough. I stayed for a couple of weeks. I was tired of it; it was over with.

I had to go out and find a real job: beer salesman! Back to beer. Jax Beer in New Orleans.

My era, the '60s, glorified football. We had fun when I was with the Colts. Those were the days. There were a lot of guys I loved. I miss John Unitas. He was funny.

I'm a candidate for two new knees. I've had my hip replaced, my back's full of arthritis, and I can't move my head all the way. My memory, I have a tendency to forget things every once in a while.

Would I do it all over again? Hell yeah! All over again.

# 26

## Carl Eller

Defensive end

University of Minnesota

Drafted, 1964 (Minnesota Vikings, 1st round)

Minnesota Vikings, 1964-1978

Seattle Seahawks, 1979

5 All-Pro seasons

6 Pro Bowls

1970s NFL All-Decade Team

Pro Football Hall of Fame inductee (2004)

Minnesota's scholarship offer was really one of the best I had. Because I was from North Carolina, Minnesota was kind of foreign to me. There was the excitement about going away to school and particularly going to a place like Minnesota.

Freshmen did not play varsity back then. As a freshman, the biggest thing I remember was when we got the announcement that we were in the Rose Bowl. Minnesota's a huge campus, and the whole campus poured out on the streets like it was Mardi Gras. The next year, I was a sophomore and went to the Rose Bowl as a player.

I was drafted by the Minnesota Vikings in the NFL draft and the Buffalo Bills in the AFL. I didn't cause a bidding war because I pretty much had my mind set on Minnesota. I lived there, liked the town, and wanted to stay. I think Buffalo knew that. Finally they came to me and said, "Would you leave and play in Buffalo?" I said I'd consider it, but I had pretty much already decided.

Most people remember the wrong way run by Jim Marshall during my rookie year, and a lot of people only remember that. What people don't remember is that I returned a fumble for a touchdown right before that. We were playing the 49ers at Kezar Stadium in San Francisco, and both plays happened in the fourth quarter. On the first of the two plays John Brodie was the quarterback. I think Jim hit him and the ball snapped out. I picked up the ball and ran for a 45-yard touchdown in Gale Sayers–like fashion. [*Laughs.*]

The Jim Marshall play was very similar, but Jim was coming from the other side. We reversed fields chasing a flat pass Brodie had thrown to Billy Kilmer. Marshall picked up the ball and kept running, not realizing he was going in the opposite direction. My thought was, "He's going to have a longer touchdown than mine." I also didn't realize he was running the wrong way at first.

Jim was our team leader and had a great career. Playing twenty years as a defensive end in the National Football League is quite an achievement.

We had some really talented players, each in our own individual way. In the beginning we kind of resented that group thing, but the "Purple People Eaters" was a name that caught on and stuck. We were very supportive of each other and very unselfish. We wanted the success of winning games, being successful as a group and as a team. There wasn't any competition in that aspect.

Going to four Super Bowls says a lot about the kind of team we had. We kept going back to prove ourselves, showing that we were not the team to accept defeat. I think that says as much about our team as any other Super Bowl team— the fact that we were a dominant team for as long as we were. [The Vikings earned four Super Bowl trips over an eight-year span.]

Those are very bitter moments, and those losses stuck in our mouths for a long time. When you get to the Super Bowl, you want to win.

I had very few injuries. I did break my thumb in a game against the Denver Broncos in Denver. I had the same injury a second time—against Green Bay, I think. Those were the only injuries I had in a game. I had a knee injury during training camp but didn't miss any season games because of it. I never missed a game, but I didn't start the game after I broke my thumb the second time.

I was traded to the Seattle Seahawks before my last season. When I showed up to training camp, Bud Grant and I had a talk, and he told me I was going to Seattle. Their head coach, Jack Patera, had been a coach with the Vikings and wanted to bring me up there because he was familiar with me.

My retirement was kind of a mutual decision, but I think the Seattle Seahawks wanted to move on after my one year there, and I didn't fit into their future. It was ultimately their decision. I was okay with it because sixteen years is a long time in professional football. A lot of enthusiasm and emotions go into it, and it's sometimes hard to keep that enthusiasm after you've been doing it for so many years.

Retirement is going great. I'm doing some exciting things. I'm the president of the NFL Retired Players Association, and we're making life better for retirees in general. That's been a real thrill for me to do that.

We're an advocacy group more than anything, but we're providing service, and a lot of it's in the area of health care and benefits. We represented the retired players during the recent collective bargaining negotiations. That's a first, and I think we were able to improve our benefits. The owners were willing to make up for some of the shortfalls over the past years for the retirees.

I think the future of the retired players is going to be good, and I think it's going to work two ways. I think the retired players themselves are going to be more vibrant in their post-football careers, but I also think it's going to be better for the fans. They're going to see the retired player in a different way. It's going to be more interactive, and they're going to be able to interrelate more on a basis where there's a relationship between the player and the general public.

# 27

## Dan Reeves

Running back

University of South Carolina

Undrafted

Dallas Cowboys, 1965–1971

Super Bowl champion (Dallas Cowboys, Super Bowl 6)

NFL touchdown leader (1966: 16 TDs)

1 All-Pro season

Head coach (Denver Broncos, 1981–1992; New York Giants,
    1993–1996; Atlanta Falcons, 1997–2003)

I grew up on a farm and had two brothers and a sister. My dad
had two brothers and two sisters, so we had a lot of cousins
who lived in the area. We used to get together and play sports
on Saturdays and Sundays. I always loved playing sports and
competing whatever season it was: football, basketball, or
baseball. I loved all three of them.

In high school I lived out in the country and went to a city
school. I started playing organized sports and was part of a
real good program at Americus High School in Georgia. We
won two state championships when I was a senior, in basketball and baseball.

I was a quarterback in football. I broke my collarbone my
senior year and missed five games. When I came back, we
ended up winning our last three games, including one against
the team that eventually won the state championship. We
had unfortunately lost a game earlier in the year that cost
us the regional championship.

South Carolina was the only school that offered me a scholarship. I signed up for that scholarship as quick as I could, before they changed their minds. Later I was selected to play in the Georgia High School All-Star Game and was fortunate enough to get the game's MVP award. I then had a lot of different choices to go to a lot of different schools, but I felt like South Carolina took a chance on me when nobody else would and decided to stick with them.

I played for a coach named Marvin Bass. He was like a second dad to me, so I couldn't have made a better decision. He was a great man to play for and a great influence on my life. I hired him on my staff in Denver and also in Atlanta.

Coach Bass was a man of integrity. His word was his bond. When I chose to stay with South Carolina, I think I showed him that I had that same type of commitment. When I first tried to hire Coach Bass in the pros, he was coaching in the Canadian League. Most guys would be there the next day if you tried to hire them from Canada to coach in the NFL.

Coach Bass said, "I'd love to do it, but I promised these people I was going to coach here. I just can't leave." He stayed there to coach that year, and I hired him the next year. He was on my staff until I got fired in Atlanta, when he was eighty-eight years old.

He was a great football coach, and we had a good football team at South Carolina; we just never had a great team. It was three years that I enjoyed. I wish we'd won more games, but you learn more about yourself and how much you love the sport during tough times.

I wasn't drafted, but two teams offered me a chance to play. One was the San Diego Chargers, who at that time were in the AFL, and the other was the Dallas Cowboys. San Diego already had many good players on offense and said they'd only try me at safety, as I'd also played safety in college. Dallas said, "We'll play you on defense, we'll play you on offense, and we'll try to find the best place for you."

It wasn't much money: a $1,000 signing bonus and $11,000 contract. That was a little less than what San Diego offered, but I felt that the Cowboys gave me a better opportunity and signed with Dallas.

They brought in over one hundred rookies to training camp, including twenty-some draft choices. Not being drafted, I played every position: safety, running back, wide receiver. I was just trying to stay around. Every day was full pads and two-a-days with a lot of hitting.

I was fortunate to stay healthy, and we had a lot of running backs end up getting hurt. I was able to play some at that position—one I had never really played before—and showed enough that Dallas kept me around.

Don Perkins was the starting fullback for the Cowboys. He taught me how to get into a stance and stayed with me after practice to work on things. He was a team player that wanted to help and just a great friend to do that. Like I said, I'd never played running back before.

Lee Roy Jordan, Dave Manders, and I lived with our wives in the same complex, and we became close. A team needs to have that chemistry where you care about each other not just on the field but off the field.

We did an awful lot of things to build camaraderie. We used to have team parties after home games. Coach Landry did a great job of making it feel like a family affair. It became an ideal place to play because we all became good friends and remain good friends to this day.

When you're a rookie, they make you do all kinds of errands and sing songs, so we went through all that hazing. If you could do that, I think the veterans were just looking for somebody that might help them get better.

We were in a blitz audible situation during one game during my rookie year. Back then if people came with a blitz it was man-to-man coverage in the secondary. If we were in a right formation, we called a 59; if we were in a left formation, 58. We were in a right formation, and our quarterback, Don Meredith, called 58.

I hollered out behind him, "No Don, 59!"

He turned around and looked at me with a grin on his face and said, "Okay. 2-59! 2-59! Hut! Hut!"

He then threw a touchdown pass to Bob Hayes. Coming off the field, Meredith said, "You smart-ass rookie, you!" He kidded me all the time about being a smart aleck.

We had an extremely good offensive football team, and I was just a part of it. We changed our offense in 1966 to be multiple formations, putting the halfback in motion to create a lot of problems for the defense. They really did it for Mel Renfro, who was a defensive back but had led the league in punt returns. That preseason, Mel played running back, and I was playing behind him. He averaged something ridiculous like 6.5 yards per carry in the preseason before hurting his ankle. I was able to come in.

We opened up the regular season, and I scored three touchdowns in the first game. We were scoring all these points, and Coach Landry decided to move Mel back to defense. I was the one who ended up benefitting from the changes we made.

I wasn't only a running back in the backfield. I'd go in motion, run pass routes, and tried to create mismatches with Bob Hayes. I understood what we were doing and had a good feel for it. Like Coach Landry said, I didn't do anything particularly well, but I was able to do a lot of things okay. He took advantage of those things and gave me a lot of opportunities. That year I caught 8 touchdown passes and ran for 8 touchdowns, so it was a balanced deal.

We had a heck of an offensive football team that was very difficult to defense because we had so many weapons. I know nobody was defensing trying to stop Dan Reeves; I benefitted from Bob Hayes, Frank Clarke at tight end, Buddy Dial at receiver, and Don Perkins at fullback. We had a lot of good football players, and Meredith was exceptional.

Meredith was a tremendous leader who enjoyed playing the game and made it fun, even to where practices were fun. He wasn't serious all the time, yet he was serious at the right time. He was an unbelievable scrambler and had a tremendous arm.

Don understood our offense, and it made him a better quarterback when we started going to those multiple formations with all the motions. If we had just won one of those games against Green Bay—we lost 34-27 the first year and got beaten on a last-second touchdown in the other one—I think there's no question Don Meredith would have gotten the credit for being the great player that he was.

He called a lot of his own plays, and you could come back to the huddle and say, "Hey Don, they didn't cover me on such-and-such." He would go ahead and use those things. I remember playing the Washington Redskins, and near the end of the game I said, "Don, they're covering me with a linebacker, man-to-man, out in the flat." He said, "Look, I'm going to run a shoot-and-go. You go out in the flat, I'll pump it to you, and then you break down the sideline."

I ended up catching a touchdown pass right at the end of the game to beat the Redskins up in Washington. You've got to have somebody that understands what you're doing and believes in you as a player to be able to do those things.

Don was great at taking information in the huddle and immediately trying to take advantage of it. He was always asking offensive linemen, "Can you handle that guy over you? Okay, if you can handle him, let's run such-and-such." He was always listening and knew which players gave good information and which ones really didn't know what the heck was going on. [*Laughs.*]

We went through a lot of difficult times, the Cowboys. We had knocked on the door in '66 and '67, losing to the Green Bay Packers for the championship and the right to go to Super Bowls 1 and 2. In '68 and '69 we lost the Eastern Conference championship to Cleveland for the right to play in the championship game. In 1970 we ended up losing the Super Bowl on a last-second field goal. That bonds you and makes you a closer football team. We finally won a championship in '71.

I had become a player/coach in 1970, and my first job was to help put in a strength and conditioning program for the Cowboys. We put it in that year and paid guys to stay in Dallas for $50 a workout. They could make $200 a week. Instead of going back home to an off-season job, it gave a player enough money to stay around. I think that gave us a bit of an edge, and that's what you're always looking for. We became a closer unit and got stronger, faster, and quicker. I think that was the start of the greatness that the Cowboys had because we went to the Super Bowl in 1970, '71, '75, '77, and '79.

My role as a player/coach was a little different, that's for sure. As soon as we got through with practice, everybody else would take a shower and go home. I'd take a shower, go back to the office, and work for several more hours, but I think that was probably the easiest part. The toughest part was when you've got close friends that you've played with for a long time, and you're now knowing who's going to be cut and who's talked about being cut. You know a lot of things players don't need to know, and you have to keep that to yourself.

Walt Garrison and I roomed together for three years before I became a player/coach. All of a sudden I'm coaching him and also real close friends with him. It was hard for me not to tell him some things that were going on. As soon as you tell somebody though, it's no longer confidential. I had to learn to keep my mouth shut.

I was kind of caught between the coaches and the players. Whenever Coach Landry wanted to know how the players felt, the first thing he'd do was come to me and say, "What do you think? Sometimes it might not have been exactly what Coach Landry wanted to hear, but you had to be honest and give a feel for what the players were thinking. [*Laughs.*] Another thing was that if you ever made a mistake, the other players would get a big kick out of it. They'd say, "What happened? You missed an assignment."

You had to understand that even if you were a coach, you were still going to make some errors and have some missed assignments. You probably understand players a lot better and are more forgiving when you're on the field making mistakes too.

It was a tough position, but it gave me an opportunity to do something I had never really thought about. Until Coach Landry asked me if I'd be interested in being a player/coach, the thought of coaching never crossed my mind.

I don't know if you have enough time to talk about all the injuries I had. The one that tore my left knee up against St. Louis in 1968 tore everything you can tear in your knee. Now they know it takes a year, minimum, to recover from that. I got hurt toward the middle of the season and then came back in training camp and competed that next year. My knee never was the same.

Prior to that I'd make instinctive moves, but it came to the point that I'd have to start planning: "Okay, I'm going to fake to the left and take it to the right." Or it would happen so quick, I'd say, "I'll just have to lower my head and get what I can." It just took away all the instincts that I had.

I knew my career was coming to a close in 1969. Calvin Hill was drafted No. 1 and was rookie of the year. I was very fortunate that Coach Landry asked me to be a player/coach in 1970, and I was able to play three more years in that role before retiring.

I've had both knees replaced, the left about four years ago and my right three years ago. Now my knees are in great shape. I wish my whole body was as good as my knees are now. I'd be a bionic man, though. I'd set off all the alarms going through the airport.

The Dallas Cowboys had a fantastic organization, led by a phenomenal coach in Coach Landry, and just an unbelievable number of players. It was a special group. You're talking about one of the greatest times for a sports team in history. It's hard to even imagine that somebody could have the times that we had as a pro football team.

If we had won a couple of those games against Green Bay and some of those we lost to Pittsburgh in Super Bowls, everybody would be talking about what a great dynasty that was for the Dallas Cowboys. It was a great organization, and you've got to give Tex Schramm, Coach Landry, and owner Clint Murchison a lot of credit for putting together a phenomenal team. The Cotton Bowl was a great place to play, and we had great fans.

We were fortunate enough to play at a great time in history for a great team. I wouldn't trade it for anything in the world, and I know everyone on our football team feels the same way.

# 28

## Walt Garrison

Running back

Drafted, 1966 (Dallas Cowboys, 5th round)

Dallas Cowboys, 1966–1974

Super Bowl champion (Dallas Cowboys, Super Bowl 6)

1 Pro Bowl

I grew up in Lewisville, Texas. We didn't have Pop Warner or Little League. If you weren't good enough to play on the varsity as a high school freshman, you'd play on the B team, which only played three or four games. I wasn't good enough, so I played on the B team. My sophomore, junior, and senior years, I played high school football.

You played all sports in a small school because there wasn't enough kids. We played football and basketball, ran track, and played baseball in high school. That's it. That was all the sports they had.

Television wasn't big on football then. You didn't get many games on TV. My folks weren't real well off, and TVs weren't available to everybody. I don't think we had a TV until I was in high school.

Jim Shoulders inspired me back then. You have no idea who that is, do you? Sixteen-time world champion cowboy. My heroes were cowboys: Jack Buschbom, Harley May, Casey Tibbs. Dean Oliver was another one. I could name a hundred of them. I wanted to be a rodeo guy. I played football because it was cool to play in high school, but I was also on the rodeo team.

I chose to attend Oklahoma State because they were the only ones to offer me a football scholarship. When you only have one to choose from, it doesn't take long to make up your mind. I also had an offer to go to Wharton Junior College on a rodeo scholarship, but that was two years, and Oklahoma State was four years. I wanted to go to Wharton for rodeo, but my dad convinced me that four years of education was better than two.

Sammy Baugh was my freshman coach. Slingin' Sammy from Rotan, Texas. That was a big thrill. My daddy was *really* thrilled to get to meet Coach Baugh. Sammy came down for three months and stayed in the dorm with us. Freshmen only played two games then, and we played against Arkansas and Oklahoma. Arkansas beat us in the rain that year. They wouldn't let us play on the game field, so we had to play on the practice field without any goalposts. You couldn't kick extra points; you had to run them. They beat us by 2 or 3 points. Everybody was down.

Coach Baugh said, "What the hell's wrong with y'all?"

We said, "Well, Coach, we lost."

He said, "You didn't lose; you just got beat by 2 or 3 points. Let me tell you about an ass kicking. When I was with the Redskins, the Bears beat us 73-0 in the 1940 NFL Championship. Now *that's* an ass kicking. Y'all got nothing to be ashamed of; you got to play."

Coach Baugh was a big ol' tall, skinny, wiry guy who chewed tobacco and spit on the field. He coached in blue jeans and boots. Sammy was probably in his fifties then and could still punt and pass the ball. People don't realize Sammy Baugh led the league in interceptions, passing, and punting the same year. Did you know that? He could punt the ball unbelievably. At practice he said, "I'm going to kick it out on the 2-yard line," and he'd kick it out on the 2-yard line.

Punters said, "I can't kick it out like that."

He said, "You can if you practice. I can kick it out on the 1-inch line."

I played linebacker in high school and my freshman year

at Oklahoma State. Then they fired Coach Cliff Spiegel and hired Phil Cutchin, Bear Bryant's top assistant at Alabama. At Alabama if you played linebacker on defense, you either played center or fullback on offense. Lee Roy Jordan was a great linebacker at Alabama, but he was also a center on offense. I had to learn to play fullback.

My sophomore year, I played linebacker and occasionally played fullback. Then they moved the starting fullback to defensive end and me to starting fullback, and I *hated* it. I got to play a little defense, short yardage and goal line stuff, but from then on I was a running back. You just try to run where people ain't. It's not that hard. [*Laughs.*]

As I played more on offense and less on defense, I got to liking it more. I was getting to play, and that's all that mattered to me.

My senior year, the Los Angeles Rams sent a babysitter to Stillwater three days before the NFL draft. He bought me a pair of boots and took me and my buddies out to eat a few times. I thought I was going to go with the Rams. The day of the draft, he was on the phone a lot. I was sitting in a hotel room with him and asked, "When do you think the Rams are going to draft me?" He said, "Probably in the seventh round." At the start of the fifth round he got a phone call. He got up and said, "The Cowboys drafted you in the fifth round. I'm out of here." He left, and that's how I found out I was drafted by the Cowboys: a Los Angeles Rams scout told me.

I was also drafted by the Kansas City Chiefs in the AFL. I told my dad, "If the money is close, I'm staying here." Gil Brandt, the Cowboys player personnel director, came up and said, "We're going to give you a brand new Pontiac Grand Prix and a $15,000 signing bonus."

I said, "Gil, one thing I want is a two-horse inline trailer," where the horses are one behind the other, making it easier on your car to pull.

Gil called Tex Schramm, who said it was okay if it wasn't

5. Walt Garrison and the horse trailer the Dallas Cowboys bought him as a bonus.

a lot of money. At that time the best inline trailer you could buy was about $3,000, and Gil said, "Okay."

They also had to fly my parents first class and put them up in a hotel to watch me play in the East-West Shrine Game. My parents traded their two first-class tickets in for three coach tickets so my little brother could go with them.

I played in the East-West Shrine Game, All-American Game, and the College All-Star Game against the Green Bay Packers. I didn't get to training camp until preseason had already started. I flew from the All-Star Game in Chicago to training camp in San Francisco.

I got to training camp and didn't know a soul; I hadn't met anybody but Gil Brandt. I got out to the stadium, suited out, but didn't know any plays. I didn't play a down, but there was Don Meredith, Bob Lilly, Bob Hayes, Dan Reeves, and Lee Roy Jordan—all these guys that I had read about. I thought, "What the hell am I doing here?"

I didn't think I'd make the team. They'd post who got cut, and I'd look and go, "Whew! Wasn't me."

Back then only a small percentage of rookies made a team. You might have a thousand going; only a hundred would make a team, and only five of them are on Dallas. The next year only three made the Cowboys. They don't have to keep you like they do in college.

People came to training thinking they were great in high school and great in college, but you're just a rookie when you get to training camp. Who are you going to replace? Bob Lilly? Bob Hayes? Don Perkins, who was maybe third in the league in rushing behind Jim Brown?

You can make the team by being an outstanding special teams player. They'll keep you because they need bodies that are expendable. I think that's how I made the team my rookie year, by covering and returning punts and kickoffs.

I was very fortunate. I came into Dallas and had one of the greatest teachers in Don Perkins, who's still my hero and one of the greatest fullbacks Dallas ever had. He told me stuff that took him seven or eight years to learn. He helped me because he knew he was going to retire within the next two or three years. If Perkins had been only two years older than me, he probably wouldn't have taught me much.

Perk taught me stuff that's not in the playbook. When a linebacker's inside, you block the end; you don't block the linebacker if he blitzes. He told me to look at the fingers on the tackles and the ends. If they have pressure on their fingers, they're coming straight ahead. If they're rocked back a little, it's some kind of stunt. If they've barely got their hand on the ground, they're pulling one way or another.

A lot of times a guy coming straight ahead will have one foot further back than the other, like a sprinter. If they're going another way, they'll have their feet square. You can tell after a while if a linebacker's going to blitz or drop back into coverage.

WALT GARRISON                                               207

I asked him one time, "Perk, why are you trying to help me? I'm trying to beat you out."

He said, "Walt, I want to win the Super Bowl. If you're better than me, you ought to be playing." I always remembered that, and when Robert Newhouse came up, I showed him some things Perk had told me and that I'd learned over my career.

Dan Reeves and I started rooming together my rookie year. He taught me not only what to study, but how to study. This was his second year in the league, and he was like a coach then. Most players learn, "Go here." Reeves wanted to know why you went there. Having Reeves and Perkins help me is probably one of the reasons I made the team. They were coaches in their own rights.

I knew I wasn't going to play much as a rookie, just on punt and kick returns. On Saturday nights before home games I'd go to the team meeting and team dinner. Then we'd be off until eleven o'clock.

A lot of the married guys would go home, see their wives and kids, and be back by curfew. I wasn't married, so I'd get in my car and meet my friend Bill Robinson at the Cowbell Arena in Mansfield, Texas, where they had a weekly rodeo. I'd get up in the rodeo and bulldog [steer wrestle ].

That lasted about three weeks. Somebody called Coach Landry and said, "Oh, that's so great that you let Walt come over here the night before a game and bulldog." So I had a meeting with Coach Landry, and he said, "NO. You won't be doing that during the season."

In the off-season though, I would rodeo in the Professional Rodeo Cowboys Association. I bulldogged, and I still wrestle.

Coach Landry said one time, "Walt, I don't know about you rodeoing, even in the off-season. There's a clause in your contract that says if you get hurt doing anything besides playing football, we don't have to pay you."

I told him, "Coach, I've been rodeoing since high school. Ignorance is what makes any sport dangerous. The more you know about it; the less likely you are to get hurt. I wouldn't get on a motorcycle because I don't know anything about them."

Coach Landry and his wife, Alicia, came to the Mesquite Championship Rodeo, where I was entered. He sat with my mom and dad. I drew a real nice steer; I think I might have placed on him. After the rodeo I went to see my parents and said, "Coach, I didn't know you were here."

He said, "I just wanted to come see what you did in the rodeo. That's not as dangerous as I thought."

I said, "It's not near as dangerous as football."

He said, "I still don't want you to rodeo during the season!"

Coach Landry was one of the smartest guys in the world. Before coaching the Cowboys, he coached defense for the New York Giants. Another guy at that time coached the offense. His name was Vince Lombardi. Two of the greatest coaches ever were on the same coaching staff. Can you imagine that?

Coach Landry could go from an offense meeting to a defense meeting, then to a special teams meeting and never miss a beat. He started the flex defense and the multiple-set offense with people in motion. He started the shotgun because quarterback Eddie LeBaron was 5-foot-7 and couldn't see over the line. Landry moved him back so he could see!

I played three years with Don Meredith at quarterback, one with Craig Morton, and five with Roger Staubach. Don Meredith was an unbelievable leader because he was so smart. The quarterback has to be in charge, and Meredith was in charge of the entire team. He would get on you if you screwed up, especially during your first couple of years, when you screw up a lot. Lee Roy Jordan would too, and he didn't care whether it was offense, defense, or on the kicking teams.

Staubach came in, and he *became* a leader. He was a rookie my fourth or fifth year in the league, but he was four years older than I was. Roger tried to outwork everybody. If you

6. Walt Garrison cherishes the ball from friend Don Meredith.

did ten hundred-yard sprints, he was going to do eleven. If you lifted two hundred pounds twenty times, he was going to do it twenty-five times.

When Roger was in the navy, fulfilling his commitment from college, he had a four-week leave while we were in training camp. He left Vietnam, went home to see his wife, and then flew to California to work out for two or three weeks.

We respected Roger before he even came to play because of that. Everybody knew he was going to be a great player.

Staubach was a great quarterback when he first got there, but he wasn't familiar with a lot of stuff that was going on and how to read defenses. That's why Roger scrambled so much in the early days. Usually a quarterback has three or four receivers, and will look one, two, three, and then to an outlet receiver. Roger only looked for one receiver. He would go one, run. He got to be a helluva quarterback, though, and he got to where he could read defenses on the go. The great ones can do it, and the other ones can't.

We had so many great players. Cornell Green was one of the greatest safeties and halfbacks I've ever played with. Why he's not in the Cowboys' Ring of Honor, I will never know because he was All-Pro at two positions. There's so many players Dallas has got that should be in the Ring of Honor that will never be, and that's a shame.

Dave Edwards. Nobody even knows who Dave Edwards is, but he was one of the greatest strong side linebackers ever. He'll never get recognized for what he did. He helped make an All-Pro out of Cornell Green because when the tight end can't get off the line, the strong safety doesn't have to cover him and that safety is free to intercept passes. Dave wasn't a flashy player, but he did his job and probably graded 100 percent on every game.

George Andrie, No. 66, was another guy like that. He'd take care of his business so Lilly could go nuts. He was a great defensive end who went to several Pro Bowls. George probably would have been the guy on the defensive line if it wasn't for Lilly. Andrie, like Dave Edwards, did his job well, and he did it every play.

I also played with Lance Alworth, an unbelievable receiver who came over from San Diego. Little bitty guy, but he could catch anything. After practice he'd get the second- or third-string quarterback to throw him about fifty passes. A lot of us were thinking that working after practice was dumb, but then we got to thinking that he was All-Pro several times, so maybe it wasn't that dumb. [*Laughs.*]

In Super Bowl 5 Baltimore kicked a last-minute field goal against us to win 16-13. That year our goal was to go to the Super Bowl, and we got beat. From the start of training camp the next year, everybody talked about *winning* the Super Bowl.

The first time you go to the Super Bowl, you take everything in and are distracted a lot. The reporters are there; you go into this big hall, and they have a table with your name on it. You've got friends down there, you've got family down there, and you're trying to practice and go to meetings. Plus you want to see everything because, "Gosh, this is kind of neat, you know?"

The second year, we went down there, and there weren't many wives that came down during the week like the year before. Those that did stayed in a different hotel. I didn't see my wife until after the game, and I think that was true for a lot of the players.

We played probably one of the greatest, most error-free games in Super Bowl 6. Calvin Hill fumbled going into the end zone, or we'd have beat Miami 31-3. Offensively and defensively it was one of the best games that I've ever played in, and that's because of the year before. From training camp on everyone was talking about going to the playoffs and *winning* the Super Bowl.

We went to the playoffs every year I was there except one; my last year we didn't go. Any team that goes to the playoffs year after year is a good team. Even when I was a rookie, the Cowboys had great teams.

Green Bay beat us twice in a row, and both of them were close games that came down to the last play. Those were good games and good games for fans and television. They're good games for the media too, who can pick you apart and tell you what you did wrong.

7. Walt Garrison's jersey from his last season and his helmet from Super Bowl 6.

People said we couldn't win the big one. It started out, "Next Year's Champions" and then "Dallas Can't Win the Big One," and then finally we won the Super Bowl.

Nothing in the newspaper ever affects your team. Newspaper writers are great, but they get paid to sell papers. So they make something big out of something that ain't. That doesn't bother the team; it bothers the public. If you have a bad game, you know it. You also know what teammates of yours made mistakes.

I've missed blocks, and you or Coach Landry don't have to tell me because I know. Of course Coach Landry *will* remind you on the next workout day about how bad you played and point it out to the entire team. That's just part of it. You can't linger on it and go into the next week saying, "I hope I don't make that mistake again."

The good players forget the bad plays because they know they're going to make good plays. They know when the game's over, it's over, and you've got a game next week. A lot of the veterans would tell the rookies or second-year guys, "Hey, man, don't worry about it." I mean, what can you do now? *Nothing.* You can drive yourself nuts is all you can do.

If a player jumps offside in a crucial situation, like Jim Boeke did when the Cowboys were on the 2-yard line against the Packers in the 1966 NFL Championship, he doesn't do it on purpose. Boeke was a good tackle; he just jumped. So now instead of it being 3rd and 2, it was 3rd and 7. I don't know of anybody that's ever played this game and didn't make a mistake. The best players probably don't make mistakes in crucial situations, but everybody makes them.

Everybody fumbles because there are big guys on the other side of that line. If they get their helmet on the ball, their head and body are stronger than your arm. I fumbled. I didn't mean to; I didn't try to; but if they hit you right, you'll fumble.

When I missed a block, man, it killed me. Not because I missed a block but because I let my teammates down. The respect you earn—nobody gives you respect in football—the respect you earn from your teammates is more important to me than the respect you earn from your opponents. I would rather have Bob Lilly say, "Great run," than have Dick Butkus say that. I wanted my teammates to know that I tried on every play, every time.

When it was 3rd and 3, I wanted the ball. You never think, "Oh my God, if I don't make this, they're going to get the ball." You always think you're going to do it. You don't always do it—I promise you, I've lost a lot of yardage—but you have to believe you can do it, and you have to believe in your teammates.

Wanting to be a good football player is the main thing, having the desire to make plays. You also have to be fearless, and you can't worry about getting hurt. If you're afraid of getting hit, you ought to take up curling.

I've had four knee operations because of football and one because of bulldogging. I also had two operations on my arm.

Probably the worst injury was tearing a ligament in my leg. I was out maybe two weeks with that, and it hurt. The fact that I wasn't playing hurt worse than the injury.

I got two concussions in one game against Atlanta. I got the first one, went over on the sideline, and sat down. I got back up, and Coach Landry said, "You ready?"

I said, "Yeah."

He said, "Okay, go in."

Then I got another concussion, and to this day I don't remember it. I went in to watch films that Tuesday, and it was like watching somebody else play. In film sessions I could usually list the plays and knew what was coming next from remembering the game. That game I couldn't remember anything.

In the pros you play everybody within your division twice a year. You get to know some of the players, and they're just like you; they're not bad guys, and they got a job to do. I never hated a player, but I did hate who they played for. I hated the Redskins, but I didn't hate the Redskin players. You hate them for sixty minutes, but before or after that you don't. After the game is over, win or lose, it's over. Later you play with those guys in the Pro Bowl. Now they're on your team.

Some of my best friends are my worst enemies. Does that make any sense? Diron Talbert's brother Don played for us. Diron would come in and play, and then we'd go to a party at a buddy of mine's house. He had to get permission from the Redskins, but he would stay over and spend the night with Don rather than fly home with the team. I hated Diron on the field because I had to block him. After the game we were friends again. That's the way you got to be.

It's like rodeo: I'll help a guy do anything, but I'm going to try to beat him too. He can ride my bulldogging horse, but I'm still trying to beat him. That's the way football is; you try to beat some of your best friends.

The rodeo and football got me a job with U.S. Tobacco the year after we won the Super Bowl. They called me after seeing an NFL Films show called *The Hunters,* about people who played football and had weird off-season occupations. Ben Davidson, the Raiders lineman, rode motorcycles and studied topography. Carl Eller was trying to be an actor, and they showed him in acting school.

The show came to Mineral Wells, Texas, to one of the PRCA rodeos I was in. They interviewed me and filmed me driving my truck in. On my dash I had a spittoon that my mother gave me when I was in college, along with a bunch of Skoal cans. All the cowboys used the cardboard on Skoal cans as notepads to write down phone numbers or dates. After seeing that, U.S. Tobacco called and offered me $10,000 to do a commercial. I thought, "Wow! That's a lot of money!"

I told Tex Schramm that I wanted to do a commercial for the snuff I used. I've never endorsed anything that I didn't use, ever.

Tex said, "I think it'd be bad for your image, Walt."

Thinking I was going to play football until I was fifty-five or so, I called U.S. Tobacco back and told them that the Cowboys didn't want me to do it, so I wasn't going to do it. Instead of getting somebody else, they waited a year and called me back—offering me $18,000. I told Tex they were offering more than the Super Bowl, which was $15,000. I said, "Besides, that is my image. Y'all have made that my image. You call me the 'Cowboys' cowboy.'"

I asked if there was any legal reason I couldn't do it, and Tex said, "Well, no, but we'd rather that you didn't."

I told him I was doing it, and it was the best move I've ever made. I made commercials until I retired from football, and after I retired, I worked full time in their promotions department. I did that until I retired from promotions about nine or ten years ago, and then they made me a consultant. This is the "House That Snuff Built" we're sitting in. U.S. Tobacco, the company that makes Skoal, they're great people to work for.

Retiring from football would have been hard for me if I hadn't had anything else to do. The promotions work I did took place all over the United States, on Thursdays through Sundays. I was on the road working while the football games were being played instead of at home thinking I could have played one more year, wishing I hadn't retired.

I probably could have played another year. In fact Dan Reeves called me after I retired. I was hunting quail at the Four Sixes ranch in Guthrie, Texas, over Thanksgiving. Dan asked me what I thought about coming back and playing because they needed a 3rd-down receiver out of the backfield. I told him I hadn't worked out, and he said, "Just think about it, and get back to me because we really need you."

My wife, father-in-law, and I talked about it, and I decided that I was going to do it. I was only going to play on 3rd down, about ten plays a game. I could do that holding my breath.

Dan called the next day and said, "You know how we wanted you to come back? You can't. The rule is that retired players have to be activated before a certain date."

They had missed it by a day. If they had activated me before the Thanksgiving Day game, I could have played, even on paper. The day after Thanksgiving, I couldn't play. In hindsight it worked out great because I would've had to quit my job at U.S. Tobacco or at least stopped doing promotions.

Sometime later my wife and I were at a restaurant. Coach Landry and his wife came in. He said, "Hey Walt! Come over here, join us." We went over there, sat with him, and he talked and talked and talked.

I said, "Coach, I've been around you nine years, and you've said more to me tonight than you've said to me in nine years."

He said, "Walt, I cannot get close to my players because it might alter my decisions on whether to keep them or trade them. I just don't get close to any of them. That's just the way I am."

It's a good way to be because you can't be friends and be

a coach. A coach has to have discipline on the team. If the players run the team, you're not going very far. Coach Landry expected you to know your job and to do it. If you did, you had a job. If you didn't, he'd trade or cut you. He didn't let personalities interfere with his job because he had a job to win football games.

The thing that I remember most about those days is that on our days off I didn't even think about doing anything unless I called Bob Lilly, Lee Roy Jordan, Dan Reeves, Cornell Green, and Jethro Pugh. We'd go hunting, fishing, or just hang out together. We did everything together. We'd all go down in a caravan to go dove hunting at Punk Helm's, a friend of Lilly's, and we'd stop at Meredith's store. Don's daddy had a general store in Mount Vernon, Texas, and we'd buy shotgun shells.

Players now, I don't think they congregate as much outside of football.

The guys I played with, I'm still friends with them today. Mel Renfro, Cornell Green, Bob Lilly—I can name forty that I'm still friends with today. I just called Bob Lilly today because it's his birthday.

The job changes when you retire, but your friends don't. That's a good thing. When you leave, you got your friends and your memories. That's it. Hopefully, you cultivated both of them.

# 29

## Ken Houston

Safety

Prairie View A&M

Drafted, 1967 (Houston Oilers, 9th round)

Houston Oilers, 1967–1972

Washington Redskins, 1973–1980

NFL interception leader (1971: 9)

4 Interception returns for touchdowns, 1971 (record; tied with
    Jim Kearney, Eric Allen)

12 All-Pro seasons

12 Pro Bowls

1970s NFL All-Decade Team

NFL 75th Anniversary All-Time Team

Pro Football Hall of Fame inductee (1986)

I wasn't overly involved in sports coming up. I was in band until tenth grade. I thought girls liked football players better than band members, so I actually started to play football to get a girlfriend. [*Laughs.*]

I was a better basketball player than football player, and I also ran track. I think it's important during high school to play all three because they complement each other. It really helped me and the guys I came through with. Quite a few guys that came out of my hometown of Lufkin, Texas, played professional sports.

Back then it was pre-integration, so you were limited in the amount of colleges you could go to. Prairie View was one of the top black schools in the Southwest Athletic Conference—the Black SWAC, as we called it. Coach Billy Nicks wanted an offensive tackle named Wiley Smith, and I went to Prairie View as part of a package deal.

Let me tell you how thick the talent was at Prairie View: Charley Taylor felt like he couldn't make the team and wound up going to Arizona State. He later made the Pro Football Hall of Fame.

There were eight or nine guys on that team who played professional football for a long time. Jim Kearney, our starting quarterback, was drafted as a quarterback by the Detroit Lions and played there for five years. He then went to Kansas City and made All-Pro as a safety. Otis Taylor played receiver for the Chiefs. I think Otis was one of the greatest athletes ever as far as a pure, physical specimen who could catch and run. Alvin Reed, my roommate for ten years in pro ball, was a defensive end at Prairie View and played tight end in the NFL.

I made All-American two years at Prairie View, at linebacker. I had a chance to go with the San Diego Chargers the year before I graduated as an outside linebacker but opted to stay in school.

The Oilers brought me, Alvin Reed, and a few more of us in for a pro day and timed us in the 40-yard dash. I was like 4.5, 4.6, but I was a linebacker. With that speed I guess they penciled me in as a strong safety from the day I walked into camp.

I never fully made the adjustment from linebacker to safety. [Laughs.] That's how difficult it was. In my fourteenth year I was still learning. I didn't think about being the best at my position; I just wanted to be the best that I could be. I never stopped learning and never stopped trying to get better.

I didn't make the Pro Bowl my rookie year, but I made it my second year. They gave me and my wife a plane ticket and $500, and for one week they fed us every night. I thought, "Whoa, they do this every year?"

The guys said, "Yeah."

I said, "As long as I'm here, why not me?"

Bernie Miller was an assistant coach for the Oilers and taught me a great deal. His technical skills were as good as or better than any person I have ever seen. He gave me the technicalities to go along with the physicality. I understood position on the field, position on the receiver, and zones on the field. He made that stuff clear to me. With what I already knew from other coaches, I became a complete ballplayer.

In 1971 I returned five turnovers for touchdowns (four interceptions and one fumble). I think that's still a record for one year.

I was looking to score every time I touched the ball. The Redskins had a planned return. Once you intercepted the ball, you ran to the sideline. In Houston I did just the opposite. I wanted to operate in the middle of the field to work against offensive linemen and running backs—people that couldn't make tackles in open spaces. Probably 90 percent of my touchdowns came on cutbacks, unless I'd intercepted one on the sideline and had a chance to run it in. What's interesting is that I never ran back a touchdown on an interception after I left Houston.

Before the 1973 season the Oilers traded me to Washington for five players. Being traded upset me because I had been told the Oilers were going to build a secondary around me. They wanted me to sign a long-term contract, which I didn't do for whatever reason.

Players are different things to different teams. That's why a player can be good at one place and go to another place and fail. Sometimes you have to understand the scheme and system a guy's in to know why he looks good.

For my first three or four weeks with Washington I was second and third team. I thought, "Why did you trade for me if you weren't going to play me?" I later understood the concept. Head Coach George Allen didn't just let you come in and step into a position. You had to earn that position so the players could respect you.

KEN HOUSTON                                                         221

I had a couple of interceptions against Johnny Unitas in my first game as a Redskin, but I think the game that solidified my career in Washington was week 4, when we played the Cowboys on *Monday Night Football*. Toward the end of the game on a 4th and 4, they threw a swing pass to Walt Garrison, and I stopped him on the 1-yard line. If you do anything in Washington against Dallas, you become an instant hero.

On the play I thought I could intercept the ball but got caught between Walt and the ball. It wasn't a great tackle; I just picked him up off the ground and wouldn't let him put his feet down. People thought I smothered him, but I didn't. Walt's a very good player.

That play was all positioning. George Allen was very thorough as to what you studied. If a player released inside, how many times did he stay inside? If he released outside, how many times did he come back inside? It was all percentages, and you learned to read plays. You could tell by the release pretty well what they were going to do. You just had to stop it.

The best way to describe playing against Dallas is to say that when you were in Houston, you didn't like the Cowboys, just from being in the same state. When you got with the Redskins, it got worse than that. You didn't like them, period. [*Laughs.*] You figure if George Allen and Tom Landry had a marble-shooting contest, they'd be breaking each other's marbles. They did not want to lose.

Off the field, guys are good friends. Calvin Hill ended up being my roommate. I knew Duane Thomas real well, and I see them all right now. During the game, however, it's survival. For 60 minutes you couldn't let up because if you didn't hit somebody as hard as you could, they were going to hit you as hard as they could.

I was going to let up on a friend of mine, Walter Payton. He was a blocker on a sweep, and I had him dead to rights. I always hit because you want to hit first, but he was just a blocker. I looked away, backed off, and the next thing I knew, he was at the top of my knees. If my cleats had not released on the ground, I would have had two surgeries on both knees. I said, "Never again."

Football is just waiting on somebody to blink. Whoever's willing to make contact and make it consistently, that's who's going to win. I was an offensive center in high school and college, so I had no fear of contact. The game is about defeating the guy you're playing against or hitting him harder than he wants to hold onto the ball.

The hits we put on receivers weren't intimidation; it was football. The only place a guy doesn't have pads is in his stomach area. If you put your head across his stomach, you don't have to grab for the football. He's got to cover it with both of his hands.

Some said I was a dirty player, but I don't think I was. If you throw that ball down, I'll never touch you. It's the ball I'm after. Just drop the ball or fall on the ground with it. The ball caused the problem. [*Laughs.*]

You can't get a person's character mixed up with football. You're out there trying to hit somebody as hard as you can. Character's a word that's pure and shows that you don't want to hurt anybody. You can't use the word "character" loosely when it comes to a sport that's trained to hurt.

My character was built with my family, not in sports. You run across a lot of different kinds of people in sports, and if you don't have character coming in, you won't have character coming out. Football players can be drinking, smoking, and playing the fool, but then you got to say what it is.

I had two knee surgeries my senior year in college, and they never healed. It still hurts. I played with those and the rest of the injuries. I broke my arm in my thirteenth year against the New York Giants in the next to the last game in the season. That was the first game I missed in my career. It was a different game then. If nothing was broken, you just felt like you were going to play and your teammates needed you.

One time we played the Minnesota Vikings in DC. I was tackling Stu Voigt, and Ron McDole was up on top of him. All the weight was on me. I couldn't fall, so I just squatted. The pain in my right knee was unbelievable. The trainer and doctor came out and said, "It's not good news. You'll probably have surgery on Monday." I came off the field and got on crutches after the game. The knee was really swollen.

George Allen said, "Why don't you come to the locker room on Monday before your surgery?" I went to the locker room on Monday, and Allen said, "I talked to the doctor, and he's going to put your surgery off until Wednesday because I want you to talk to the other safeties." I was the signal caller, so I said, "Okay," and talked with them.

During the next couple of days the swelling went down a bit. I'm still on crutches but walking with one foot on the ground and slightly touching it with the other foot. Allen said, "I talked to the doctor again. The surgery's going to be season ending. I don't want you to rush it. Stay around this week and talk to the guys. You can have the weekend when we go to the game."

I said, "Okay."

Thursday I put the crutches down and walked with a limp. Coach came by the sidelines and said, "You're walking. Can you jog?"

I said, "I don't think so."

He said, "Let me see you."

I jogged but just barely, with a limp. I was afraid I would damage it even further.

That evening he called and said, "Houston, I want you go to St. Louis with us. You don't have to dress; just help me on the sidelines." I agreed because by then he'd put off the surgery a whole week.

I go to St. Louis and to breakfast with him. Allen said, "I didn't turn your name in on the injured list. The team's going to get fined if you don't suit up. I just want you to suit up." I suited up and was out on the field during warm-ups, just jogging, not doing anything.

Allen called me to the sideline and said, "I want you to do me one favor. Go get taped. I promise St. Louis isn't going to throw at you. When I introduce the starters, I want you to go in."

I'm thinking, "This man is crazy!"

He said if it seemed like I got injured in this game, the team wouldn't be in trouble. I went into the game, played the whole game, and from that day to this one I've never had surgery.

Now that I look back, it was probably the fourteen years that led me to retire, but I thought I had another year. Some things happened in my fourteenth year that I didn't understand as an older player. I probably overreacted and ended up retiring—probably prematurely, but I opted out.

They put a little column in the paper with the fifteen or twenty Hall of Fame finalists for 1986. I remember cutting that out, thinking, "How do I preserve this?" because I wanted my kids to know that I was nominated.

I was the most shocked guy in football when I was elected. I didn't see myself as a Hall of Famer, and I didn't understand the significance of being a first-ballot Hall of Famer. There are so many guys that probably should be in there but may not get in because of pure numbers. I was inducted in 1986, on the day that the Challenger exploded.

I saw so many guys in my fourteen years that could have played my position, but it was already my job, and there are a limited amount of jobs in the NFL. That's why when you get there, you become better and better and why it's so difficult for somebody to take your job.

After retiring, I went into the school system and became a coach, coaching in pro ball and at the University of Houston. I'm still in education, as a counselor. I've been an alternative counselor for almost twenty years in the district.

I always thought I was going to be a teacher—that's what I went to school for. I played football but never got into being a football player. Pretty well every year the most money I would take out of my contract was what a teacher would make because I was going to quit. I actually left the team three times my rookie year, and they talked me into coming back. I enjoyed it, but I played without having to have it. I think that was the difference.

# 30

## Elvin Bethea

Defensive end

North Carolina A&T

Drafted, 1968 (Houston Oilers, 3rd round)

Houston Oilers, 1968–1983

8 All-Pro seasons

8 Pro Bowls

135 consecutive regular-season games

Pro Football Hall of Fame inductee (2003)

I'm from New Jersey. I ran track and played soccer in junior high. The New Jersey rules said you couldn't play football until the tenth grade. One of my best friends said, "We're going to try out for the football team."

I didn't know what football was, had no idea. I went out and made the JV that morning, and by that afternoon they put me on the varsity squad. I had no idea what I was doing; I made it because of my size. I was like 235, 240 in high school.

The toughness came from my father. He didn't let up on you; you worked. Football and track, he called that foolishness. That's how toughness was instilled in me—the way I grew up, the things I had gone through. I was the first of nine children. We had to raise chickens. I worked in construction, wherever I could help out the family. I worked in a junkyard in high school and knew right then that's what I didn't want to do.

In 1964 I was the state champion in the shot put and discus. I had about twenty different scholarships between football and track. I really wanted to go to Villanova for the shot put, but my grades weren't where they should have been.

My mother made the decision that I go to North Carolina A&T. She went to school with Mel Grooms, one of their coaches, who was also from Trenton. I came home after work on a Saturday, and next thing I know, I'm in the station wagon with Coach Grooms and his family, off to North Carolina. It was all my mother's doing. As they say, "Always do what your mother tells you." It was a good move.

Going to a black school was different. Back then segregation was a big thing in the South. Our high school's offensive line included two blacks, an Italian, and a Polish guy. As far as segregation is concerned, we knew nothing about it. Then I went to college at A&T, where four students sat in at Woolworth's in 1960 to protest segregation and Jesse Jackson became student body president. I was just thinking about going to school and knew nothing about "You can't go here."

In college I learned more about toughness. Our motto used to be, "If you go to a black college, you can make it anywhere in the world." You found out who you were and what you were made of. Just being moral and finding out the world is tough out there. Going to a small school, you found how tough it was. Everybody talks about going to all these big schools, but it taught me a lot and I found myself going to a small school.

Our facilities were antiquated. [*Laughs.*] Very, very antiquated. For weights we'd get a metal bar and those gray concrete bricks, slide the bar in the hole, and fill it with cement. We had no idea what the thing weighed, but that's how you'd do your bench press.

Now when you do your two-a-days you expect for your clothes to be washed by the time you come back in the afternoon. Not at A&T. You came back in the afternoon, and the same stuff you took off was the same stuff you put back on. Wet, smelly—that's what you'd put on. The only thing you got was a new jock.

We'd travel to play Florida A&M. From Greensboro, North Carolina, through South Carolina, Georgia, and Florida, you drove all the way through and couldn't stop at a hotel. I'll never forget one time we stopped in Georgia and told the guy we wanted to go to the bathroom. He said, "Go around out back." We go out back, look around, and it's a big ol' field. That was where you went.

You never stayed in a hotel for road games like you do today. A good example of that was the University of Maryland–Eastern Shore, where Art Shell and Emerson Boozer attended. The school was in a little town called Princess Anne, Maryland. You slept in a train depot the night before the game. The train would come, blowing the whistle, waking you up. They gave us old army blankets, and that's what you slept in: old, green wool blankets that made you sneeze. We didn't know any better; we thought it was fun. Then you had to go out there and play a game.

We shared our home stadium with a AAA baseball team. To get to the game we didn't ride; we walked about a mile to the stadium. Half of the stadium was a dirt field. If you fell down, lime was all in your face. We didn't think about it; that's what you dealt with. That's where mental toughness came in.

My last year, scouts would come around. I saw scouts from Kansas City, San Diego—basically all black scouts—and they would say, "We're looking at you to be No. 1." Gil Brandt put out the word that I was going to be No. 1 for Dallas. I was all excited when the draft came up and waited to hear from Dallas.

The evening of the draft, somebody yelled out, "Bethea, the Houston Oilers are on the phone." I had no idea who the Houston Oilers were. They told me I was their third pick, and I said, "I'm waiting for Dallas to call me; they said I'd be No. 1."

I signed for a $15,000 salary and a $15,000 bonus, so $30,000. I gave half of that to my parents. In 1968 it seemed like a lot of money.

My first car was a Dodge Charger that cost $8,000. Oilers owner Bud Adams owned the Dodge dealership, so the money he gave us, we just gave it right back. Everybody on the team had a Charger. [*Laughs.*]

Training camp was from hell. It was at the Schreiner Institute, a prep school in Kerrville, Texas. Every day was 100 degrees or close to it. By two o'clock you'd walk out across that field and see heat waves coming up off the ground. Many times I thought, "What did I get into?" We were going wide open, in pads. Back then it wasn't just shoulder pads; it was full gear.

They gave you handfuls of salt tablets without knowing what it did to you. You'd lose 8–10 pounds of water weight a day. You'd gain it back that evening after drinking all the fluids. It was hell, but that's where the toughness paid off.

I was drafted as an offensive tackle, but in college I played four positions: guard, tackle, defensive end, and linebacker. I never left the field and played sixty minutes, both ways. The Oilers had me play half the practice on offense; then they'd put a red shirt on me and I'd play defense. For $15,000 they got a hell of a deal. They got two players.

I played offense through training camp and the preseason games. We were paid $50 per preseason game. That's before taxes now. It came out to about $43 after taxes. When you traveled, you got a five and two ones as a per diem, along with a Coors beer.

During my rookie year we were playing Buffalo, and one of our defensive guys, Gary Cutsinger, was getting beat up pretty bad. I was standing on the sideline, waiting to go in on offense, and the head coach tells me, "Bethea, you're in!"

I said, "Well, the defense is on the field."

He said, "On the field, now!"

I didn't have time to get scared or think about it. I just put on my helmet, lined up, and took off. I had a good game. Stew Barber from the Bills told my teammate Billy Shaw, "I don't know who this rookie is, but he's giving me fits over here." From that day on, I never looked back.

My rookie year I was just excited to be there, but my second year I started learning the game. I had the physical ability, but it was a mental thing remembering the calls and not ignoring them. Whatever was called on defense, whether it was the wrong defense or not, you played the defense that was called.

Watching game film really helped. I'd carry one of those projectors in a big ol' box and take it home with me. I know Ken Houston and Garland Boyette did the same thing. That's where you became a professor of the game, learning what the other team is doing and what you're going to do to stop it. Watching the down distances and what formations they were using, that's where being a smart football player came in. Learning all those things helped you make fewer mistakes by having an idea of what you're up against. That's where being a real professional stands out. They go in prepared.

I did so well the first year that I got a $1,000 raise to $16,000—to help me pay off that car. [Laughs.] After my second or third year I made the Pro Bowl. I got an extra $1,500 for making the Pro Bowl as part of my contract. I had what a lot of what they called "if clauses" in my contract. They'd load you down with them: if you made so many tackles, if you made all-AFL, if you made the first team. They were incentives, and you'd work your butt off to get them. The Pro Bowl itself paid $1,000 for the winner and $750 for the loser. We would take each other's heads off for that extra $250.

You had to work during the off-season. I lived in North Carolina my first two years, 1968 and 1969. There weren't many companies that would pay six months on/six months off. The only thing back in Greensboro, North Carolina, was the Marlboro cigarette company. That didn't pay enough, so I moved to Houston in 1970. I worked with Zendler's clothing store in sales from 1970 to 1978.

In the '70s most teams were afraid of the Steelers. We couldn't wait to play the Steelers because it brought out the best in everybody. The better teams—the Dolphins, the Patriots—you knew they had great teams, and you didn't want to get embarrassed. You'd get yourself up mentally in preparation during the week.

In 1978 we were the AFC wild card going into Miami. We weren't even supposed to come into the locker room, much less go down there and beat them. We went down there, and they had Bob Griese, Larry Csonka, Jim Kiick and Larry Little. Going into that game, we didn't care who you were. We went down there to kick some butt, and that's what we did. It was a defensive game and we beat them 17-9.

We had to go to New England the next week. We went up there and had to go up against Leon Gray, who I'd say was the best offensive tackle I ever faced, and John Hannah, who's in the Hall of Fame. They had a helluva team. We didn't care. We beat New England in Foxboro.

We then played in the AFC Championship in Pittsburgh. It drizzled the whole game. You could look at the net where the guy kicks the ball and see icicles coming off of it. We didn't have any heaters when you came off the sidelines. They might have had one little blower, and that was it. We went into the locker room at halftime, and the trainer didn't have any dry T-shirts for us to change into. We lost 34-5.

Coming back to Houston was the thrill of my life. They took us with a police escort from the airport to the Astrodome. We got in the dome and couldn't believe it. There were sixty thousand people waiting for us. Here you are, a loser, and they still had the place packed. Our head coach, Bum Phillips, made his famous quote, "This year we knocked on the door; we kicked at the door; next year we're going to kick the son-of-a-bitch in!"

Next year came and we again played at Pittsburgh for the AFC Championship. Mike Renfro caught the ball for a touchdown that would have tied the game at 17 at the end of the third quarter, but the officials said he wasn't in bounds. Everything went downhill from there, and that's when all the talk about using replay to decide calls started. We lost that game 27-13.

They again gave us a police escort all the way from the airport to the Astrodome, and for the second straight year the people packed the dome to greet us.

Looking back, we had something going and didn't realize it as a team. Joe Greene made that statement to me too. He said, "You guys had no idea what you had."

On the field it's a different story, but Franco Harris, Joe Greene, L. C. Greenwood, Dwight White, Terry Bradshaw—we all were friends. One year we didn't go to the playoffs, but we beat Cincinnati for Pittsburgh to get in. The Steelers sent us all Samsonite briefcases. That's how close we were.

We had that war-on-war against each other at game time, but when we'd see each other out of that uniform, we were friends. Once it's over, it's over. You took the veil off, and it was back to reality. It wasn't difficult; it was just a game. There were a few that couldn't turn it on and off, but to the majority it's just a game. Go out there and do the best you can against your best friend, and go back to work at practice on Monday.

The way you practice is the way you play, and the way you play is the way you practice. I always practiced hard and set a goal. Every week I gave myself a challenge to be better than last week. One play better, one tackle better, one sack better. I'd always push for that one more.

On the sideline you're nervous before each and every game. They play the National Anthem, and when they get to the last note, "The home of the brave," you know it's all-out war. You put everything you got into each play. The game's physical, but it's mental too. It was a mental challenge of focusing on the individual in front of me. "What is he going to do? What play are they going to run?"

It's about going out there with a mental attitude and knowing when a play is over, it's over. Get back up; now here we go again. I get down in my stance and try to figure out what keys they're giving. The guard would give away if it's a sweep by how he put his hand down. If it was going to be a pass, he'd just put his hand on the ground. If it was going to be a run play, he'd have it solid. You'd always watch where his foot was. You're talking a split second now.

There's so many things on that field that you blank out the crowd. I'm looking at the guy in front of me, and at the same time I'm looking at the ball in my peripheral view. I'm anticipating the count, but I don't hear the quarterback going, "Hut, Hut, Hut!" He can "Hut!" all he wants, but until that ball moves, I can't jump; otherwise I'm offside.

I have the defense that they called in the huddle; now I got to think about the linebacker calling "Red! Red! Red!" or "Strong Left!" or "Zip! Zip! Zip!" I'm listening to all this back here, and at the same time my outside linebacker, Robert Brazile, and I have our own call going among ourselves. If he calls, "x-x-x!," I'll go upfield first. If he doesn't call it, I'm covering his area and he's taking my position. Now if my mind is not there and I don't hear it, we'll both go inside, and somebody goes around and scores.

At the same time I'm looking to see where the back is lined up, if the tight end is on my side, and worrying if that tight end and guard are going to double team me. You're like a computer watching all these things happen in split seconds.

There are rules according to your position. If the tight end and guard double team me, the rule is to just fall down and make a pile. I'm out of the play but at the same time I'm taking two guys, and a linebacker can go in and fill. If I don't make that pile and the lineman straightens me up, the tight end can block me into the linebacker, taking the linebacker out too.

Another rule is once you're upfield and the play goes the other way, you take an angle in case the play cuts back across.

You can't catch the play on the other side, but if you take that angle, the runner may break three or four tackles, and you just happen to be the last guy going that way to cover. You meet him right there and knock his nuts off.

Your talent works hand in hand with following those rules. Following them 100 percent will show up whether it's the Super Bowl or the preseason.

I've had thirteen operations [points to four scars on left knee]. My first year I had a medial, then a lateral there, cartilage taken out, and I had another one back behind my leg. And this is the good leg! [*Laughs.*] [Points to scars on right knee.] This was '69, this was '70, and then '71 back here.

I hear guys say, "I blew my knee out, and that's why I couldn't make it to the pros." Hey, my knee: they took the cartilage out of here, and they'd spray this sticky stuff called "Toughskin" on it. In '69 they started taping me directly to the skin. I'd get to practice early, and they'd take the tape and put it directly on my skin to give it support so it wouldn't wobble. You'd go to pull the tape off, and you'd pull off the skin and everything. I did that for every year I was there. That's how bad I wanted to play. I've also had to have operations on both ankles. I broke my finger in New England and had it opened up for the knuckle.

I broke my arm, a compound fracture, in Oakland in '77. Mark van Eeghen came around the corner on a sweep, and I was going to bring him down with a forearm club. I clotheslined him, but he ducked his head and came right across. Broke both bones, crack! It didn't hurt at the time. I was down on a knee, moving it around, and next thing I know, they got a cast on me.

In about 1975 I played with a cracked sternum. Trying to breathe, oh man, *with a hairline crack*. They built me a big pad to wear to cushion it, and I said, "Let's go play." Otherwise you were going to sit on the bench.

Once playing Detroit, I was chasing down a play that was

8. Elvin Bethea's third finger is permanently bent sharply to the right from NFL action.

away from me, and all of a sudden a guy came back and hit me. I went up in the air, and all I saw was the lights. I came down on my right shoulder and broke or dislocated it. That was painful. They said, "If you get it operated on, it's going to hurt worse." I told them not to worry about it. I never did get it put back in place. I got a big ol' hump here.

The next week, we played Denver. The pain was still bad, and they gave me what they called a TENS unit, wires they harnessed underneath my shoulder pads. It would pulsate and give me an electric pulse—kind of like sticking your hand on a lawnmower. I could turn it up or down and turn it as high as I wanted to stop the pain.

Well, my shirt got wet. We didn't think about *this*. When the shirt got wet, one of the leads came off, and this thing's shocking the hell out of me. I'm on the ground rolling, reel-

9. Interiors of Elvin Bethea's helmets. On the left, suspended cloth straps and a rubber bridge that would often pierce his forehead. On the right, hard rubber and foam.

ing in pain. I was trying to turn it down and trying to get at it because it was stuck underneath my shoulder pads. They had to pull all of this stuff out to get under it to cut it off. I went to the sidelines, put on a dry shirt, stuck it back on, and said, "Let's go!"

That's football. That's what real football was. I don't care what it was, you wouldn't come off the field.

We played with concussions; we had no idea what a concussion was. All I knew is you'd get hit, and all you'd see was little light stars. The trainer would come over ask if you were okay, crack one of those smelling salts, and stick it under your nose. You'd jump up, and those stars would go away.

Against Cincinnati I lost everything. I couldn't move from the neck down. Kenny Anderson is going back to pass, and I'm putting my head down trying to tackle him. Next thing I know, Kenny steps forward, and here's Curley Culp. Curley weighed 300 pounds, and I weighed 265. We hit head on, and I'm out. I'm laying there and couldn't move nothing. It was just like being in a vacuum, looking up. People said, "Move your feet, move your fingers." Nothing. They said I was out twenty minutes.

I didn't know about this until after, but every team has an emergency vehicle waiting. After my feeling started to come back at the hospital, they told me, "The emergency vehicle at the game didn't work, so you came over in a hearse." That night I rode back home with a collar on, drinking a Coors beer, and I played the next week.

We were a bunch of misfits: alcoholics, drunks, and a lot of things we can't talk about; we had the whole bunch. One guy would sometimes show up drunk and once showed up at a practice meeting with a baby. He had stayed out all night, and his wife had to go somewhere and made him take the baby. Coach Wally Lemm's talking, and the baby's in the back crying. That was my second year. I couldn't believe it.

I remember one time in the early '70s, maybe mid-'70s, getting on the team bus after a game. Black guys would get on one bus, and the white guys would get on another bus. I don't know if it was a mental thing. It wasn't a team thing; you could get on any bus you wanted to. One day I just happened to get on the first bus that came to me, the bus the white guys got on. Somebody yelled out, "Hey, ain't you on the wrong bus?" That set me off. I don't know what I didn't say. When I got finished, everybody knew I didn't play that. I busted my ass out here for a team sport, and you're telling me that? *No*. I was captain at the time, and from that day on we had no more problems.

There were some guys you had questionable thoughts about. You could feel something, but you just couldn't put your finger on it. They'd go hunting for alligator and come in with a noose in the locker room. You'd walk in and find a real alligator with a noose around its neck. We had some guys that I always kept my eye on and didn't say much to.

My last year was '83. Going through training camp in San Angelo, Texas, was an ass kicker. It was hot as hell, and I was thirty-seven years old. We're running wide open, and I'm just trying to hang on. I did fifteen years, and I said, "That's it."

I talked to Channel 13 and told them, "I'm finished."

Eddie Biles was the head coach that year. He called me after I told everybody I was retired, and they had this big retirement thing for me. Coach Biles asked, "You want to play another year?"

I said, "No, I've had it."

He said, "What would it take to get you back?"

I said, "I'm not coming back."

He said, "Well, think about it."

I had made $240,000 the previous two years. Biles called me the next day and said, "What will it take?"

I said, "$300,000." Not knowing I was *way* under.

He said, "Let me get back with Ladd Herzeg [the general manager]."

Ladd called me and said, "I don't think we can do that."

I said, "Well, I'm not interested in going back anyway."

Next afternoon I got a call asking, "When are you going to come and sign the contract?"

I signed the contract, but I was way under because Mark Gastineau and Joe Klecko from the New York Jets had just signed $1 million dollar contracts for their rookie year. Here I'm getting $300,000.

They told me I only had to play certain downs and help with coaching Jesse Baker. I thought, "Oh, that's easy."

About three-quarters of the way through the season, they fired Eddie Biles and hired Chuck Studley. Studley told me, "You don't have to practice anymore. You can just travel now."

That sort of hurt. I finished the year out, and for the last game they let me suit up. Then I packed my jersey and everything else in a case. I was glad to get out of there. After sixteen years of getting beat up and ornery, all the operations and injuries I had, it was time.

When football was over, it was over. I cut the cord and never looked back. That was just part of my history, and life goes on. I went to work with Anheuser-Busch.

People started to tell me, "You're going to be in the Hall of Fame."

I'd say, "I don't know what the Hall of Fame is."

I honestly didn't know. Then I'd see all these other guys going in and think, "I know I was better than him; I went to 8 Pro Bowls, and this guy only did this." Still, I never thought in a hundred million years that I would go in. If you didn't play in New York or California, don't even think about it. How many from Dallas had even gone until the past few years? I played on teams that were 1-13 two years in a row. I said, "There's no way."

I never really paid attention until 2003. I was working with Budweiser and going to a meeting in St. Louis. I got a call from a friend of mine at Channel 26 in Houston. He said, "You made it in."

I said, "Made it in what?"

He said, "The Hall of Fame."

I said, "Don't play with me. I'm in a cab in St. Louis, and I'm headed to a meeting right now."

He said, "I need you to go to the Fox news station there."

I said, "I don't have time for all this."

He said, "Go put your clothes on and get down there."

I said, "You're not kidding me now? I'm going to have to put my stuff in the hotel and check in before I go there."

I went to the station. They interviewed me and told me I was one of fifteen finalists for the Hall of Fame. The inductees were named at the Super Bowl, which was in California that year. They asked me to fly out there, and I said, "I'm not spending the money to go out there for you to tell me I didn't make it. I'll stay home."

10. Elvin Bethea looking sharp in his Hall of Fame blazer.

The Monday before the Super Bowl, they sent the finalists a round-trip ticket for the finalist and his wife to go to Hawaii, to introduce him as a Hall of Famer at the Pro Bowl. All fifteen of us got a letter with a first-class ticket to Hawaii to use if we were chosen. I had a whole week to look at that ticket sitting on my desk.

The afternoon of the voting, a reporter came over and asked, "Can I sit in your house and wait for the call?"

I said "No."

My wife said, "*Definitely* no."

He sat outside.

A call came. The caller ID said, "Pro Football Hall of Fame." I picked it up and heard, "This is John Bankard. I'm head of the Hall of Fame and wanted to tell you you're the 181st football player to go into the Hall of Fame."

Everything that's led up to this—all the injuries, all the 1-13s, all the training camps—all of that has come down to this, and you're saying, "I can't believe this." I held that ticket, and I said, "We can hold onto this ticket now. We're going to Hawaii!"

The thrill that gives me goose bumps today is the presentation in Canton. Ah, man, it gives me bumps every time I think about it. You go up on the stage, the entrants come in, and you're on the stage with the other inductees. You're standing there with your sports jacket on, and as the proceeding goes on, each and every Hall of Famer that's there comes up on stage. That's when you feel like you want to melt right through the ground.

They take that jacket off you and put the Hall of Fame jacket on. I think that's the highlight. Then every Hall of Famer comes up and shakes your hand to welcome you to the club.

Deacon Jones shook my hand and said, "It's the one team you can't be cut from."

It can't get any better than that.

# 31

## Bob Griese

Quarterback

Purdue University

Drafted, 1967 (Miami Dolphins, 1st round)

Miami Dolphins, 1967–1980

2-time Super Bowl champion (Super Bowls 7 and 8)

NFL player of the year, 1971

NFL completion percentage leader (1970, 1977, 1978)

NFL touchdown pass leader (1977)

5 All-Pro seasons

8 Pro Bowls

Pro Football Hall of Fame inductee (1990)

We didn't have peewee football. The first organized football I played was in high school, at a new Catholic school called Rex Mundi.

The coach said, "What position do you play?"

I said, "Well, I've never played organized football before. I like to catch the ball."

I ran one play at wide receiver. He came back and said, "Why don't you try the next play at quarterback?" I think he had read newspaper clippings that I had been a pitcher in baseball and knew I had a good arm. I was a pretty good pitcher in Little League and Pony League. Throwing a ball came naturally, but I really didn't learn how to throw a football until I got to Purdue.

I was not highly recruited and only had two schools to choose from—Indiana and Purdue. I just liked Purdue and the coach, Jack Mollenkopf. That's basically why I went there.

Besides playing quarterback, I was the placekicker for three years and punted. We played USC in the 1967 Rose Bowl and won by one point. We were seniors, and that was the first time Purdue had ever gone.

The draft wasn't like it is today, where it's on ESPN. Hardly anybody knew when the draft was. I went over to the Athletic Department on some March or April day, and one of the coaches passed me in the hallway and said, "Hey, did you know you got drafted by the Dolphins?"

I said, "Oh, that's nice." [Bob was the fourth-overall pick in the draft.]

For a few years you could get drafted by two teams, an AFL and an NFL team. That was a little leverage. Our draft in 1967 was the first combined draft, so there was nobody else to negotiate with. There weren't agents back then either. I just had a friend who helped me negotiate a contract. Teams could give you anything they wanted. Even after you played your first contract out, if you didn't sign with your original team, there was nobody else to sign with because there was no free agency.

I worked at a bank the first off-season and then got my real estate license. It wasn't like today, where players make so much money that their off-season work is their off-season conditioning program.

I didn't start the first game of 1967, but the quarterback that did got hurt. I played in that first game and started the rest.

Everything was challenging. I was a rookie starting on an expansion team in its second year of existence. We weren't very good, so I had to scramble a lot. I was a pretty good runner—not because I wanted to be but because I *had* to be.

Coach Shula came in 1970. He gave an interview and said, "One of the first things I want to do is get that young quarterback Griese to stay in the pocket." The first time I saw him I said, "Hey, you give me a pocket, and I'd love to stay in it."

With Coach Shula, it didn't take long. Before he came we were 3-10-1. His first year we were 10-4.

We played Kansas City on Christmas Day in the 1971 AFC divisional playoffs. They were the powerhouse of the league, and we were just upstarts. We hadn't won anything; we hadn't done anything. We weren't at their caliber yet, but they kept missing field goals, giving us opportunities to stay in it. Our attitude was, "If they're not going to win it, let's go out and win it." [Miami won 27-24 in two overtimes, still the longest game in NFL history.]

We lost Super Bowl 6 to the Cowboys. The last time Coach Shula saw us after the Super Bowl he said, "We're going to have to work as hard the following year to get back to where we were before we lost the Super Bowl." We all knew 1972 was going to be a tough year coming back.

Right from the start, Coach Shula pounded on us, "You've got to take care of business every game. You never know which game is going to matter."

We played the Chargers in week 5. I suffered a broken leg and a dislocated ankle on my right side. I'd followed through with a throw, and Ron East fell on my lower leg. The doctors didn't know how long it would take to recover, and I didn't expect to be back that year. I just wanted to be healthy as soon as I could so I could play with my boys.

Back then the playoff game locations were decided ahead of time. In other words, as long as Pittsburgh was in the play-offs, they were going to host the AFC Championship in 1972, regardless of how many games we won or lost. Even though we were undefeated, we still had to go up there to play. Today it's decided by who has the most wins.

Coach Shula had seen me in practice; I was practicing pretty well. I actually had an advantage over a lot of guys because I hadn't been wearing down. I wasn't worn down physically, I wasn't battered mentally, and I wasn't bruised from taking sacks. When Coach Shula came at halftime of the AFC Championship and said, "Are you ready to go?" I was not surprised.

I said, "Yeah."

We went in and made some plays. We moved the ball in the second half, while in the first half we hadn't. We called the plays back then, and it was just calling the plays at the right time. Our punter, Larry Seiple, ran from punt formation, making a key first down. I hit [Paul] Warfield over the middle on a slant route; he brought it down and went 52 yards. [The Dolphins beat Pittsburgh, 21-17. The halftime score was 7-7.]

I don't think we were talking about the record before Super Bowl 7 or after. Once you get into the playoffs and you're 14-0, then you better go undefeated. [Laughs] We didn't try to go undefeated; it just happened. When we won the championship, it wasn't "Hey! We were undefeated!" It was, "Hey, we won the Super Bowl, and we're champions!"

We didn't think anything about the fact that we went undefeated. We thought that if we did it, somebody else would do it in the coming years. Then five years passed, ten years passed. The Steelers won the Super Bowl four times in the '70s and didn't do it. Neither did the Cowboys with Roger Staubach. Ten years passed, fifteen, twenty years. San Francisco with Joe Montana and Steve Young . . . all these good teams; none of them were able to go undefeated.

As time went on we realized, "Hey, this must be something special," even though we didn't think it was anything special when we did it. All we wanted to do was win the Super Bowl.

The following year we were 15-2 [including playoffs] but actually had a better team. A lot of the players were back. We were confident and just another year older. We got beat a couple of times, but everybody's pointing for you, and you got everybody's best every week. It wasn't even close in the Super Bowl. We beat the Vikings 24-7. [It was 24-0 until 1:35 left in the fourth quarter.]

My fourteenth year was 1980. We were playing the Colts, and I got hit by a defensive end. He hit me as I was throwing and kind of took the arm backward as my muscles came forward. Because it was midseason, the doctor said I couldn't play the rest of that year. Back then if I'd had the surgery, I wouldn't have been able to play the following year either. I couldn't play without the surgery. I decided, "Well, if I can't play the following year, I'll just retire and be a coach with Coach Shula."

I told all three of my sons, "Don't plan on doing what I did because it probably won't work that way. I just kind of slipped through the cracks. Pick a good college, get a good education, and if you want to walk on the football program, that's fine."

What Brian did was all his doing. I didn't want to put any pressure on him. [Brian Griese quarterbacked Michigan to a national championship in 1997 (Michigan and Nebraska were recognized as co-national champions) before playing eleven years in the NFL.] I was a broadcaster with Keith Jackson, and we did a lot of Brian's games his senior year at Michigan. I'd been catching heck all year from the writers about calling a fair game with Brian on one side.

We broadcast the Rose Bowl Game, and Michigan played Washington State. Washington State was Keith's alma mater. Now Keith was catching all of these questions: "Hey, your alma mater's Washington State and you're doing the Rose Bowl?" I was kind of laughing at him.

Brian had a good game, and Michigan won. Near the end of the Rose Bowl Keith Jackson said, "Whoa, Nellie. You want to know who the MVP is? I'm standing right next to his proud daddy."

# 32

## Rocky Bleier

Running back

Notre Dame

Drafted, 1968 (Pittsburgh Steelers, 16th round)

Pittsburgh Steelers, 1968, 1972–1980

4-time Super Bowl champion (Super Bowls 9, 10, 13, 14)

I grew up in Appleton, Wisconsin, not too far from Green Bay. Football wasn't as big as it is today, but by 1960, when the Packers lost the championship game to the Eagles, people had their favorite players, they would wear their green and gold, and this kind of fever kind of grew. My dad had gotten some season tickets, and I went to a couple of games, not a whole lot, but you'd watch them on television.

I attended Xavier, a Catholic high school. From my sophomore through my senior years we dominated the Fox River Valley Conference. We never lost a football game and were the state's No. 1 ranked team in both football and basketball in 1962. I made All-State and was selected to the Parade High School All-American Team.

There was a guy in Appleton named Russ Skall who had gone to Notre Dame, walked on as a football player, and played special teams. When I was a junior in high school, he took my dad and me to the Wisconsin–Notre Dame game in South Bend. We left about four o'clock in the morning because Russ wanted to go to the team mass and team breakfast. We missed the mass but got down to campus for breakfast. Huey Devore was the interim coach, and we went over just to say hi to the coach. Huey Devore said, "Young man, if you'd like to come here, you have a scholarship to the University of Notre Dame."

I go, "Oh. Thank you very much." [*Laughs.*] I didn't know how to react to that.

That was Huey's last year. Ara Parseghian came in at the beginning of 1964.

I decided to only visit three schools my senior year. My first recruiting trip was to Notre Dame. We played basketball with the other recruits. It gave them a chance to see your physique, your ability to play, how coordinated you were, and your quickness rather than overall speed.

The following week, I went to Wisconsin. I met Head Coach Milt Bruhn, and he brought in the jazz band director in case I wanted to play in the band. I had played trumpet in high school. He said, "We can work that out, blah, blah, blah." This was a big pitch. [*Laughs.*]

There was another All-State running back in Wisconsin named Jankowski. Coach Bruhn said, "You two will be my starting running backs by your sophomore year."

A friend of the family had gone to Boston College. I went out to Boston College and loved Boston. Not Boston College necessarily, just Boston. I had just read all this history about the American Revolution, and this is where it was.

I came home and had to make a decision. I did what every good Catholic boy is taught to do—go to church. And then I did what my mother wanted me to do, which was to go to Notre Dame. [*Laughs.*] Really I made that decision. Dave Hurd, the Notre Dame recruiter, had given me a piece of advice: "Make your choice based on what school you'd like to go to and graduate from if you'd never played football." It was one of those decisions you make and see what happens.

My junior year was 1966. Michigan State was the second to the last game for us and the last for Michigan State. In the polling for the "mythical national championship" we were ranked first and they were second. This was the first time in years the two top-ranked teams actually played at the end of the season to give the semblance of a championship game. It got blown up to being called "the Game of the Century."

Whether you're playing in a big NFL game or a big game in college, it's all about preparation. You take on the mannerisms of your coach and his approach. If he is a person that puts pressure on himself and demands excellence from himself, *you're* going to feel the tensions.

Ara Parseghian and Steeler coach Chuck Noll both had the same philosophy. You play how you prepare and how you practice. It's not a matter of trying to get up for a big game; it's a constant building of your confidence. From the first day of practice, the first game through the last game, it's a constant building of *you*. Chuck Noll said, "It's not my job to motivate you. It's my job to take motivated people, show them what needs to be done, and prepare them for the contest at hand."

Ara was the same, but at the college level motivation's more important because he can't fire you. Ara would build the groundwork for the upcoming game, whether it was against Michigan State or a weaker team.

We would play Saturday and review on Sunday. After the review Ara would give a little tidbit about the upcoming opponent. They might not have won a game all season, but he would plant something like, "They have an All-American candidate." By Thursday you thought you were playing the national champion. The preparation for the Michigan State game wasn't any different.

We took the train up from South Bend to East Lansing, and along the way you could see a change from Notre Dame fans along the side to Michigan State fans as the train went by.

I remember walking into that stadium, and that was the first time that I ever experienced the movement of airwaves. It was packed as we were introduced, and it was like I could see the air move with the cheering that had taken place. It was, for me, obviously a memory I haven't forgotten. We all went, "Whoo." But once the game starts, the game starts, and we were well prepared.

It's always how you deal with the intangibles. Nick Eddy, our All-American running back, got hurt coming off the train. He slipped on the train tracks, wrenching the arm he had previously hurt. He wasn't able to play. Terry Hanratty, our All-American quarterback, got hurt in the first quarter. Coley O'Brien, the backup, became the starter. George Goeddeke, our offensive center, got hurt in the first half. Tim Monty, a sophomore, was inserted and played the majority of the game at center.

I always tell people the toughest guy in that game was Tim Monty. When Goeddeke went out, Michigan State moved Bubba Smith from defensive end to nose tackle to take advantage of the smaller, inexperienced player. Here's Bubba at 280 pounds, and Monty's maybe 215. Tim would come back to the huddle, and his helmet would be screwed on backwards with mud and muck caked on it. *But* Bubba Smith never got through. We had the ball last, ran the ball, and ultimately ran out of time. The game ended in a tie [10-10].

Michigan State had a barefoot kicker who had kicked 50-yard field goals, and Ara didn't want to give them the opportunity to win the game. His thought was that if we could control the ball and maybe get into position for a field goal, then that's the way we would play, rather than chucking the ball downfield, trying for the big play, and ultimately either turning the ball over on an interception or having to punt. Ara received much criticism for settling for a tie when in actuality the game had been tied for a while.

In that game I caught a pass over the middle and got hit by linebacker George Webster, right in my kidney. After the game I'm in the john going to the bathroom, and I see this red stream of urine coming out of my system. I was put in the hospital with a lacerated kidney and missed our last game, at Southern Cal. We beat Southern Cal, 51-0, on national television, which clinched for us that mythical national championship.

My senior year, we played at Georgia Tech in the second to last game. Bud Carson was their head coach and ultimately came to the Steelers. He became the defensive coordinator in the early '70s and created our defenses.

Right before the half we had the ball down on the goal line. I carried the ball into the line, got stuffed, but wasn't down. I slid off the hole and turned backward, pushing and falling into the end zone, scoring the touchdown. I felt this hit and a little twinge on my left knee. It gave a bit as I ran off the field. We checked it at halftime. The doctors gave the typical knee flex back and forth. My other muscles, because of the game, controlled it. The doctors said, "It looks okay."

I started the second half. We had a lead, and I was taken out of the game in the third quarter to let other people play. We flew back, and my knee started to swell. It was sore after the adrenaline left and everything relaxed. They checked it on Monday and said, "You need a knee operation."

It was a partially torn ligament. The final game was in Miami, so I went down with my leg in a cast, just to be a part of it. That was a very emotional time for me because it was my last game and I wasn't playing. We won that game against Miami, and they gave me the game ball.

We didn't have the exposure coming out of college that you do today. There weren't mock drafts, and there wasn't a combine. I received several letters of interest: "If we draft you, would you play for the Saints?" They asked your height, weight, and 40 time. You filled it in and sent it back.

I'm 5-foot-9 1/2. I go, "All right, 5-foot-10. Hmmmm . . . how about 5-foot-11? You can't tell the difference between an inch and an inch and a half. Five-eleven sounds better."

Weight: I weighed about 195 pounds my senior year, so I put down 200.

Forty time? I never ran the 40! I didn't have a 40 time. So

I extrapolated down to 40. In high school I ran the 100, and my best time was maybe 10.4 seconds. That would make 50, 5.2. Okay, 40? Four-six . . . five? Four-five. That sounds reasonable, 4.5. That was *really* good back then. I ended up running the 40 in like 4.8. [*Laughs.*]

At that time there was a three-day draft, seventeen rounds. There was a family in South Bend that we seniors became friendly with, a big Notre Dame family. We'd be invited to their house and were there Sunday night—my roommate, Danny Harshman, Tom O'Leary, three or four of us. We're sitting having a gin and tonic, and the local late-night news comes on. The sports comes on and they say, "In the draft today the Pittsburgh Steelers drafted Notre Dame running back *Bob* Bleier in the sixteenth round."

That's how I found out. My real name is Robert, but I've always been Rocky. I guess they just said it the proper way.

When I came to the Steelers, they didn't know what to do with me. At Notre Dame I played right halfback, which was also the flanker spot. I was a pretty good receiver, had good hands, and could run routes. In training camp I was with the other rookie receivers and thought, "I'm not a receiver; I'm a running back."

A couple things happened that first week. One rookie running back lacerated his foot prior to training camp and couldn't practice. A couple other people got hurt in training camp.

We had a scrimmage with the Cleveland Browns rookies. We needed a running back. I moved back to the backfield and had a pretty good scrimmage. Afterward I switched between running back and flanker.

Things I learned at Notre Dame helped me tremendously. Most people are right-handed, and get down in a right-handed stance no matter what side of the ball they're on. One of the things Ara taught was when you are on the right side of the ball, you get in a left-handed stance. When you're on the left side, you're in a right-handed stance. The reason is that if you're on the offensive line, pulling to the left on the right side of the ball, it's easier to push off your right foot in a left-handed stance to get around the center. If you're in a right-handed stance, you have to drop your left foot. That one step might make a difference between a hole being open or closed.

It's the same way if you're on the right side as a flanker. At that time there were no standup receivers, and everybody had to be in a three-point stance.

In camp the Steelers said, "On the right side everybody has to get into a left-handed stance." Guys were bitching and moaning. The coach goes, "Can anybody get into a left-handed stance?" I'm the only one that raised his hand. I think that was an impressive moment—a little checkmark for that coach.

They had just changed the rules on crackback blocks [a block a receiver usually performs, cutting back inside, often surprising the defender]. A flanker back now had to make sure that his head and shoulders were in front of a linebacker's thigh pads.

The coach said, "We want you in a left-handed stance so you're in a position to push off your right foot without cheating in. If you cheat in, that might give away that it's a crackback. You don't want to give the defense an idea."

Like Notre Dame, the Steelers ran out of the I formation. The coach goes, "Bleier, how did they do it at Notre Dame?" At Notre Dame the first step is a crossover step, not a lead step. If you're going to your right you take your left, cross over, and then plant your right. At the exact same time the quarterback spins and takes a drop step. You're both in the right position, and your gut is open rather than your leg coming across to possibly cause a fumble. You also could cut up, in, or out as the ball's given to you. You're in a position of power rather than trying to do chop steps. Not that the Steeler veterans bought into it, but I think the reasoning earned me another checkmark.

We played an exhibition game at San Diego. Don Shy was the starting running back, and I was backing up Don. Don got hurt the first play, and I was inserted in the game. One play was a quick pitch to me to the left. There was no room to turn up, so I stopped, reversed field all the way to the right, and picked up 30 or 40 yards. Well, it could've been 20, but to me it was like 30 or 40. [*Laughs.*]

The following week it was another quick pitch to the left. There wasn't a hole, so I started to juke and stutter step. I got tackled for no gain. Bill Austin, our head coach, pulled me aside and said, "You don't have the speed to juke. Put your head down and pick up what you can."

I thought, "He's right." I don't have those Gale Sayers moves. It was a lesson, understanding what you can and cannot do.

Toward the end of training camp we were leaving a meeting, and Austin said, "This letter came in the mail to you, and it was accidentally opened." It was my 1-A classification notification.

He said, "We think you're good enough to make this team, so we'll take care of this for you." Whatever that meant. My assumption was they'd get me in the Reserves or National Guard. During the early '60s they would have articles in the papers about Packers Paul Hornung and Boyd Dowler going to Camp Randall for their two-week Army Reserve. I thought that was the natural course: you make the team, and they get you in the Reserves.

In October Bill said, "We got a problem."

Basically there were no Reserve openings. It was 1968, the height of the war. We had the most people in Vietnam during that period—five hundred thousand. All the Reserve and National Guard units were full.

He said, "Don't worry, we got time. We called your draft board, and they're not going to draft until the end of the season."

When I got a draft notification, the only thing I could do was change draft boards, which I did, but that just delayed the process. In December I got my draft notification to show up the next day.

I went through basic and advanced training and was sent to Vietnam. I was in the country four and a half months when we were on a patrol. A sister company had been hit, and our responsibility was to get them out of their hot spot, which we did late that evening. On the way out we ran into an ambush. We were carrying some of our dead out of that area and had to leave them to get out of this ambush. We headed back to locate those bodies, taking a break early in the morning, moving out of a wooded area to an open rice paddy. We were a reinforced platoon, thirty of us at the most.

I carried a grenade launcher, and our point man was maybe 40 yards in front of me. He saw enemy activity across the rice paddy and hollered. Shots were fired. Suddenly a machine gun leveled the area, and everybody jumped to the left and the right of the rice paddy. I jumped to the left, crawled to the end of that rice paddy, and saw the machine gun nestled in the bushes. Four guys were pinned in the lower rice paddy. My responsibility carrying the grenade launcher was to get fire power on the machine gun's position. As I breeched a grenade, I got hit in the left thigh, probably by an AK-47. I pulled back behind some bushes to get cover. I launched fire power as that was my responsibility, regardless of whether I'd been shot. I did that until those guys that were pinned down got out.

Most of our guys were on the right side; I was on the left. The medic came over, and he and I crawled back to our commanding officer 40 yards away. Now guys were in a firefight in the field, and finally they crawled back after twenty or twenty-five minutes. We left three guys dead in that field.

We didn't know what we'd run into and set up an L defensive position. They probed our perimeter and then a timed grenade came flying through the air. I caught it out of the corner of my eye. It hit my commanding officer in the back, bounced off of him, and rolled to where I was. As it rolled by me, I leaped in the opposite direction. As I leaped, it blew up through my right foot, my knee, and my left thigh. I blew up into the air and landed on top of my commanding officer.

Next we were in a firefight with those who had probed our perimeters. Our commanding officer got hit, our lieutenant got hit, our forward observer got hit, our medic got hit, our captain got hit, and our other lieutenant got hit. Our sergeant took over and popped smoke because we didn't know what our location was. The gunship came in.

We think we either wounded or killed the enemy leader, so they stopped and withdrew. A sister platoon fought its way to us and dragged us out that evening. It took about six hours to get out of there. I had been hit twice. [Rocky received both the Purple Heart and Bronze Star awards.]

In the hospital I asked the doctors about playing football. They said I would never play again. Their thought was, "Don't worry about it; you'll have a normal life. You'll be able to walk."

It wasn't as if I didn't believe them, but I had some experience with injuries. I had that knee operation, that lacerated kidney, and we all have bumps and bruises playing in the backyard. The lesson learned is that in time those injuries heal. Later on you're back out playing. As I looked at my war injuries, it wasn't as if I'd lost a leg or a foot. They were still there. Damaged, yeah, but we've all been damaged before.

I got a postcard two or three days later. The postcard had two lines: "Rock—Team's not doing well. We need you. [*Signed*] Art Rooney." Mr. Rooney was famous for sending postcards. He always carried a postcard in his pocket and would just jot a note to somebody. You get one, and you go, "Somebody cares." I think that's the biggest thing—*somebody cares*.

I had an operation in January of '70 that took me out through February. In March or April I started working out. I started running—well, limping—in the morning. I'd hit the gym after getting done with my army responsibilities. I'd go home and run sprints as best I could.

In July I got released from the army and went to Pittsburgh. *And there's a players' strike!* The rookies were in camp. I stayed out of camp for a week because I wanted to support my fellow striking veterans. Eventually I asked the veterans, "Would you mind if I go into camp?"

They said, "Go ahead."

The camp took its toll. Although I had my strength and body weight back up, my speed was not anywhere close. My desire was to be able to play, so I went through all of training camp. On the last cut Head Coach Chuck Noll said, "I think you should go home, do whatever's necessary to get yourself back in shape, and come back *next* year."

I was crushed. Not that I didn't expect it, but it was just that [*sigh*] somebody had said "No" to me for the first time ever. So I begged Chuck. I said, "Are you sure? Can I practice with the team today?"

Either I wore him down or he just said, "Oh, my goodness. Go ahead." I went to practice because I didn't know anything else to do. That's how badly I wanted to play.

The next morning Dan Rooney called and said, "We want to put you on injured reserve and have our doctors take a look at you. Maybe you can come back toward the end of the season and help this team."

I had another operation. Scar tissue was built up, and they went back trying to loosen it up to give me more flexibility in my foot and toes. It gave me a chance to kind of be there, sit in meetings, and watch practice. It bought me that year.

I went home, back to the gym, and got bigger and stronger. Right before I came back, I twinged a hamstring working out. The first week of camp I pulled the hamstring and was out for three weeks.

Thank God they had six exhibition games. I got a chance to come back and play special teams in some, including the last one against Cleveland. On my way back I started to get sick. I came down with strep throat. On Tuesday I called our trainer and said [whispers], "My throat. I can't talk."

At practice Wednesday the trainer said, "Are you going to be ready for Sunday's opener?"

I said [whispers], "Yeah, don't worry; I'll be ready."

They made a move and put me on the taxi squad. At that time you had three moves during the year to move people up and down. At the end of the season they moved me up. The last three games, I got to sit on the bench and play some special teams. I always believed "Out of sight, out of mind." At least I'm hanging around. That was 1971.

I came back bigger, stronger, and faster in 1972. I was the leading ground gainer during the exhibition season and made the team. I never carried the ball in the regular season, but I got to play special teams.

Coming back in 1973, I weighed 218 pounds, bench pressed 465, and squatted 600. They had watched this development over time. I was the leading ground gainer during the exhibition season again and got to carry the ball once that season.

In '74 I again was the leading ground gainer during the exhibition season. In the first regular season game Franco Harris got hurt, and Frenchy Fuqua became the fullback. I became the backup to Frenchy. That was a big deal.

The fourth game was against Houston, and Frenchy gets banged up. I'm inserted in the game with Preston Pearson. Right before the half Preston breaks one 43 yards. We get to play the second half and win the game.

Frenchy's still banged up the following week. I get to start at fullback against Kansas City and have a good game [86 all-purpose yards and a touchdown].

The following week is a Monday night game. Franco's healthy, so he's going to start at fullback. At the pregame meal running backs coach Dick Hoak says, "Franco, you and Rock will start tonight." I was kind of confused because nobody told me I was going to play halfback. We start that week, win that game, and I start the remainder of 1974.

The reason I got a chance to start was that Chuck Noll had told our backfield coach, "You have a weakness in your backfield. Who is your best blocker?"

"Bleier."

Noll said, "Start him."

My backfield coach at Notre Dame had said, "Anybody can run with the football. You give it to a two-year-old and what are they going to do? Run! To be a complete back you have to catch, block, and know your assignments." That always stuck in my mind, so the opportunity went all the way back to college, learning the fundamentals and not being afraid to block. It got me a starting job, and the rest becomes history.

I ran for 98 yards in the 1974 AFC Championship at Oakland. We scored 21 points in the fourth quarter to win, earning us a trip to Super Bowl 9 against the Minnesota Vikings.

Chuck had been to a Super Bowl before, which was great. He'd been on the Colts staff for Super Bowl 3. He told us [*very relaxed manner*], "Listen, here's our week's work: We'll go down to New Orleans on Sunday. We'll have Sunday off; we'll have Monday off. We'll start our regular week's work Tuesday. Now Tuesday's also media day, guys, so you'll have pictures taken and questions by the press. Each day we'll have to have a press day, but we'll control it. It'll be in the morning before practice. The media will ask you questions because they have a job to do; they got to write stories for their hometown papers. You're going to hear the same questions time and time again. I would like you to just make up different answers. Have fun with it. It's not a big pressure deal."

We went down to New Orleans and had Sunday and Monday off. Those who wanted to go to the French Quarter and stay out all night could get it out of their system.

We put a play in specifically for me to take advantage of weaknesses in how the Vikings defensive line played and read. The play was called "Dive 34 Sucker." Everybody went to the left, and I came back to this open hole on the right.

It was a sucker play against Doug Sutherland, who out of that Purple People Eater defense was probably the most disciplined. Doug read his keys and did everything perfectly. When that guard pulled, Doug was in his hip pocket, creating a hole. Alan Page was supposed to take an inside charge to fulfill that hole, but if you set it up as a pass, he would take an outside charge.

We had our offensive tackle drop back in pass protection, and everything else pulled to the left. I gained 17 yards the first time we ran that play. Franco would have scored, but I got 17. [*Laughs.*] We ran it again and picked up about 12 yards. We ran it again and picked up like 9 yards. We ran it *again*—now I'm getting nervous—and picked up about 8 yards.

Now it's in the fourth quarter, 3rd and 6, in plus [Vikings] territory. We need to pick up the first down to hopefully run out the clock. Quarterback Terry Bradshaw comes into the huddle and says, "What do you guys wanna run?" In unison the whole offensive line goes, "Sucker."

I'm thinking, "How dumb do you think Doug Sutherland's going to be? We can't run that five times in one game."

Doug responds a little late, and we squeeze out the 6 yards. We win our first championship with a 16-6 victory.

The following season our first game was against San Diego and defensive tackle Louie Kelcher, the biggest man in the NFL. It's the first game, so what's the only game film they watched? The Super Bowl.

We run Sucker probably the third play of the game. Louie wasn't going for it. All of a sudden there's an eclipse of the sun, and things go dark in my arena. Louie proceeds to separate me and the ball with one stroke of his forearm. We scrap the play.

The following week we're playing Kansas City and put in "Dive 34 *Wham* Sucker." The "Wham" was Franco running into the defensive tackle as added protection. All week long Franco practiced his blocking. Although he improved, he just kind of runs into somebody—a "titty blocker," as they called them.

Before the game Dick Hoak comes up to me and says, "We're going to make a change."

"What's that, Coach?"

"In Wham Sucker you play fullback and Franco moves to halfback."

I go, "Dick, that's not fair! It's my play. You're giving it to Franco because he can't block?"

So because of Louie Kelcher they take the play away from me, and I'm running into defensive tackles. [*Laughs.*]

The Super Bowls were one game out of a series of games. It wasn't the biggest game because each playoff was big. If you didn't prepare enough to win those games, you would have never reached the Super Bowl. It's one play here or one play there that makes the difference, the execution of that play or the luck of that play.

The first Dallas game in '75 [Super Bowl 10]—that was a back and forth game. We came up with some big plays: Lynn Swann down the middle . . . Lynn on the sidelines . . . Lynn deep in the end zone. . . . It was a breakout game for Lynn on national television. Those passes were caught and not dropped. That made a difference.

Bradshaw got knocked out of the game in the fourth quarter. It was a pass play with a blitz coming from the outside. Cliff Harris and Larry Cole both hit Bradshaw, *but* he threw a 64-yard touchdown to Lynn, giving us a 21-10 lead.

Dallas goes down to score a touchdown, and now Terry

Hanratty's our quarterback. Time's running out. We bring up the ball to their 42-yard line, and now it's 4th down and 8. The Cowboys use their last time out. We're ready to punt the ball, you know?

They had blocked one of our punts earlier. Hanratty goes over to the sideline during the time out and Chuck gives him a play. I'm thinking, "What's he calling? Well, if we throw it downfield, it'll eat up some time, possibly pick up a first down. If they intercept it, it's like a punt."

Hanratty comes back. I say, "What'd he say?"

Hanratty just shakes his head.

In the huddle he says, "Full Right Split. Eighty-four Trap. On 2." A strong-side tackle trap, and *I* run the ball. I'm going to myself, "Are you freakin' nuts?"

We break the huddle, and Hanratty says to me, "Run out as much time as you possibly can." [*Laughs.*] I'm not a run out guy. *Franco* is a run out guy.

The ball's snapped, the guard pulls, there's no hole, and bam! I pick up two yards . . . four seconds off the clock.

I'm feeling personally responsible to put us in this position. I'm on the sidelines watching Roger Staubach, one of the all-time great two-minute quarterbacks, come into the game and systematically move the ball down the field.

Staubach throws into the end zone; clock's ticking down. Another throw into the end zone; clock's ticking down. He throws again, and it's intercepted by Glen Edwards. We win the game.

What made the difference? Our plays, execution, Glen coming up with that big interception. If Lynn drops a couple of those passes, we're not in a position to score. If Bradshaw overthrows or they get to him before he releases the ball, we might not win. It's all those little games of inches that make the difference.

The same thing happened against the Cowboys in Super Bowl 13. It was 14-14, nearing the half. Mel Blount had just intercepted the ball, and we moved into plus [Cowboys] territory. We were on the 7-yard line, and it was 3rd and 1.

We called 1-18, a play-action play. My responsibility was to act like I was going to block the linebacker and then go down the line of scrimmage. The first shot was to hit me very quickly down the line of scrimmage—an arrow, they called it. I was to pick up the first down and get out of bounds. The secondary receiver was the split end.

The ball was snapped, I go down, and linebacker D. D. Lewis read it as a run. He jumped across to contain it, taking my path away. I dove inside of him to avoid him. All of a sudden he read it was a pass play and had me in man-to-man coverage. He spun to the outside, momentarily losing sight of me. I drifted backward as Bradshaw rolled to his right. I drifted into the end zone, and Terry's and my eyes met. Bradshaw released the ball and I thought, "He's overthrowing me."

I leaped in the air, hoping I could get a finger on it, maybe knock it down a little bit. As I went up, *thump*! I felt it stick to my hands. I came down into the end zone, and we score. That gave us a lead we never relinquished and gave me the cover of *Sports Illustrated*.

We had a 35-17 lead in the fourth quarter. The Cowboys quickly scored twice, but they were running out of time. The last score made it 35-31, setting up a desperation onside kick.

I'm the center guy on the onside kick. I'm not any different than anybody else. I *dare* anybody else to say anything differently; I'm saying to myself, "Don't kick it to me. I don't want to be the goat." They kick it to me. [*Laughs*.] I fall on it, hold on to it. The biggest hit I got that whole game on that last play, as they tried to dislodge the ball.

That next year Sidney Thornton became the starting running back with Franco, and I was the third guy. I was still playing, but everybody wants to be a starter—it's your identity. Sidney got banged up, and I started the remainder of the season, including the playoffs and Super Bowl 14.

At a Super Bowl 14 press conference a reporter asked, "Do you ever think about retiring?"

I said, "No. Why?"

"They say go out on top. You didn't start this year, and you're getting older. It's a legitimate question."

"Well, maybe it's always in the back of your mind, but you don't think about it." But I started thinking about it. That's what triggered it.

We won the Super Bowl, 31-19, over the Rams. After the season they made a movie about me called *Fighting Back* as I pondered whether I should or shouldn't retire. The local producer says, "You can't retire! You got a movie coming out. You have to be playing. We'll have farewells for you in Cleveland." [*Laughs.*]

I didn't base my decision off that, but I decided the next year, 1980, would be my last. The Steeler motto was "One for the thumb" [a fifth Super Bowl ring].

I said to Dan Rooney, "I think this will be my last year. I wanted to let you know if you need to make some decisions. Do you think I should tell Chuck?"

I didn't really want to tell Chuck. Chuck was the type of guy who'd say, "If you're thinking about retiring, then you've already retired. So why don't you just leave now?"

Dan said, "Maybe we should wait." [*Laughs.*]

As time ticked away in each game my last season, it was a closure.

My last game at Three Rivers Stadium was very important to me as a player. It happened to be "Rocky Bleier Day" because they announced it was my last home game. We played Kansas City.

Where it was throngs of people for years waving the Terrible Towel screaming, "Here we go, Steelers," it now boiled down to the fact that we weren't going to the playoffs; it was a disappointing season, it was December in Pittsburgh, and it was cold. There was polite applause as we were introduced. [*Laughs.*]

The game was a pillow fight. It was like we said, "You're guests here, and we're not going anyplace. Why don't you guys win?"

"No, you guys are the home team. You should win."

"No, go ahead."

We got the ball with maybe four minutes left in the game, trailing. We had the ball on our 20-yard line, 80 yards to go. It could've been 8 yards to go to score, and I don't know if we could've made those 8 yards. That's the way we'd been playing.

Bradshaw came into the huddle and said, "Let's make something happen."

For some reason it was like every Trojan War movie: out on that last final charge, into death's throes we go, outnumbered by thousands, but the old war horse came alive.

We started to move the ball. Franco went off left tackle, picked up 6 yards. I picked up 2; he got a first down. We had a quick screen to John Stallworth and picked up 6 more. Franco off the right side, we pick up another first down.

Bradshaw dropped back and hit Calvin Sweeney up to the 45-yard line. He dropped back and hit Bennie Cunningham up over the 50.

Two-minute warning.

All of sudden, in a game that had no cheering at all, we could hear pockets of fans going, "Offense! Offense!"

Bradshaw decides to give me the ball six times in a row. He hasn't given me the ball six times in a *game*. The offensive line does a wonderful job of opening holes. We go off tackle, up the gut, and we do sweeps. Now that "Offense!" chant turns into, "Rocky! Rocky!"

We get down to the 11-yard line.

In everybody's childhood, playing in the backyard, whether

it be baseball, basketball, or football, we all have dreams putting ourselves in a position to win the championship game. You're on the basketball court by yourself; you're in the corner, the clock's ticking down, and you take that one final shot. Is it good? Yes! And you win. You make all the sounds of a crowd.

Now we're on the 11-yard line with twenty-eight seconds left on the clock. Bradshaw calls a trap to the left side with me carrying the ball. We break the huddle, we line up, the ball's snapped, and the clock ticks down: 28, 27, 26, 25. I get the ball into my gut. I look for the hole, and it becomes the biggest hole I've ever seen in the twelve years that I've played. I move up into the hole. The clock's going 24, 23, 22. . . .

The linebacker scrapes and hits me. I keep my feet. I am now ten black jerseys pushing me toward the goal line! I'm racing toward the end zone; the clock's going down: 21, 20, 19, 18. . . .

I look up, and I'm 4 yards out. I see a defensive back coming up fast. I leave my feet to dive over into the end zone. He leaves his. Our two bodies, hurdling one another. Clock's going 15, 14, 13. . . .

We collide mid-air. We come down. The ball crosses the goal line. And we win the game!

Not that it was the Super Bowl, not that it got us to a playoff, but it was my crowning feat. I got to score the winning touchdown in my last home game. From a retirement point of view it was another step, something you could take away and have a memory of.

Before free agency and large contracts you had to prepare for the day when you weren't going to play. You made nice money, but it wasn't enough for the rest of your life. We always had an off-season job, trying to figure out what may happen. I worked in an investment banking firm and in the insurance industry. Most of it was playing around trying to decide what career I might want in the real world.

I got a job with the local NBC station. I covered the Steelers, so the year following my retirement I was back in training camp, being part of it, getting recognition as a former Steeler. It took me four years to realize that's not what I wanted to do, but it helped the transition.

The interesting thing about leaving the game is that we live in a society where nobody teaches you how to retire, especially from a game when you're a young man. It's always the philosophy of "Set a goal, have a vision, etc."

With the majority of athletes things are always done for you. You have a coach; you go to practice; everybody tells you what to do, where to go, what time to be there, what bus to be on, what we'll have to eat at the team dinner. Everything is organized for you. Now you have to face a decision on your own, and it's made for you either by injury or by getting cut because you're not good enough to make the team. It's a reality of the game that everybody goes through.

How you deal with that specifically becomes very important, and it's not easy. Sometimes it takes time to be able to see what you're going to do with the rest of your life. What you really want to do with the rest of your life is continue to play this game.

# FOURTH QUARTER

*Players Whose Careers Began in the 1970s*

The merger greatly enhanced the NFL, and the 1970s launched the league's popularity into the stratosphere. The Super Bowl became an American cultural fixture, the screws driven in by classic games between the wildly popular Pittsburgh Steelers and Dallas Cowboys. Whispers that football was overtaking baseball as America's pastime got louder as league attendance topped 13 million[1] and television revenue increased exponentially.

Despite the league's wealth player salaries remained comparatively low. While Marvin Miller skillfully negotiated on behalf of baseball players, football players trudged behind.

The "Rozelle Rule," conceived in 1963 after Carroll Rosenbloom's Colts signed R. C. Owens away from the 49ers, forced teams signing free agents to compensate a player's original team. Both teams needed to reach an agreement or Commissioner Rozelle would send players and/or draft choices from the new team to the original club. The courts struck down the discouraging rule, under which only 19 percent of players who played out their options signed with a new team.[2]

Despite the victory players didn't gain significant changes toward free agency. Instead a "Right of First Refusal/Compensation" section nestled its way into the Collective Bargaining Agreement of 1977. Players could hypothetically play out their contract and sign with other teams. After terms were agreed upon, a player's original team had seven days to match the new offer. Instead of stopping there—a plausible gain for players—the agreement reverted back toward the Rozelle Rule. The signing team had to compensate the original team a number of draft choices proportionate to the player's worth, determined by his new salary. The clause also survived the 1982 CBA negotiations.[3]

In 1977 St. Louis Cardinal Norm Thompson signed with the Baltimore Colts. In 1988, eleven years later, Wilber Marshall became the next NFL player to sign with a new team.[4]

The NFL hatched Plan B free agency in 1989. Teams protected nearly two-thirds of their roster from signing with other clubs unless compensation was paid to a player's original team. Under Plan B the top thirty-seven players from each team were still denied free agency freedoms that baseball players had won a decade earlier. Full free agency rights weren't granted to NFL players until 1993.

### Pro Football in the 1970s Timeline

1970   AFL/NFL merger takes effect; league divided into National and American Football Conferences. Baltimore Colts, Pittsburgh Steelers, and Cleveland Browns each take approximately $3 million to join AFL teams in AFC. All three major television networks pay to broadcast the new super league's games, netting $185 million for the league.[5] NFL players negotiate $12,500 minimum salary for rookies, $13,000 for veterans.[6] Median salary for U.S. males with four years of college: $12,144.[7]

1971   NFL attendance tops 10 million.[8] Ed Garvey becomes NFL Players Association executive director.

1972   *Mackey v.* NFL filed; players hope to win true free agency.

1974   Players conduct off-season strike to no avail. New television contract scores estimated $269 million.[9]

1975   Players lose confidence in NFLPA; about 50 percent elect to skip union dues.[10] December arbitration ruling decimates Major League Baseball's "Reserve Clause," opening gates to free agency in baseball.

1976   First class of baseball free agents hits market. Reggie Jackson signs with Yankees for nearly $3 million; Bobby Grich signs with Angels for $1.5 million. Average annual salary for twenty-four free agents: $200,696; for Major League Baseball: $52,300.[11]

1977   Super Bowl 11 attended by 103, 438. Player shares—winners: $15,000; losers: $7,500—remain equal to Super Bowl 1, with paid attendance of 61,946.[12] Despite favorable decision in *Mackey v.* NFL,[13] NFL players don't win free agency in new Collective Bargaining Agreement.[14] Estimated average NFL salary: $30,000.[15] Median salary for males with four or more years of college: $17,391.[16]

1978   New television contract worth $646 million.[17] Fran Tarkenton, NFL's highest-paid player, earns $275,000.[18] Tarkenton retires after the season as all-time leader in completions, passing yards, and touchdown passes.[19] Baseball free agent Larry Hisle, an excellent player before injuries truncated his career, begins play under new $3 million contract with Milwaukee Brewers.[20] Hisle led American League in RBIs in 1977, the only time he finished as a league leader in any statistical category.[21]

1982   Seven weeks of regular season lost to player strike. NFL players return still lacking free agency rights of other sports.

1987   NFL owners sign replacement players to play regular-season games during player strike. Strike concludes without owners conceding free agency. New television contract reportedly worth $1.4 billion through the 1989 season.[22]

1989   Art Shell becomes the NFL's first African American head coach of the modern era

1993   NFL free agency era begins.

## Notes

1. NFL Communications Department and Seymour Siwoff, *2012 NFL Record and Fact Book* (New York: Time Inc. Home Entertainment, 2012), 534.

2. John Mackey et al. v. National Football League et al. 543 F.2d 606 (1976); Justia.com, U.S. Supreme Court Center.

3. Bruce H. Singman, "Free Agency and the National Football League" (1988); http://digitalcommons.lmu.edu/elr/vol8/iss2/2; accessed September 12, 2013.

4. Steve Springer, "NFL Preview 1988: Marshall's Jump Isn't a Great Leap for NFL: Linebacker's Move to Redskins Not Followed by Mass Exodus of Players," *Los Angeles Times*, September 3, 1988.

5. Steve Wulf, "Out Foxed," *Sports Illustrated*, December 27, 1993.

6. "History." NFL Players Association official website, https://www.nflplayers.com/about-us/History/; accessed September 12, 2013.

7. Claudia Goldin, contributor, *Historical Statistics of the United States: Earliest Times to the Present, vol. 2, part B: Work and Welfare* (New York: Cambridge University Press, 2006).

8. NFL Communications Department and Siwoff, *2012 NFL Record and Fact Book*.

9. Wulf, "Out Foxed."

10. NFL Players Association, "History."

11. Leigh Montville, "The First to Be Free," *Sports Illustrated*, April 16, 1990.

12. NFL Communications Department and Siwoff, *2012 NFL Record and Fact Book*, 484.

13. *John Mackey et al. v. National Football League et al.*

14. Singman, *Free Agency and the National Football League.*

15. Wulf, "Out Foxed."

16. Goldin, *Historical Statistics of the United States.*

17. Wulf, "Out Foxed."

18. Fran Tarkenton, "Fran Tarkenton: NFL Is Loved, but Brain Injuries Threaten Its Future"; TwinCites.com; http://www.twincities.com

/sports/ci_24007325/fran-tarkenton-nfl-is-loved-but-brain-injuries; accessed September 12, 2013.

19. Gary Gillette, exec. ed., *The* ESPN *Pro Football Encyclopedia*, 1st ed. (New York: Sterling Publishing, 2006), 1285–1287.

20. Robert H. Boyle, ed., "Scorecard," *Sports Illustrated*, December 5, 1977.

21. John Thorn, Pete Palmer, et al., eds., *Total Baseball*, 6th ed. (New York: Total Sports, 1999), 951.

22. Wulf, "Out Foxed."

# 33

## Jack Youngblood

Defensive end

University of Florida

Drafted, 1971 (Los Angeles Rams, 1st round)

Los Angeles Rams, 1971–1984

5 All-Pro seasons

7 Pro Bowls

1970s NFL All-Decade Team

Pro Football Hall of Fame inductee (2001)

I had a passion for football as a kid and was fortunate to be gifted with the ability to play in high school, college, and later with the Los Angeles Rams. It's an accumulation of passion once you learn you have the ability to play that game.

When [head baseball and assistant football] Coach Dave Fuller offered me the scholarship to Florida, I weighed 200 pounds soaking wet—*maybe*. Over the next four years I put on about 15 pounds a year. That was through weight training and a wonderful cook named Loasey. She was our training table cook and fed us so well. At night she'd put out cookies, milk, and ice cream. We'd run down about ten or eleven o'clock and get a midnight snack. [*Laughs*.]

My defensive line coach talked to some scouts, and they said I'd be a middle-round draft pick. There were seventeen rounds then.

The *Gainesville Sun* asked me to come down on draft day and watch the draft come across their teletype. I go down to the *Gainesville Sun*, and the teletype's ticking off. I see Jim Plunkett come off, Dan Pastorini come off, and John

275

Brockington come off. I'm thinking, "This is going to be a long day."

It got to pick fifteen or sixteen, and the phone rang. They answered it and said, "Jack, the coach of the Los Angeles Rams wants to speak to you." I put my hand over the receiver going, "Who's the coach?" [*Laughs.*] Of course it was Tommy Prothro; he'd just been hired. He said, "Youngblood, we're going to draft you."

I said, "Thank you, Coach. I appreciate that." I had absolutely no clue I'd be drafted that high.

I reflect back on the youngster who began this game and realize that if I hadn't had Merlin Olsen and Deacon Jones teach me how to play the game, I wouldn't have turned out to be the player that I did. In fact I remember this explicitly: Merlin and Deacon both put their arms around me that first year and said, "Kid, you can play. But we're going to teach you *how* to play."

We played a 4-3 defense then. There are differences in the sizes and types of players that play in the 4-3 as opposed to the 3-4. The 3-4 is basically a linebacker-dominated defense. Bulk is the major emphasis on the 3-4 line. We switched to a 3-4 late in my career.

Speed and agility is the fundamental in the 4-3. When you rush the quarterback, you keep your rush integrity so that you can keep him in the pocket and pressure him at the same time. You also cut off angles to the running game. When a running back's got 5 yards to deal with, he can go any way he wants. When he has only 2 yards to go, you got him where you want him.

The key to the game that's been there forever is making the quarterback throw the ball before he wants to. Anytime they put us in the prevent defense—what we called three-man—it didn't work. We'd been pressuring the quarterback all day long, and then they put three on five. I mean, I'm carrying a gun to that fight. [*Laughs.*]

When rushing a scrambling quarterback like Roger Staubach or Fran Tarkenton, you had to be careful, keeping him in the pocket and putting pressure up the middle. You had to really recognize your lane integrity because both of them would jump out of the pocket if you pressured them. It killed your defense when you gave them that much more time.

I broke my leg in the 1979 NFC divisional playoffs against Dallas. I went to the locker room and told my doctor, "Tape this damn thing up. This is the fifth time we've been in this position to move on in the playoffs. I'm not going to give it up now. I've got to try and play."

My doc said, "I can't do that."

I go, "Why not?"

"You got a broken leg. I can't do that."

"Yes you can. We've got to tape this thing up and see if we can play."

He goes, "I don't know how to tape."

We got the trainers in there, and they taped me up. I went back in and chased Roger Staubach around on a broken leg. That wasn't any fun, but I still recorded a sack. We won that football game after they had knocked us out of the playoffs two times prior. That put us in the NFC Championship Game for the fifth time. We beat Tampa Bay, and that put us into Super Bowl 14 against the Pittsburgh Steelers, the first time we had made the Super Bowl.

We kept Terry Bradshaw in check for the most part, but Terry had all the tools in the world and a phenomenal offensive line. He also had two fantastic receivers (Lynn Swann and John Stallworth), three if you count Franco Harris coming out of the backfield. He also had Rocky Bleier, and his tight end (Randy Grossman) wasn't bad, so he really had five receivers. We kept him pressured, but Terry threw the ball up a couple of times, and those receivers made huge plays.

Playing with the broken leg was one thing, a matter of pain and function of the leg. The most debilitating injury

I had was the nerve damage against Cleveland in '78. Calvin Hill came around the corner, and I went in to make the tackle like we were taught to do, with your face in front, driving through with your legs. Calvin Hill had this high knee action, and his leg caught me just perfect. It stretched that nerve in my left shoulder. That may be the most excruciating pain I've ever experienced.

During the season you try to maintain your strength. I worked out the Friday morning before leaving for that game, bench pressing 300 pounds, ten times, that kind of thing. We got back Sunday night. I went into the locker room Monday morning and said, "Something's wrong here."

I lay down on the bench, and I could not bench press 135 pounds. My left arm was just shot, and the atrophy set in because of the nerve damage. It was brutal. I fought through it, learned to compensate, and played the rest of the season.

Playing with those injuries wasn't about being tough. It was passion—passion for the game. I like to think I'm tough enough to help my teammates and play well on the football field, but it was a matter of passion. Once you learn you're really good at something and you like it, that creates an intensity to do it over and over. You don't ever want to quit. Unfortunately, we've got terminal bodies. [*Laughs.*] The mind says, "Yes," and the body eventually says, "No."

There's some serious issues we're dealing with right now. Thank goodness we're dealing with them because it's obvious that we have some critical issues with our retired players. The brain injury issue is one of the most important because not only does it affect your abilities, it limits your life.

We've come a long way in a lot of things. For example, we didn't know how to go to the moon in the 1950s, and now we do.

We didn't know that we were going to have this kind of reaction to the contact that we had. There were symptoms when you got out of the game and later in life, but you didn't connect it back to the cause. Now we have. We understand that multiple blows to the head cause problems. We need to heal people. Taking drugs, masking the symptoms, that doesn't do anybody any good.

I've looked at some therapies. I'm promoting one right now that needs to be in every locker room in the country. It doesn't address the symptoms; it addresses the issues, the imbalance of the brainwaves. It gives the brain the energy that it needs and wants to balance itself. That's healing.

# 34
## Otis Sistrunk

Defensive tackle, defensive end

Did not attend college

Undrafted

Oakland Raiders, 1972–1978

Super Bowl champion (Oakland Raiders, Super Bowl 11)

1 Pro Bowl

I played football, basketball, and track in high school. I never sat on the bench; I always started, even as a freshman. I had two scholarship offers, but I didn't have the proper clothes and decided to join the Marines. Football always crossed my mind in the Marines because that's what I was about: football.

After the service I played football in Norfolk, Virginia, with a Continental League team called the Norfolk Neptunes. The Continental League was like AAA baseball. After playing there for three years, I got a shot to go into the NFL. I had tryouts with the St. Louis Cardinals, Washington Redskins, and Los Angeles Rams. I was picked up by the Rams. I was with the Rams for a week before getting traded to Oakland for a seventh-round draft choice.

My first regular season game was played on the old turf in Pittsburgh. When the Raiders and Steelers played, we would always go after each other. We were about the best two teams in the AFC at one time. The fans called it a rivalry, but I never considered it a rivalry. I'd call it just a good, tough football game.

We, the Raiders, played in several big games with historic plays. I'll try to recall some for you. I got old, so I don't know if I can do it or not. [*Laughs*.]

We played at Pittsburgh in the 1972 AFC divisional playoffs, which ended with what's called the "Immaculate Reception." I was at defensive tackle and was in the backfield chasing quarterback Terry Bradshaw. We almost got to him, but he just happened to turn and throw the ball. After he threw the ball, the next thing I saw was Franco Harris going down the field.

We thought it was a good pass, but I don't think he caught the ball. I didn't see the ball hit the ground, but after looking at the replay and hearing some of our defensive backs say the ball hit the ground, I think the ball hit the ground. Also my teammate Jack Tatum said the ball didn't touch him; it touched Frenchy Fuqua of the Steelers. [NFL rules prohibited an offensive player from catching the ball directly after it had been tipped by a teammate.]

In the 1974 AFC divisional playoffs we played the Miami Dolphins in Oakland, after they'd won the last two Super Bowls. Clarence Davis made what I think was one of the best catches ever in the NFL to win the game for us. That is called the "Sea of Hands." I was on the sideline between the 20- and 25-yard lines. It was amazing that C. D. caught the ball and held on to it with Manny Fernandez after him. I remember thinking we were going to the Super Bowl. That was one of the biggest plays in Raider history.

In Super Bowl 11 Willie Brown ran back an interception for a touchdown. You might've seen the close up of him while he's running down the sideline. I chased Fran Tarkenton before the pass, but after Fran threw the interception, I started running downfield to block. I couldn't catch Willie and saw that nobody from Minnesota was going to catch him either. I just slowed up and said, "Hey, we got this game." I think that put a knot on it. We knew we had it won then. [Brown's interception made the score 32-7 in the fourth quarter.]

My personal highlight from that game was sacking Tarkenton. Any defensive lineman that played against him will tell you that it was the toughest thing to catch Fran in the backfield.

Some say the officials missed calling a Bronco fumble in the 1977 AFC Championship. I don't remember that play that well. I just know we lost against Denver when we should have beaten them. That was a big backbreaker for us. But, you know, that was a long time ago. When you lose, you don't remember much. I even forgot what the score was.

People put a label on our team, but I don't feel it was accurate. Just because we played hard doesn't make us gangsters. I think it had something to do with the silver and black uniforms we wore. Everybody used to say the bad guy in the western wore the black hat, and the good guy wore the white hat. In pro wrestling the bad guy always wore black, and everybody else wore different colors.

When I played, the character of the Raiders was very good. One of the most important things to us was working with kids. Phil Villapiano and I used to go to the schools and talk to kids three to four times a week. Phil and I used to fly back to Oakland in the off-season just to work with the kids. John Matuszak also used to go to the schools. We tried to teach them to stay in school and listen to their fathers and mothers, their ministers, and their teachers. We told them, "Try to be a better person than you are today," and "Don't be a follower; be a leader." That's the best thing in the world to tell a kid.

Contract negotiation with Al Davis was very short because he'd take care of his players. Here's the most important thing to know in professional sports: if you take care of your players, they'll take care of you.

We also felt we had the best coach in the NFL in John Madden. He is one of those coaches that if he told you to run through a wall, you're going to try to run through it.

Football's a rough game, and I wish I'd played golf. Golf would have been easier. In football, a lot of guys got concussions, and a lot of guys had to retire because of injuries. You don't go out there to mess around; you got to go out there and play. It's a tough sport, and you can get hurt. A lot of my friends got hurt. You never know what can happen.

I played in high school, then in Norfolk, and then in the NFL, where you get hit more than in the Continental League. Over time it's tough because of the wear and tear on the body. All of a sudden my knee just got bad. I asked the good Lord to help me make my mind up. I had an operation and retired.

Working for the military is my life now. It's been thirty-two years, and I'm going to retire next year. I'm not ready to retire because I love the military. I look up to every soldier, Marine, navy, and coast guard member. When they go and fight, I look up to those guys. They're something special.

The Raiders are still the same today because we're just like family. Ted Hendricks, Phil Villapiano, Willie Brown, Art Shell—we talk to each other at least once a week. You try to find out what the next guy's doing. If one of the guys I played with in the '70s calls and has a problem, somebody's coming to his aid.

Football was a life. It was my life. I wanted to play football, so I chose football. What I loved best was meeting a lot of good friends and still meeting with guys I played with and against.

A lot of guys looked at it about money, but I looked at it about the love of the game. It was about getting out there and winning. The thing about it is, you spend the money, and the money's gone. But when you win the Super Bowl, the ring stays. The ring belongs to me.

# 35

## Conrad Dobler

Guard

University of Wyoming

Drafted, 1972 (St. Louis Cardinals, 5th round)

St. Louis Cardinals, 1972–1977

New Orleans Saints, 1978–1979

Buffalo Bills, 1980–1981

3 Pro Bowls

I went to a Catholic grade school. My eighth grade graduating class was eight students. They didn't have organized sports, so I was never exposed to them. I didn't even know you needed a jock strap. Everyone else in town went to public school, so I was kind of an outsider to begin with. I got into football in high school. I was looking for acceptance in the school and to become part of something, besides trying to get out of work.

My family had an institutional food distributorship. After school I unloaded trucks and made up orders for the next day. I felt if I got involved in sports, I wouldn't have to unload trucks. My dad was pretty smart though; he just left them there until I got home.

Hauling those crates around did a lot to build up my muscles. I had the advantage of doing manual labor, while most kids weren't afraid of work. They could take a nap right beside it. [*Laughs.*]

I had a lot of scholarships to different areas—many in California. When you got done with the SAT and the ACT exams, you had to do another essay part to get into one of the California universities. Well, after eight hours, I said, "Screw it. I've got scholarships to other places. I'll pick one of them."

At that time Wyoming, Arizona, and Arizona State were all in the WAC [Western Athletic Conference]. Wyoming had been the leader of the WAC for a long time. I visited Arizona and Arizona State but figured I may as well go to the winning team.

I had Lloyd Eaton as a coach through my junior year. He was a great coach and took Wyoming to the 1968 Sugar Bowl.

My sophomore year, 1969, was the one hundredth anniversary of collegiate football. We were getting ready to play BYU, and the blacks on the team wanted to wear black armbands during the game to protest the Mormon religion's policy of not allowing blacks into their ministry. Eaton said, "You protest by going out there and beating them."

The players showed up at practice wearing black armbands and were all kicked off the team. That became national news as "the Black Fourteen Incident." We had to dress up a cheerleader for the game because he could snap long.

Recruiting really suffered the following years. Eaton left, and Fritz Shurmur came to coach. They had to rely on getting players from Montana and Wyoming. Those guys only played eight-man football, so we didn't have a real good class. When I was a freshman, we had a great class and 115 people on full rides [scholarships]. When I finished four years later, there were just 11 left out of those 115.

When I was drafted, I was out climbing mountains. I didn't even know the draft was going on. When I got back, a guy from the newspaper called and said, "You've been drafted by the St. Louis Cardinals." I said, "St. Louis Cardinals? Why the hell would a baseball team draft me? I haven't even played baseball."

The reporter said, "Are you serious?"

My roommate said, "There's a football team too!"

I said, "No, no, I'm joking; I know it's the football Cardinals."

I didn't want to sound like an idiot—I *am* an Academic All-American.

The reporter said, "What do you think about that?"

"I guess I'll give that a shot until I have to find a real job."

It wasn't like my childhood dream had been answered. I played football to keep my scholarship and get an education. I grew up in Twentynine Palms, California, and we only got two channels. I never remembered watching a lot of football on Sundays.

At training camp I was an outsider again. The top draft choices all came from Alabama, Michigan, UCLA, and USC. They kind of looked down at me, and I had to fight my way through it.

The Cardinals didn't bring in fifty rookies. They brought in the bare minimum because Bill Bidwill was somewhat cheap on that. We only had about eight offensive linemen, so we had to service the plays for the defense too. Usually the rookies serviced the defense.

I flunked my physical because they found a heart murmur. I went back to St. Louis to take some tests, and they found I'd probably had it since I was a kid. It was no big deal. I missed two weeks of training camp because of that. When I came back, the veterans hated my guts because I'd missed the two hardest weeks of training camp. These guys had to run all day on both offensive and defensive plays. They were not kind to me.

I came out and thought we were a team, trying to give the coaches a good look, but you'd get knocked on your ass because everybody wanted to look good. I finally went out and played like a game every single practice. Some didn't like that, and I got into a fight every single day.

I was out there on a Saturday, and the first game was on Sunday. I counted fifty-three players [the number of players on a roster] and said, "Wow, I guess I made it." At the end of practice that day my offensive line coach, Bill Austin, said, "Head Coach Bob Holloway wants to see you."

I thought, "Either he's going to congratulate me on making the team or, better yet, tell me I'm starting."

I went up there, and Holloway said, "You got caught up in the numbers."

I said, "I was out at practice and counted everyone. I counted exactly fifty-three, and that's what you can keep."

He said, "In the process of counting those fifty-three players, did you happen to count yourself?"

That, I had neglected to do. I was cut.

In the second game of the season Chuck Hutchison went down with a knee injury. They brought me back, and I started. Can you believe I was cut and then eight days later I was a starter? Not a good one at that particular time, but I was starting.

At the end of the year Chuck Hutchison came back. There used to be an unwritten rule that you couldn't lose your starting position through injury. Plus he was a second-round draft choice, so they had some money invested in him. They put him back at that position.

Don Coryell became our head coach my second year. Coryell brought some young coaches like Jim Hanifan, Joe Gibbs, and Rod Dowhower. They all became head coaches elsewhere.

At training camp in '73 Hanifan told me, "Conrad, keep working hard, and the first chance I can get you in there, I will." I worked my ass off, but Chuck Hutchison wasn't making any mistakes. He was a pretty good football player.

We went to scrimmage the Minnesota Vikings. On a scrimmage you don't have special teams. You flip a coin and see who goes on offense. They run twenty plays against the opposing defense, and then the other team runs twenty plays.

We won the coin flip, and Hutchison ran onto the field with the first-team offense. He ran back to the sideline saying, "Does anybody have a chinstrap?"

Hanifan said, "Dobler, get in there!"

Chuck Hutchison never walked on the field again.

CONRAD DOBLER                                                           287

Now it doesn't make a difference how he lost his chinstrap; the point is that opportunity presented itself. [*Laughs.*] I tell people I wish I had been smart enough to have stolen his chinstrap. I'm sixty-one years old, and to this day I carry a chinstrap in my briefcase to remind myself how easy it is to lose your career over something that simple. The simple things in life are the most important.

We only won four games that first year with Coryell, but we could see the improvement. We lost a lot of games early, but we scored 30 or 40 points. When you put together a team, you have to have the team buy into your system. No one had bought into Bob Holloway's system.

I grew up as an offensive lineman with Dan Dierdorf and Tom Banks teaching me the game and with Jim Hanifan teaching us to be better football players, better people, better husbands, better fathers, and better citizens.

We spent a lot of time together. You learned a lot of football off the field. You learned a lot of love for each other. I'd take a bullet for them, and they would for me.

We knew as an offensive line that you could look to your right or left, and your teammate would do everything possible to make sure their guy didn't get a sack. On defense it just takes one guy to make the tackle. In order for us to make the play go, it takes all five of us.

It's important to know how your teammate is going to react. If I'm playing next to Dierdorf and his defensive end is crashing down, I know Dan is going to take him, and I got to drop off and slip around the back of him. If someone hasn't played much with Dan, that player doesn't know Dan is just going to bury the defensive end when he slips. The new guy's probably going to get caught up in traffic, lose a knee, or not get his man.

If we have a zone on but Dierdorf gets tied up man-to-man, I know he's not going to turn that guy loose. He knows

I'm going to take the guy that would have been his man. We had this big trust and faith in each other.

We tied an NFL record by allowing only 7 sacks one season. Two of those sacks weren't even against us. They sacked our field goal kicker on a bad snap, and on another a back forgot to pick up the outside blitzing linebacker. In reality the five of us only gave up 5 sacks the entire season. They give that many up in a game now.

Three things allowed me to play with the necessary intensity and discipline to succeed: pride, fear of failure, and fear of letting my teammates down. I wanted to prepare. I always say, "Proper Preparation Prevents Piss Poor Performance"—the six P's.

Know who to get. If you knew you were supposed to pull to the outside and pick up the corner, you had a chance of being successful. There's going to be times he's going to knock you on your ass, but you still have a chance because he may fall over the top of you. Not a beautiful block but effective. If you forget to pull, you don't have a chance of being successful.

The notorious play I got labeled with was just folklore. Everyone's nasty out there; I just got stuck with the reputation. I think it started in 1977, when *Sports Illustrated* called me the dirtiest player in the NFL. If I'd been four years older, I might have been called "Mean Conrad Dobler," and Joe Greene might've been called the dirtiest player in the NFL.

I think the reason that I got that reputation is because I fought every day at practice. I took offense in them saying, "You're just a dumb shit from Wyoming." I wanted to prove that this dumb shit from Wyoming was going to kick your ass. I was cut once. I wasn't going to get cut again unless it was because I was no good, not because I wasn't tough. So I fought and fought. Isn't that the best technique in the world?

As much as people say I was the dirtiest player in the NFL, I did my part to make the game safer.

On play-action passes you have to sell the run. Most guys would come out like they were run blocking and then come back into a pass protection drill. I wasn't real good at run blocking because I'd lose my balance. I learned to come off and strike the defensive tackle in the facemask so I could keep my balance and a squat position.

At a rules committee meeting Redskins coach George Allen started complaining about me striking the facemask. Coryell said, "Well, if you want that, you guys can't use the head slap anymore." That was my part in getting the head slap rule reversed.

I didn't mind the head slap. I was quick enough and studied martial arts, so I could get my hand up and block it. When you blocked it, it opened up their rib cage, and you could take out a nice piece of rib.

Most people would try to avoid the head slap and move the head away. Then you get the end of it, like a horse kick. If you walk right behind a horse, he can't kick you. If you're two feet away when he kicks and gets fully extended, he's going to knock you on your ass.

I would move into the head slap because they couldn't get the full pendulum swing. I do have a lot of ringing in my ears now, but I don't know if that had to do with the head slap, the banging of heads, or the concussions I received. It's probably a combination of all of them.

When you get a concussion, a lot of times you see stars, and sometimes you just go blank. Sometimes you get up, and it's like you're walking in a fuzzy, cloudy area, like you're driving in fog. One time, I lined up in the defensive huddle. They said, "Get the hell out of here and on the other side of the line!"

There was some steroid use around. My roommate in St. Louis, Bob Young, was the strongest man in the NFL. I used to watch him inject steroids in his room. He died of a heart attack from using them.

Most players took bennies and things of that nature. You'd take them to keep you alert, just like No-Doze or something like that. They'd get you fired up and keep you from having butterflies.

Whether it's in business or sports, everyone's looking for that edge. Everyone wants an edge whether you're a stockbroker or a banker, a candlestick maker or a baker. The stock brokerage company makes money because they know something before you do—they have the edge.

People talk about the steroid era in baseball. What they should say is this is the steroid *testing* era. Not that everyone is using them—just that everyone's getting tested. Versions of steroids have been around for hundreds of years. There's no way to say whether the great players from back in the day didn't use some sort of enhancer.

Steroids give you the energy to work out longer, and you lift more. You get excited, so you're lifting more, getting more excited, and putting more weight on the machines. Would you have gotten that way if you worked that hard without them? Yeah, probably. There's some physical attributes in taking steroids to enhance the growth of the muscles, but the growth of the muscles only happens if you put the time in to work those muscles. You can't take them and just sit there. How much is it because of the steroid use, and how much is it because of the extra work you put in?

One problem we had in St. Louis was that Coryell knew how to beat a defense, but he didn't know how to build one. I have a picture in my office with nine of us Cardinals who made the Pro Bowl. There's only one defensive person—Roger Wehrli. The other eight were offensive players. That's why we never made the Super Bowl.

When Coryell was fired, I spoke out against management and said, "If they fired Coryell, they'll probably trade me."

Somebody said, "If he wants to get traded, we can accommodate him."

They said they thought my knees were bad and I might become a liability. When I got traded, it didn't hurt my feelings. I got more money in two years with the Saints than I made in six years with St. Louis.

When I went down with a knee injury, St. Louis said, "We knew he was going to go down." Well, they didn't know crap.

I got my knee caught on the turf, and Bill Bergey of the Eagles rolled over it and took it out. I had them tape it up, went back in, and played on torn cartilage. That was just the stupidest thing in the world. I then tore my cruciate ligament and chipped the top of the bone, which never heals. I turned a six-week injury into one I never recovered from.

When I went to New Orleans, Archie Manning was sacked 60 times the year before. When I was there, we gave up 17 one year and 18 the next. It was the first time the Saints ever won more than 5 games; we went 7-9 and 8-8. Every time I'd pull for a sweep my eighth year, I was dragging a leg, but we led the league in the least amount of sacks.

The Saints traded me the day before training camp opened in 1980. I was traded to Buffalo because Joe DeLamielleure didn't want to play for Buffalo head coach Chuck Knox. Knox said, "We'll get Dobler up here as a stopgap, and that will force Joe to come in to camp." After two weeks Buffalo traded Joe to Cleveland, and they were stuck with me. I played two years there, not officially, but good enough to get a line to again lead the league in the least amount of sacks.

When I was traded to Buffalo, Joe Ferguson had been sacked about 50 times, but we had a winning record two years in a row. I didn't do it by myself, but I contributed something and got the guys to play as a team by saying, "The only award we're going to get at the end of the year is having the least amount of sacks of any offensive line."

The last two years I played, I never even practiced. I'd watch, run a couple plays to stay warm (Buffalo didn't have an indoor facility), and then play on Sunday.

I'd go in Sunday at 7:00 a.m. for a game at 1:00. It'd take me that long to get ready. My knees were so bad that I *had* to start. I could have probably gotten a couple more years as a backup, but once I got warmed up, if I sat down too long, I would get so stiff that I couldn't go in and relieve anyone. I had to go from the locker room to the field and play every down, or else I wouldn't even be able to walk.

Forget about walking the day after a game. Every night during the season I slept with ice packs on my knees. I had to put my hands against the wall in order to bend them enough to get in to take a shower.

Nowadays my shoulder comes out a lot, even when I'm putting coats or shirts on. I have to walk my fingers up the wall in the morning to put it back in. I'll tell you what—that'll wake you up!

I have to get my shoulder replaced, but every time I have a surgery, I have to go on the IV for three weeks, twice a day, for $1,000 a day. I'm just so tired of the IVs, and I'm tired of the surgeries. I've had nine total knee replacements. I take antibiotics every day because I have MRSA, which will never go away. I've had maybe twenty knee surgeries all together. The nine knee replacements I've paid for myself. Add two of them together, and it's more than what I made in ten years in the NFL.

I'm 99 percent disabled, and the NFL hasn't done a damn thing for me. But let me tell you something: even if workers' comp decided to give me $20 million, it's not going to make up for what's been done to my body. There's no amount that's going to do that. Now that I have the opportunity to maybe go see the pyramids, climb Mt. Everest, or ride my bike around, I can't do it. I can't even get up a flight of stairs.

All the things you wanted to do in life, you can't. I can't get down on the floor to play with my grandkids. It would take me twenty-five minutes to get back up. I used to take my kids, cross my legs, and they'd sit on my ankle and ride on my foot—horsey rides, you know. I wouldn't imagine doing that for my grandkids.

Minimum wage for a rookie now is more than I made all of my ten years in the NFL. I'm not talking about a Pro Bowl player or a starter. I'm talking about a player who just makes the team and gets a great seat at the game.

Dan Dierdorf was telling me about an offensive tackle holding out because he was a franchise player. The tackle came in two or three days before the first game and played the first two games. In those twelve days he made more than Hall of Famer Dan Dierdorf made in thirteen years. That gives you a perspective of what we made.

We all had jobs in the off-season. I sold cars for a long time. I was actually pretty good. I made more money in my rookie off-season selling cars than I made playing ball. I almost didn't go back to training camp.

Everyone asks if I'd do it again, and I always used to say, "Yes, and it has nothing to do with the money." I've gotten older and rethought that. I say, "Yes, I would play it again, but it has something to do with the money." People ask what I mean.

Most of your injuries are compounded when you go back out and play after getting injured. Even though you rehab, going back and playing makes you more susceptible to another injury or damage to the knee later in life.

If I was making today's money, I would have had plenty of money to quit after my first or second knee surgery. The money has a lot to do with it because most of us could have gotten out after four or five years.

# 36

## Joe DeLamielleure

Guard

Michigan State University

Drafted, 1973 (Buffalo Bills, 1st round)

Buffalo Bills, 1973–1979, 1985

Cleveland Browns, 1980–1984

8 All-Pro seasons

6 Pro Bowls

1970s NFL All-Decade Team

Pro Football Hall of Fame Inductee (2003)

I'm from a family of ten, and I'm the ninth of ten. My four older brothers played football, so I'd play with those guys. I went to a Catholic school that graded A for athlete, B for boy, and C for coed. I thought I'd better play athletics.

For college I got recruited by everybody. Ted Hendricks was my host at the University of Miami, and they took Chuck Foreman and me to Super Bowl 3 between the Jets and Colts. That was my first recruiting trip, first plane ride, first time out of the state of Michigan, and I got to see the Super Bowl—the most historic one of all.

As a kid growing up in Detroit, I watched guys like Bubba Smith, Gene Washington, Clinton Jones, and George Webster play for Michigan State, and that's when I started loving football. The reason I went there was because those guys were my idols.

I had Duffy Daugherty as a college coach. He was a humanitarian and recruited black players before other coaches would. He said you had to have three bones to play football: a backbone, a wishbone, and the most important one—a funny bone.

I played for Buffalo Bills coaches Lou Saban and Jim Ringo in the Senior Bowl. They wanted to draft me, but some of the scouts said I was too small. I weighed 245.

That year they had one of the longest first rounds in draft history. Al Davis told me Oakland couldn't decide between me and Ray Guy. I thought I'd go to Pittsburgh because all the Michigan State coaches were there. The Steelers told me they would pick me unless J. T. Thomas was available. Thomas was available, and Buffalo picked before Pittsburgh's next pick. Otherwise the Steelers would have picked me in the second round. I missed four Super Bowls because of that.

I was the last guy picked in the first round. It was like one o'clock in the afternoon, and I think that's when they started putting time limits on picks. I was glad to go to Buffalo because it was close to home and I got to play with O. J. Simpson.

My rookie year, 1973, O. J. broke the single-season rushing record with 2,003 yards. I had just come from Michigan State, where we broke the single-game collegiate record on All-American Eric Allen's 350 yards rushing. I thought that was just how it was. Little did I know how hard it is to break those records.

When I was traded to Cleveland [in 1980], I went from a running team to a passing team. There was an adjustment, but we had the two Pruitts, Mike and Greg, and they were great running backs. Calvin Hill was there too. We also had great receivers like Reggie Rucker, Dave Logan, and Ozzie Newsome. It was probably the best offensive team I played on, and our nickname was the Kardiac Kids.

Playing in Cleveland was great because as a kid growing up in Detroit, I'd go watch Jim Brown, Leroy Kelley, Gary Collins, and all those guys play against the Lions. Cleveland is a flagship NFL team to me because they had the best teams in the 1950s.

Cleveland's about a hundred miles closer to Detroit, where my wife and I grew up. It was really good because my dad could watch the Browns games via satellite in the bar he owned. My only fear was that Gary, Indiana, would get an expansion team. Then I would have been all the way around the lake. [*Laughs.*]

You want to play against the best. I played against Joe Greene and Jack Lambert. The rivalry we had in Cleveland against the Steelers was great. It was like the Buffalo-Miami rivalry, except we would win. When I was in Buffalo, we didn't beat the Dolphins.

The league then either found a giant leap in evolution, or they found steroids. The heaviest I ever weighed was 260. At age thirty-five I wasn't going to take a pill or an injection to play a game. I'm not saying all the guys were using, but in the early '80s, that's when steroids changed the game.

By '85 I was too small to play, and that's why I retired. I never had an injury, never missed a game, and never missed a practice. I quit because I wasn't big enough to play anymore.

Many radio talk show hosts say, "This guy didn't get a [championship] ring, and only guys who get rings should be in the Hall of Fame." I disagree with that totally. We couldn't trade teams. There was no free agency. You played as long as you could for the team you were on.

My mother always said, "Bloom where you're planted."

I got the Forrest Gregg Award in 1977, given to the best offensive lineman as voted by the defensive players. We were 2-12.

You played your position like you were a carpenter, electrician, or painter building a house. I just did my job as an offensive guard, and I did it the best I could.

I was lucky to play with two MVPs—O. J. and Brian Sipe. I was on the leading rushing team and the team with least number of sacks allowed.

I wish the current guys would understand the history of the game. The current kids, you ask them, "Who's the first African American in baseball?"

They'll say, "Jackie Robinson."

Ask them, "Who's the first African American football player?" and they don't know.

Football integrated from 1920 to 1928 and again in 1946, with guys like Bill Willis and Marion Motley—before Jackie Robinson integrated baseball. The African Americans who played in the '40s, '50s, and '60s, they had to do everything.

I think the union's been a con job forever, including now. They don't represent us; the guys who built this league are not taken care of. We had sub-poverty pensions before, and now with this new agreement [2011] we're up to poverty, with no disability. I think this new legacy fund is a bigger joke than ever. We get $108 a month for every year that we played. My pension for thirteen years in this league is about $30,000 per year *before* taxes.

The NFL should be ashamed of itself for allowing that union to not take care of the guys who built the league, the most profitable league in the world. We have a fund for destitute Hall of Famers [the Pro Football Hall of Fame Enshrinees Foundation], and that kind of union carelessness is sick.

[Former union leader] Gene Upshaw had over $2 million in his checking account, $15 million from deferred income from the union, two houses—one in Virginia and one in Lake Tahoe—eight luxury vehicles, and a thirty-two-foot boat. That's a union leader? Give me a break. I grew up in a bar in Detroit, where the factories were open from 7:30 in the morning until 2:30 at night, seven days a week. We know what unions are; they take care of the common man.

I'm not going down without a fight. I don't care if they got an agreement or not.

I try to make a difference for the retired guys. When I go to my grave, I don't want people to just say, "He was really a great football player." I want my family and people to say, "He was a great humanitarian. He was a good man who made a difference."

[While this book was in production, Joe walked from Rich Stadium in Buffalo to the Pro Football Hall of Fame in Canton, Ohio, raising awareness about the cost of prosthetic limbs. In 2009 he rode a bicycle two thousand miles from East Lansing, Michigan, to Matamoros, Mexico, to raise funds for an orphanage.]

# 37

## Billy "White Shoes" Johnson

Wide receiver, returner

Widener University

Drafted, 1974 (Houston Oilers, 15th round)

Houston Oilers, 1974–1980

Atlanta Falcons, 1982–1987

Washington Redskins, 1988

NFL punt return touchdown leader (1975, 1977)

1 All-Pro season

3 Pro Bowls

1970s NFL All-Decade Team

1980s NFL All-Decade Team

NFL 75th Anniversary All-Time Team

The white shoes go back to high school, when everybody wore black shoes. A buddy of mine and I were just talking in the summertime, and he said, "I got an idea; why don't you do this?"

I said, "Why not? The only thing Coach can do is stop me from wearing the shoes."

My friend helped me get the shoes dyed with the help of a real cobbler. I had two or three pairs made. They looked brand new. You couldn't tell they were black shoes dyed white.

I decided to take the challenge, wearing them to school and practice one day. Coach questioned me about them because he wasn't one to like things like that. I told him that they made me run faster. I had a good scrimmage, and he never said another word about them.

At the time I matriculated into college, it was called PMC

[Pennsylvania Military College]. My sophomore year they changed the name of the school to Widener University. I played for who I think is one of the best coaches in college football, let alone Division 3: Bill Manlove. Playing for Coach Manlove was really a treat. You wanted to do well just for him.

We had just got some new facilities, the program had turned around, and it was great. We had guys other than myself, like Joe Fields and Jack Klotz, who played pro ball. It was a good brand of football, and you played it because you wanted to play it.

There are a lot of Division 3 programs doing well today. You ask those ball players, and they'll attest that there's nothing like playing Division 3 ball. Great competition out there.

The touchdown dance was also on a dare. Well, it wasn't quite a dare, but I said something that I shouldn't have said about an opposing team in college. They were talking a bunch of negative stuff because they were from a division higher. You know, bulletin board stuff, incendiary remarks. I said if I were to score, I was going to dance.

My guys said, "No you won't."

I had to be true to my words, so when I scored, I danced. And I've been dancing ever since.

For the NFL draft Randy Grossman and I both went on Tom Brookshier's show. I got a call that the Oilers had drafted me. I was elated coming from a Division 3 school, as a guy of my stature and my size. Randy got a call and as a free agent signed with the Pittsburgh Steelers. We both came into the league at the same time, and he walked away with four Super Bowl rings. And I'm still in search of.... [*Laughs.*]

I wasn't supposed to make it. I wasn't even supposed to be in a professional football camp. Guys were bigger and more talented across the board than in my collegiate division. I was blocking linebackers in college that were 215 pounds. Shoot, now some of the corners and safeties were 215.

I just played like I played before. I had nothing to lose and everything to gain. That's how I looked at it, so there was no pressure on me. I just did all I could do.

I think if a young man can learn how to catch the ball that's punted or kicked to him and has confidence that when he gets the ball he can make something happen, he'll be a solid punt returner. To me that's what it takes.

You also have to want to be a good punt and kickoff returner. A lot of guys have the ability, but they don't want to do it. That's the difference that makes it—enjoying it, ingratiating yourself to that job. For me it was another chance to get the ball, and I felt as though I had the advantage when I got the ball.

You think you'll never get hurt and that you're invincible. I had three injuries and recovered from every one of them. It's all part of the game, and you continue to work hard. Then it's a challenge to come back. Every time you come back, if it happens again, like it happened to me, you say, "Gosh darn." You fight to come back again and say, "It'll never happen again."

It makes you appreciate where you are as an athlete and of how much you take for granted when you're healthy. It also makes you work hard without any complaints.

I haven't missed a beat since I retired. Football's great, but it's only part of your life. I'm a guy who played football, but football doesn't define who I am. I'm in a new chapter in my life.

# 38

## Doug English

Defensive tackle

University of Texas

Drafted, 1975 (Detroit Lions, 2nd round)

Detroit Lions, 1975–1979, 1981–1985

4 All-Pro seasons

4 Pro Bowls

All-time NFL safeties leader (4; tied with Ted Hendricks and
Jared Allen)

A lot of football players are shaving in the eighth grade
and kicking everybody's butt. I was the tall, skinny guy, all
Adam's apple and elbows. I was the last one chosen and sat
on the bench. I got cut in the eighth grade. My sophomore
year, there was a varsity JV and a B team. I was third string
on the B team. My junior year, I managed to make varsity.
By midseason I was playing but not starting. The first game
I started in my life was the first game of my senior year in
high school.

When Texas offered me a scholarship, I probably didn't
understand what an incredibly lucky deal it was to play for
one year and receive a scholarship offer from Texas. Pat Pat-
terson, the defensive line coach at Texas, saw something in
me that he wanted to coach.

To turn down a scholarship from Texas and go to a lesser
school—so that maybe the competition wouldn't be as stiff—
would have been like putting your tail between your legs and
doing something less than what you know is right. I accepted
the scholarship out of fear—fear of feeling like I had backed

11. Doug English's College Football Hall of Fame induction ball.

down from something and fear of having to live with that the rest of my life.

If you learned something from Coach Darrell Royal about football, you learned it about life, and vice versa. He made it first things first and real simple. Every position had three or four things that you had to be able to do. If you were going to play a certain position, you had to be good at those specific things. It didn't matter if you could do all this other great stuff.

Those three objectives for each position were designed to fit with the objectives of everyone else on the field. When you put it all together, it was dominant. It was a great synthesis of the collective pieces becoming greater than the total sum. It was a great example of how to do business, live your life, and play football. That was Darrell probably more than any other coach.

My senior year, we had this freshman named Earl Campbell. You might have heard of him? That was 1974, the first year freshmen were eligible to play varsity. Earl would race the fastest guys on the team. He'd be three steps ahead of them at 20 yards, but then they'd beat him at 40. It was unbelievable how fast his first three steps were.

Coach was looking for a way to get Earl into the game, so he put him on the punt block team. He basically said, "Earl, line up on the ball—and follow it."

We were playing Arkansas in a really tight game. We had them backed up, having to punt right before the half. Darrell sent out the punt block team, and Earl came trotting out.

Back then the punt formation included two upbacks. The upback on my side crossed over to block on the other side, and my guard blocked out. Earl and I were both free.

Earl *was* a few steps ahead of me. [*Laughs.*] He almost caught the ball before it hit the punter. Earl blocked the punt, it bounced into my hands, and I ran it all the way—about three steps—into the end zone. That was my one touchdown.

After the season I played in the Senior Bowl rather than the Hula Bowl because they paid you. With the Hula Bowl you got the benefit of a week in Hawaii. The two coaching staffs that lost in the NFC and AFC Championships were the Senior Bowl coaches.

The San Francisco 49ers staff coached our team. After the game 49ers defensive coordinator Paul Wiggan goes, "Hey, Doug, you want to go have a beer at the hotel?" I'm sitting there having my beer with the coach, feeling pretty cool, and he goes, "Doug, I want you to know the San Francisco 49ers are going to draft you in the first round if you're still available."

I thought, "You are kidding me! If I'm still available?!? San Francisco?!? Outstanding!" I was excited, but between that night and the draft Wiggan became the head coach of the Kansas City Chiefs.

If you were going to be a top draft choice, there was a tradition of getting a keg and having a draft party. On draft day a bunch of my teammates were over, and we're waiting for the phone to ring. Of course I wasn't drinking; I wanted to be sharp for my new employer.

The first round came and went, and San Francisco drafted another guy. Second round comes and goes, third round comes and goes, and the fourth round comes and goes. The guys are looking at me, and I'm sitting there like I'm a loser. Every once in a while the phone would ring, and some buddy of mine would say [*mock voice*], "Ah, this is Tom Landry with the Dallas Cowboys. We just drafted you." Finally my lawyer/agent calls and says, "Oh, by the way, did you know Detroit drafted you in the second round? They want you to fly up there as soon as you can."

I'm like, "Somebody hand me the atlas. I've got to figure out where this is."

I got a $40,000 bonus my rookie year. Veterans could not believe I got that kind of money. I got $25,000 $30,000, and $35,000 a year after that. It was the biggest contract the Lions had ever given a second-round draft choice.

Detroit was the perfect place for me. I had unbelievably good coaches every step of the way. Plus in a blue-collar town they like that you're on the pro team, but if you want to cash a check, you're going to need two IDs. If you want a beer, you're going to pay regular price like everyone else. I'm thankful that's where I went because it was a grounding experience.

My first pro game in 1975, my head was kind of spinning. It was a preseason game and the first game ever in the Silverdome. They didn't quite get the Silverdome finished in time, and panels were missing in the ceiling. During the pregame I'm all nervous, psyched up, and beating my head against the wall. I look out, and their punter and our punter are trying to kick balls through the holes in the ceiling. [*Laughs.*]

The ceiling was air-suspended cabling with canvas or nylon patches between the cables. An air-blowing system blew air into the stadium, which inflated and held up the roof. When you went into the stadium, you had to go through revolving doors and pressure locks. If you ever opened a regular door—like the door that led to the tunnel and locker rooms—it would blow you back if they didn't have the opposite door shut. We learned to lean into that door when we opened it.

My first three years, I was coached by Fritz Shurmur, who later was defensive coordinator for the Green Bay Packers in two Super Bowls. At that stage in my career he was the perfect coach for me. Fritz demonstrated foot and hand placement, and I was learning the mechanics, specifically about the technique of moving mass and leverage. After Fritz left, Monte Clark came in as head coach and brought in Floyd Peters. Floyd was the defensive line coach in San Francisco, which didn't draft me.

Floyd had created what they called "the Gold Rush" in the mid-'70s. The 49ers led the league in sacks and shortest amount per carry on run plays. He came to Detroit, created what they called "the Silver Rush," and we led the league in sacks and fewest yards per carry.

Once Floyd got a hold of you, he had your butt in the air, head down, weight on your hand, and you were throwing your body. I remember him chewing on me, "Quit rassling with those guys!" It was exactly what I needed. I started going to Pro Bowls every year because Floyd was coaching.

We did a lot of crazy things on the field, and he loved it. He never chewed on us for a personal foul or being offside. He figured if we were really coming off, we were going to be offside. If we got in a fight or two, he understood it was because we were aggressive. Floyd had this great expression, "Win when you can, lose if you must, but always cheat." [*Laughs.*] He wasn't telling us to be sorry humans; his point was to do whatever you had to do to get your job done.

We'd get in those games when it was just working. We'd knock the quarterback down almost every time, rush his passes, and get three and outs.

One of the phenomena about sports, particularly football, is that you play on your subconscious level. Only your subconscious is powerful enough to manage the reactions and thousandth-of-a-second decisions you have to make. Fear and thinking too much—which comes from being scared—put you on a conscious level.

Sometimes you see a team make a few mistakes. Soon they're thinking, and the coach is yelling at them. That pushes it into a conscious level, and they're moving slower and making bad decisions. It's like they're working off their CD-Rom drive instead of their hard drive.

The cool thing about when you're on is that everyone gets into this relaxed, throw-your-body-and-let-your-feet-take-it-from-there style of play. Everything works. I can almost remember those games by heart, when our biorhythms were right and theirs weren't. We weren't big winners in Detroit, but those were my victories.

Some All-American and All-Pro guys get big reputations because they play on winning teams. If you watch them, they're pretty average until they get ahead. Once they get ahead, they don't care. They're just throwing their body, their reactions and subconscious carry them, and they're All-World. We used to call them front-runners.

Those golden six years—five with Floyd and one with veteran defensive line coach Eddie Kayak—were the best of the years. We were a unit. We stuck together and were loyal to each other.

We had Al "Bubba" Baker, one of the great stories in the NFL. I think he was a nineteen-year-old rookie, All-Pro. He didn't have the classic long legs, short waist, and broad shoulders. He was more of an angular block, a tall, lean guy. He was fearless and had a strong mother that he talked about a lot.

The veterans were used to pushing rookies around, but Al didn't back down from anybody. He was my end, and we had a ball rushing the passer and going to Pro Bowls together.

We had another defensive end, Dave Pureifory. We lost him a couple of years ago to pancreatic cancer. Pureifory said he was 6-foot-2, but I think he was more like 5-foot-11 and weighed 260. He had two or three black belts in martial arts. He was the most imposing, intimidating guy from his stance that I'd ever seen. We used to call him "Devil," for the Tasmanian Devil. He was like the cartoon character, a little whirlwind that would lacerate opponents, giving 6-foot-8, 350 pound guys fits.

This is what I love about athletes at the professional level: you get this marriage of unique qualities that are paired together in one athlete. Pureifory was just savage on the field, but to sit and talk with him, you'd swear you were speaking to a philosophy professor. He was a deep, thoughtful, and wise man.

He was great for Bubba Baker because Bubba could have gone off. His career could have been cut short by killing somebody in a bar fight or who knows what. He could have gone any number of ways, and he'll be the first to tell you that. Now he's one of the most upstanding, coolest people you'll ever meet. I think part of it was due to Floyd, part was due to the relationship we had on the defensive line, and part of it had to do with Dave Pureifory. I remember seeing Bubba going "RRRR!" and Dave sitting on a stool, quietly talking to him, gently waving his hand, slowing Bubba down.

Every team in the NFL has a culture. The NFC Central Division was old school, very old franchises: Green Bay, Chicago, Detroit. Minnesota was fairly new, but they got it. They called it the black and blue division because most of the teams wore black, purple, or blue.

We all gravitated toward where the line had to dominate to win, you tackled hard, and it wasn't pretty. Each team had their own culture, but we had a physical, old school disposition altogether more than the other divisions. That's where the term black and blue also comes in.

Playing against Walter Payton twice a year was wonderful and horrible at the same time. One thing I loved about Walter was that he wasn't mouthy. Chicago had a few players who got kind of obnoxious. Their best players were not mouthy, but their also-rans could be.

Walter was a terror when he had that ball or when he was blocking. He worked so hard, and I respect the way he approached the game even more than his ability. When you tackled him, you could feel his knees hitting you in the ribs all the way to the ground. You knew if you released your grip in the slightest, he would be on his feet and still running. He fought you *all* the way to the ground. When you hit the ground, he'd relax. If he got up before you did, he'd help you up. He'd say, "Good job" in that high voice. That's why they called him "Sweetness."

The time leading up to the players' strike in 1982 was kind of like looking at the extended forecast and seeing we got this huge storm coming and we may get 12–14 inches. You say, "Well, do I board the windows?" But it may not happen.

We learned that we were probably going to strike, and then there was a strike. Most of us were like, "Oh good; we get to go fishing. We'll go home, and they'll let us know when it's over."

The NFL Players Association has hurt NFL players more than anything, including opposing linemen. It's like there's a dark and a positive side of unions, and the bad side formed the NFL Players Association.

The opposite would be the baseball guys. Their union was formed by their agents, lawyers, and representatives. They understand supply and demand: earn your way, and use whatever markets you've worked for to negotiate. Being free market thinkers, they got free agency in the early 1970s for a very few. It was a big hurdle to get there, but after a few guys got there, salaries went through the roof for everybody.

While baseball's union hammered out free agency and then tried to lower the hurdle to it—figuring everything would take care of itself, which it did—the football guys were being led by Ed Garvey, whose whole deal was wage scale. He went to twenty-eight billionaires and said, "Right now your salary expense is 52 percent of your gross. We'll take that 52 percent and pass it out according to *our* needs."

The owners said, "Get out of my office!"

That's why we had a strike. Garvey asked for something that they weren't about to give him, and even if they did, it'd be horrible for the players. Consequently we struck until things fell apart, and they just took whatever the NFL gave us.

The strike deal was frustrating to me because I had to lose a paycheck and see the league go downhill and my world under assault because of a small group of naive guys that didn't know business. I'll strike for something that works, something I believe in, but for wage scale?

I played ten years in the NFL and started taking my pension a couple years after I turned fifty-five; that same ten years in Major League baseball is worth four times more than an NFL pension. Why? Because business people ran the baseball union, and our football union was run by non-business people. It wasn't until free agency [1993] that anybody started making any real money in the NFL. Salaries went up several-fold within a few years.

I'm not sure which play it was in which I got the neck injury that ended my career. It was against the Bears in Chicago. The Lions identified a play where a guy cut me, and I came down face first on the turf. I never argued, but I think it may have happened earlier in the warmup.

I started getting tingling in my hands, and then my right leg experienced a lot of numbness. A couple of times, I was running, and it was almost like I stepped in a hole and I just fell. I played through the third quarter. In between the third and fourth quarter, I told the trainer about it. His eyes got wide and he said, "You're not going back in the game."

Language was rough, and we were excitable. I screamed an obscenity and said, "Yes, I am going back in!"

He stood up there and said, "You are not going back in that game!"

"Yes, I am!"

About that time someday runs up, jerks the helmet out of my hand, and takes off running out of the stadium. I start running after him, and the trainer grabs me. I'm dragging him along, and he's got his got his finger in my face, saying, "Doug, look at me. You're not going back in the game."

It suddenly occurred to me that the ball boy took my helmet. They had a "steal their helmet" signal for aggressive players to get them out of the game. Apparently somebody had given the fastest ball boy word to steal my helmet. I couldn't go back into the game with no helmet. I thanked the trainer later. He probably saved my life.

I went to the hospital the next day. They operated and said it was an absolute miracle that I wasn't dead or paralyzed. It wasn't a broken vertebra; it was a ruptured disc mashing on the spinal cord nerve. Spinal cord nerves are about the consistency of crab meat, so they're very easy to damage. Once you bruise the spinal cord, it no longer sends signals through the bruised area.

Because the Ford family made sure we had the absolute best medical care you could get, I had this wonderful operation. I walked out of the hospital two days later, and I've had a great neck ever since. I just can't run into people with my head anymore. Yet everyone I'd heard of that had a neck injury was in a lot of pain and didn't have such a good outcome.

The operation I received on my neck in 1985 has been done with regularity only in the past ten years or so. When I had my neck injury, orthopedic surgeons would do neck operations literally with a chisel and a hammer. They'd unzip the back of your neck and chip away. No one recovered. You were in pain the rest of your life. That always stuck with me. Who your doctor and hospital are when you get hurt could mean life or death and certainly pain or no pain.

Like so many NFL guys, I got asked to host a celebrity golf tournament. After my injury I met Kent Waldrep. He got hurt playing for TCU against Alabama and is in a wheelchair. He started a foundation, and we switched the recipient of the funds from the golf tournament to the Kent Waldrep National Paralysis Foundation.

I've received a lot of inspiration from Kent and hundreds of other people in wheelchairs, people who have superhuman strength of character to get up each day and spend two hours just to get out of bed and into their wheelchairs. I'm now president of the Lone Star Paralysis Foundation.

By my fifth year, 1979, I'd developed knee problems in both knees. I had to tape every day for practice and for games, to the skin, from my toes to my crotch. Afterward I'd peel that tape off and take pieces of skin with it. The next day I'd tape back over those scabs.

My right shoulder was to the point that I could hardly lift my arm. I'd probably begun my neck injury that would end my career six years later. I was getting stingers, and my whole right arm would often feel like it was literally on fire. You hear about guys having stingers, and you have no idea what that feels like. I've had probably a dozen of them, and there is no worse pain than your nerve system turning against you.

Physically I was beat up. We were 2-14 that year. I had never experienced a losing season like that, even in high school. We literally fought our way out of the bars at night, fought in the locker room, and fought on the field; it was just horrible.

I always heard about what a great game football was, but I never thought it was that great. I started because my friends were doing it and just kind of kept going. Practice, road trips, conditions, the heat, the injuries—it's just kind of miserable.

I thought, "Why am I playing this game?"

After the '79 season I said, "I hate it, and I'm never going to play it again." I quit and took a job opportunity that put me in London during training camp. I wrote a letter to the coach and told him of my decision. I deeply regret that. I regret not telling him up front early on so he could replace me or do whatever he needed to do to make plans. I left him hanging and wasn't mature enough to understand how important it was.

I didn't feel important after that 2-14 season. I certainly didn't think football was important. Looking back, I can see that even after a debacle like that, it was still important, and I should have done better.

I had eighteen months off and was able to watch the game for the first time from outside the forest. I learned what *is* important about sports and what *is* important about football.

No matter how much you win or don't win, the only thing that's important about any success in sports is that it gives you a forum and a chance to make a difference. When a kid comes up and asks you for an autograph, you look him in the eye, let him know you're happy to see him, and say, "I'll be happy to sign that for you." While you're signing it, you say, "Are you making good grades?"

His eyes get really wide, he looks at his mom, and she's like, "Told ya."

Then you get a letter from his mom three weeks later saying, "Johnny has brought home homework every night, and his grades have gone to all A's in all his subjects because you asked him if he was making good grades."

It took me fifteen seconds to make a difference. Why? Because I can run into people real hard with my head. It's crazy.

Life's not math. Things don't add up. For some reason people in our society value sports figures. It makes absolutely no sense to me, but because they do, you can really do some good.

For the foundation I can ask somebody, "We have this fundraiser, and I need a tent and a car." A lot of times what gets those for us is that I played football. Versus the fact that

12. Doug English with his Powerdrive training equipment, currently used by the University of Texas, the Detroit Lions, and high schools throughout Texas. www.PowerDriveTraining.com.

we're taking people that were told by their doctor they'd never walk again, and six weeks later they walk out of the recovery center. And it does matter in many cases; I don't want to overstate this.

I hate the word "celebrity." It gives me the creeps when people talk about celebrities because most celebrities I know are not nearly as inspiring as the guy who puts in a twelve-hour day building fences, working on cars, or driving a truck to take care of his family.

I like the word "character"; I like the phrase "hard work." I like sacrifice, I like empathy. I like people that beat the odds and outwork the other guy. A lot of that goes on in football, and *that's* what's important.

Just being a good football player—it's a game. It's people running into each other. It doesn't make one kid healthier or smarter. The only important thing about being a great athlete is you can take that acclaim and do some good with it.

# 39

## Louie Kelcher

Defensive tackle

Southern Methodist University

Drafted, 1975 (San Diego Chargers, 2nd round)

San Diego Chargers, 1975–1983

San Francisco 49ers, 1984

1 All-Pro season

3 Pro Bowls

Super Bowl champion (San Francisco 49ers, Super Bowl 19)

In Texas if you're big, you're going to play football. I grew up in Beaumont and was more interested in baseball. The Little League president lived next door to us when I was seven. You had to be eight to play peewee league, but I was bigger than most of the kids. He stuck me in baseball a year early.

I started playing football in junior high when it was seventh, eighth, and ninth grades; the ninth grade hadn't moved to high school yet. I broke my ankle playing baseball the summer after my ninth grade year.

Going into high school, we met the PE Department and the coaches. You were given a card to check what sports you were going to play. I only checked baseball.

Our coach said, "Who's Kelcher?" I stood up. He said, "You're playing football."

Sophomore year we went 0-10. We only won two games the rest of my career in high school. My senior year, I'm going, "This is not fun."

I really didn't think about football past high school. My whole world was Beaumont, Texas. My dad was a hardworking, blue-collar guy who worked as a machinist for thirty-some years. I thought, "I'll get a refinery job or something."

Schools started recruiting me though. All of the Southwest Conference schools called except Texas. My first question was, "How did y'all find me? You don't heavily recruit a guy who only wins two games in high school."

I started talking to my dad and mom about how it was an opportunity and that a college scholarship was something to look at. I decided to take three or four trips. My mom's side of the family was from Arkansas, and there was a big push from Mom and Grandma for me to be the token one off to Fayetteville.

I visited Arkansas. I remember flying Frontier Airlines out of Dallas on a prop job. Joe Gibbs recruited me; he was at Arkansas with Coach Frank Broyles. I'd made my mind up that I was going to Arkansas.

Hayden Fry called and wanted me to visit SMU. I didn't know who Hayden Fry was, but he was a real personable guy and talked everything up. I decided to visit SMU. It was my last visit, and I had a great weekend in Dallas. I think the Cowboys were in the Super Bowl, and everything was popping.

You get into some situations and you know what's right. SMU felt right to me. I didn't know anything more except Hayden was a great coach, and I loved talking to Bum Phillips, the defensive coordinator. I went home and broke my mom's and grandma's hearts and said, "I'm going to SMU."

Freshmen still weren't allowed to play varsity. It was the last year we had a freshman football team. We never saw the varsity much except on Mondays. We called it the Toilet Bowl, and the freshmen would scrimmage the redshirts and guys who didn't play on Saturdays. We only played five games as freshmen. Jerry Pettibone was our coach. We'd practice, but it was just to keep us busy. We had graduate assistants for coaches and no curfews.

My sophomore year, we got into the big leagues with Hayden and Bum and went 7-4. There was a lot of politics going on, and they fired Hayden. Here we are 7-4, and I lose Hayden and Bum. Dave Smith came in for the next two years. We were 6-4-1 both years in the old Southwest Conference days.

On draft day a reporter from one of the papers was doing an article on getting drafted. Up to that point I heard three or four teams say they were going to draft me. I'd never heard from San Diego. I picked up the phone, and it was Tommy Prothro. He had a unique vocal delivery and said, "Kelcher, this is Tommy Prothro, and you've been drafted by the San Diego Chargers."

I said, "Okay. Where are you guys at?" I didn't even know where San Diego was.

They flew all the draft choices in. At the time I didn't realize it, but that was probably one of their stronger drafts. Gary Johnson was a No. 1; Fred Dean and I were No. 2s.

The lucky part for us was that they had a big scandal the year before with a team doctor prescribing drugs to players, and they cleaned house. We had the opportunity to come in and play immediately. We had ten or more rookies on the team who were playing.

My first year, we went 2-12. I'm thinking, "Here we go again. I'm right back into high school." We hung in there, though. San Diego was a beautiful place to play, and I grew with the new team.

Our owner, Gene Klein, hated Raiders owner Al Davis. I don't know if it was from football or business dealings, but there was no love lost between the Chargers and Raiders. Klein said that Al Davis caused him to have a heart attack— that shows you how deep it went. The Raiders had been kicking the Chargers butts for years when I got there.

The Coliseum in Oakland was a horrible place. I remember my first year traveling to Oakland, and the Raiders had a nice locker room with a carpet, everything good. Our locker room: my jersey, my pants, all my stuff was hanging on a hanger on a nail. Back then you'd do what you could do to get into somebody's head.

I remember standing on the sidelines looking up in the stands, and there was a Charger fan waving a Charger banner. Some Oakland fans behind him lit it on fire. [*Laughs.*] You expected it. Nothing surprised you.

In 1977 our quarterback, Dan Fouts, was hurt, and we played the Raiders in San Diego with a quarterback named Cliff Olander. In that game I fell on Ken Stabler's leg and hurt him. He went out, and they didn't really have any quarterbacks after him.

We beat the Raiders, who were defending Super Bowl champions. It was just one of those things that wasn't supposed to happen. The rivalry got even more heated once we beat them.

The funny thing about football is that years later you become friends and drinking buddies with the guys you hated. I started going to Stabler's golf tournament. I'd see Ted Hendricks at functions, and we'd have a beer together. That's the great thing about the fraternity of football: once it's over, it's over.

I think fans take it to heart more than the players. I've never gone out on the field with the intention of hurting somebody. You're going to play hard, there's going to be some cheap shots that today they'd suspend you two games for, but you don't intentionally try to take somebody out. It's kind of a closed fraternity, and you don't want to be the guy that ended anyone's career.

In 1978 we had a team meeting. Gene Klein came in, and Coach Prothro held a piece of notebook paper that said, "I hereby resign effective [this date]."

Klein said, "I'd like to introduce you to the head coach of the San Diego Chargers: Don Coryell."

Coryell was a great players' coach. Things turned around, and we started being really competitive. Offensively quarterback Dan Fouts and the guys were scoring a lot of points. Defensively we held our own. The camaraderie between the team and the fans grew. It was a special time.

I was fortunate enough to have Gary Johnson next to me, with Fred Dean and LeRoy Jones. We were affectionately known as the "Bruise Brothers." In 1980 Gary, Fred, and I all went to the Pro Bowl. It was the last time three defensive linemen from the same team have gone.

Dan Fouts used to kid us about defensive line meetings. Offensively they'd have all this offense to learn from Coryell and were in meetings for hours. Dan said he walked by our defensive line meeting and our coaches said, "Raise your right hand. Raise your left hand. Okay, you guys are ready!"

We played at Miami in the 1981 playoffs and started out with a 24-0 first quarter lead. Right before halftime Duriel Harris caught a pass and lateraled back to Tony Nathan, who went in for the score. The hook-and-ladder deal. That touchdown started the ball rolling for them. [The Chargers led 24-17 at halftime.]

The hook-and-ladder was a great call on their part. You went for the one guy, then the other guy swung by, and at the last second the ball flipped to him. I was like everybody else; I was trying to chase the guy with the ball. All of a sudden our offensive goes idle for a while, and everything's working for them, like it did for us in the first quarter. Hey, we got a game. Then it just becomes who blinks first in the second half. We get tied up; they go ahead; we tie up; we go ahead; they tie up.

In the fourth quarter the Dolphins were ahead and driving. They handed off to Andra Franklin, and I was fortunate enough to get a hand in there. He fumbled and we recovered. I don't know if Andra was just tired or if I was just expending everything I had.

It was one of those things that happens playing football. You run the same play a hundred times, and he never would fumble. It was just the right moment. It was good for me because I helped turn the tide, and that's what we're out there for—get the ball back to the offense and let Dan and them do what they do best.

I remember the Dolphins missing a field goal. I can still smell and see it—where the defensive line drove low, getting in the ground to get the offensive line to go down, so maybe the tall guys could get up with their hands. There's just certain things in that game that stuck in my mind and faces that you recall.

Our kicker, Rolf Benirschke, had a 27-yard field goal attempt in overtime to end the game. Back then you had the clips on the shoulder pads. I had already unclipped mine, was ready to celebrate, and he missed it. I'm like, "Are you kidding me?"

Now I'm scrambling to get my padding and jersey ready. Rolf ended up making a field goal later, and we won 41-38.

From a fan's standpoint it was a great game to watch. From a player's standpoint a lot of energy was expended. Both teams threw everything they had on the field. I've never been more tired after a game. You had these adrenaline rushes, playing and sweating, and it was hot in Miami.

I told Billy Shields and Eric Sievers, "Man, you got a lot of mileage out of that picture of y'all carrying Kellen [Winslow] off the field." You know with, "He's so tired."

I used to give Kellen a lot of heck about that: "Me and Ed White laid out there for twenty minutes waiting for somebody to come get us. Nobody came. They turned the lights off in the stadium and started stealing our shoes and socks. We finally had to get up and go in. We were so tired."

I think the Miami game kind of culminated the 1981 season. We had a really good team, a really good spirit, and some great players. Dan and the offense showed that in the end they could come back. I'm glad Rolf came through finally. [*Laughs.*]

If you go back and look, everybody had a contribution. It wasn't like this guy did everything that day. It was a team effort, and that's what really made it special. A fumble here, a first-down catch here, a tackle here, and a stop there.

We went from Miami to Cincinnati the next week and to 59 degrees below zero with the wind chill. Reality set in real quick. I woke up that Sunday morning, walked over to the window at the hotel, and my nose stuck to the window. I thought, "It's cold outside." And it just got colder.

That sort of weather is not really copacetic with the passing attack. The ball was as hard as that floor. For Dan it was like throwing a rock. Your mind starts playing games. There was ice on your facemask. I had a beard then, and it was completely frozen, spit coming out like icicles. We got behind, and with our offense it's hard to play catch-up in that sort of weather.

I remember the second half: they opened the tunnel, and that wind came off that river. I had never felt cold like that in my life. They had a big-ass back named Pete Johnson, and I remember thinking, "Oh my God, they're just going to run him." It was like tackling myself.

Defensively we could have done a lot better, but again, we're from San Diego. We weren't used to cold weather. That game broke my heart. Once we beat Miami, I thought we had a really good launching pad to the Super Bowl.

I wish we had won the Super Bowl in San Diego because it was like family there. There was no free agency in the '70s and early '80s, and a lot of us played together eight or nine years. People got married, and our kids grew up together. Like any sort of work environment where you're with people daily, you're with your teammates more than your own family—and they become family.

It just wasn't meant to be, and you go on. We were thankful to get where we were. Unfortunately there's a winner and a loser, and we just happened to come up short on some of those games.

In the off-season Fred Dean started having contract problems, and they traded him to San Francisco. They brought in a new defensive coordinator who decided to go to a 3-4 defense, so somebody's being left out. There was a lot of animosity, and it just wasn't working. I said, "I'm beating my head here," and was going to retire.

My first few years in San Diego, Joe Gibbs and Bill Walsh came through as offensive coordinators. When Fred Dean went to San Francisco, our offensive line coach and assistant equipment manager were also there with Walsh. The offensive line coach called me and said, "Bill wants to know if you want to play some football."

I said, "Well, yeah," and went to San Francisco for the '84 season.

San Francisco owner Eddie DeBartolo treated players differently than Gene Klein did. Gene was a good guy, but like coaches are players' coaches, I think Eddie was a players' owner. "You win for me, and I'll spend whatever it takes to get there facility-wise and travel-wise."

When I was in San Diego, there used to be Pacific Southwest Airlines, and the team scrunched into these little seats. In San Francisco we flew on 747s with five seats between the next guys. It makes a difference, and you appreciate it. Eddie was going to win, and he was going to make sure there were no excuses.

San Francisco was real special. Life is easy when you're winning. We won Super Bowl 19 after the '84 season, beating Miami in Dan Marino's only Super Bowl appearance.

Afterward, I said, "It's time. I've played ten years, and I got a ring. Instead of the game telling me when to get out, I'm going to tell the game." I retired after the '84 season.

I feel so fortunate because I was able to enjoy my career with two Hall of Fame quarterbacks: Dan Fouts and Joe Montana. Dan was a hard guy and expected a lot out of the guys around him. A consummate professional, he was all business on game days. With our offense we always felt like if it were 40-38 and we stopped them with twenty seconds left, our offense could score. I'd come off the field, Dan would be coming on, and I'd go, "Can you do something? We got you twenty seconds!"

Joe Montana is one of the nicest guys you'd ever meet. I have a lot of respect for him, with who he was at the time and what he became. There wasn't any class differential. He was just a normal guy in the locker room and on the field.

We weren't playing for big bucks, although I thought it was a lot of money for a twenty-one-year-old kid from Beaumont. The difference is that guys today are coming to training camp today with money in the bank, and we were coming to training camp to get paid. We were glad camp started because a veteran's pay was $400 a week, and that went a long way. We had bills to pay.

I'm one of the lucky ones. I got to play a kid's game and make a comfortable living at it, and I met my wife and lifelong friends. I owe the game a lot. I'm sitting here because of what I did back then. I have had a blessed life as far as that.

I'm like you now; I'm a fan. I'd say I enjoy high school and college football more than pro right now. The simplicity of high school is fun. I really enjoy the smaller schools. If I see stadium lights on in the middle of nowhere, I'll stop to see who's playing.

I can watch a game, and the feeling will come back. As a player, I don't think you ever get over that: wearing your jersey in the hall, listening to the coaches, the emotions. I still get chills thinking about it. It's instilled in you.

It's funny how the longer you're out of the game, the less ego you have. We all have our fifteen minutes of fame, and it'll be gone. All you have is the memories, and you try to make as many good ones as you can.

# 40

## Chris Bahr

Kicker

Penn State University

Drafted, 1976 (Cincinnati Bengals, 2nd round)

Cincinnati Bengals, 1976–1979

Oakland/Los Angeles Raiders, 1980–1988

San Diego Chargers, 1989

Super Bowl champion (Super Bowls 15, 18)

NFL extra-points leader (1982, 1983)

1 All-Pro season

My dad, Walter Bahr, captained the U.S. national soccer team and was a member of the 1950 World Cup team. England was the favorite to win, and the United States knocked them out of the tournament with a 1-0 win. They made a movie about it called *Miracle Match*. The game wasn't really a big deal here, but it was a big deal in England. Professional soccer wasn't much money back then, but my dad played in various leagues on the East Coast.

As kids messing around, we played all sorts of sports. Among all of it we kicked some. During the summer of ninth grade, the high school football coach saw me kicking in the park with his son and asked me to come on out. They let me kick a football on Friday evenings and play soccer the rest of the week.

Had they ever told me I had to choose, I would have continued to play soccer and given up football. I had much more say in the outcome in soccer. In football you sat around and never kicked if your team didn't score. Fortunately I didn't have to choose.

I went to college at Penn State. For two years I played both soccer and football. My first season with the football team, we were the first team to go 12-0. We only lost five games in three years.

I had three 55-yard field goals at Penn State. It's not that difficult to kick the ball 55 yards, although obviously there's accuracy involved. More than anything else, it's having the opportunity to do it. Guys are kicking a lot more long field goals now because they're allowing them to. Sebastian Janikowski has hit some very long field goals, some at the end of the half. They wouldn't try a 60-yard field goal in the middle of the first quarter because you're not going to give up the ball on your own 45. A lot of it is circumstance.

I was drafted about where I had expected. I expected one of two teams; the one team passed, the Bengals went next, and that's where I ended up. My first year salary was $29,000, and I got a $42,000 signing bonus. Contracts for my position now are in the millions.

A lot of guys have kicking talent, but I think the biggest thing is keeping an even keel. You can't get too high or too low. Every kick is a new experience, and you have to put the last one out of your mind. There are a lot of guys with the leg strength and accuracy, but a lot of talented guys can't do it in a game.

I'm not sure that the pressure to kick a game-winning field goal is any different than it is all game long. It doesn't mean you're not nervous—it's a good nervousness and you try to use it—but you're nervous on every kick. They can change the entire momentum of the game.

If you go on an 80-yard drive from your own 10 and miss a short field goal, it deflates your whole group. The opening drive is always a key drive to score on. A lot of kicks are just as important as a last-second field goal. It just appears more important because of the ramifications of missing. I don't know if I was any more nervous on those late kicks than I was in the first quarter.

CHRIS BAHR

If the snap's perfect, it's easier to hold. If it's a perfect snap and hold, that makes it easier to kick. If the snap isn't real good, it's up to the holder to make it better. If he doesn't make it better, it's ultimately up to the kicker. A bad snap or hold makes it tougher, but you can certainly adjust.

It comes down to this: I'm the last one. There's the snap, the hold, and then me. I always had the philosophy that we made field goals and I missed them. I took blame for all the misses.

Wind is the toughest thing to kick in. All you can do is pick a line and hit it. The wind's probably going to move the ball, but you don't know if the wind's going to stop while the ball's in mid-flight. For the most part if the wind's coming from the right, you're going to aim toward inside the right post and allow for a little bit of wind. You don't always aim for the center. You *never* aim outside the post. [*Laughs.*]

Certain stadiums had odd winds. Places on water were a little tougher: San Francisco was hard, Chicago could be hard, and Cleveland was tough. Oakland was a little tough because the field was so soft all the time. It's certainly easier kicking on turf than it is on grass. You always get a perfect spot on turf, so you don't have to worry about it being down in a hole.

Cold affects distance, and there's nothing you can do about it. What makes a ball go is compressing it with your foot, and then it decompresses to take off. In the cold you don't compress it as well. The coldest weather I ever played in was when the Raiders played Cleveland in a playoff game. The wind chill factor was minus 37. That was pretty nippy. [The Raiders won 14-12, later winning Super Bowl 15.]

Kicking on the hash marks doesn't make a huge difference now. The hash marks are basically right on the goalposts. In the old days those hash marks were a lot wider. They moved them in to help offenses and inadvertently helped the kickers.

The Bengals released me after the 1979 season. Al Davis once told me that he originally wanted to draft me but waited too long. The Raiders were the first team that called when I was free. I visited the Raiders and Tampa Bay and chose the Raiders.

We weren't any badder than anybody else. We got that reputation, but we were no different than most teams. We just had eye patches on the guy on our helmet.

I think most players like when their team's hated in opposing cities. The game's livelier and there's more passion in the stadium. To go into a place fervent about beating you makes it more fun.

In 1980 we were the first wild card team to win the Super Bowl. Every team in the AFC playoffs was 11-5 that year, and the seeding was determined by tiebreakers

Things went our way, and we were playing well at the time. We got to play the wild card game against Houston at home. The next week, at Cleveland, we intercepted a pass late. At San Diego early on we had a ball that was tipped and ended up right in our receiver's hands for a 65-yard touchdown. We then beat the Eagles 27-10 in Super Bowl 15 at New Orleans.

We made about $36,000 extra for the entire playoffs. We earned an extra three grand for the wild card game. If you didn't play in the wild card game and had won the Super Bowl, you'd have won $33,000 total. I don't know how it works now, but back then you made a little more winning the Super Bowl as a wild card than as a division winner.

I was the safety with the Raiders on kickoff coverage. Now they keep guys other than the kicker as a safety. I had a responsibility to follow the initial wave within about 10 or 15 yards. I made eight tackles in 1980.

I don't think I ever had a kickoff returned for a touchdown. There may have been one with Cincinnati in a preseason game, but I don't ever remember a touchdown being scored in the regular season.

We'd known the Raiders were going to move to Los Angeles for a long time. They had been in court for a couple years,

CHRIS BAHR

and we were pretty sure it was going to happen. I liked the Bay Area; everybody did. I think a lot of people were disappointed to go, but the team went, and you went with it.

The 1983 Los Angeles Raiders were a really good team. When we didn't turn the ball over, no one played with us all year. We didn't have a close game in any of the games that we didn't turn it over. There was a six-game stretch where we turned it over a ton and had some issues. In the playoffs we didn't turn it over at all. [The Raiders trounced opponents 106-34 in the playoffs, including a 38-9 Super Bowl triumph over defending champion Washington.]

Our two cornerbacks, Mike Haynes and Lester Hayes, were voted the top cornerback tandem of all time. We had Marcus Allen in the backfield, Todd Christenson at tight end, and a real solid defense.

In the Super Bowl Marcus Allen reversed field on a play and went 70-some yards for a touchdown. He made the choice to go back the other way, things broke, and it turned out to be a highlight reel. When you look at it later, it was a pretty special run, but during the game you have the same reaction to all the big plays that happen. There's an excitement when you score, and when someone returns a kickoff or catches a long pass for a touchdown, you have the same emotions. Marcus had a 5-yard touchdown run in that game that was probably just as slick.

I played my last year, 1989, with San Diego. It was a different environment traveling with San Diego as opposed to the Raiders. When the Raiders went to Seattle, it was so loud you could barely hold a conversation. With San Diego in Seattle you could hear real well. People didn't sit on the fence with the Raiders; you either loved or hated them. San Diego was an opponent you wanted to beat, but the game dictated the crowd's reaction.

After that season Bobby Beathard came into San Diego as the new GM. He said he was going with a young group and wanted to have a young kicker. Back then guys didn't realize that kickers could kick into their forties and be just as effective. I had a couple of possible opportunities, but I didn't push hard to find another team.

It was a great time, the years I spent in the NFL. Other than talking to you and occasionally doing a function now and again, I don't think about it anymore. Louie Kelcher and I have become friends over the years, and the game's so far gone that we don't talk about football.

I've been out of football for twenty-three years. It's way in the past. It was a great time, it's over, done with; move on.

Life's great. I've got two kids. One graduated from college a year ago. I've got one going to college this year. I like where I live, I like what we're doing, and life goes on. Football's just a short little stay.

*Overtime*

Two contrasting myths seem to encircle NFL players of previous eras. The first is that they earned a paltry wage. While it's true their salaries weren't enough to set someone up for life, the average NFL salary stayed consistently comparable with those of other jobs. Even the minimum salary in 1957, $5,000, netted more than what many Americans brought home, although several players noted they made more at off-season jobs. Perhaps it is more accurate to say that players earned a disproportionately low wage compared with league revenues, their importance to the NFL's success, and the health risks associated with their occupation. Nobody pays to watch owners play football, and not one of them has suffered a torn ACL watching from his luxury suite.

The second myth is that ballplayers blew their money, and those in current financial straits have only themselves to blame. Money management skills, however, vary among individuals. Subpar pensions and football-associated medical costs appear to possibly be larger factors. Another factor appears to have been that players entered into the conventional workplace perhaps 5–15 years after their college peers had begun building their own careers, honing skills, learning new technologies, and accumulating both seniority and retirement benefits.

Thankfully many of the men presented here succeeded

in business after football. A major difference between these men and today's players is that players of the '60s and '70s *had* to become successful afterward. Not having the financial luxuries of substantial free-agent contracts necessitated immediate career adjustments after football.

Many still work to support themselves. Lee Roy Jordan operates a lumber company. Conrad Dobler works in the medical industry. Louie Kelcher runs a regional trucking business.

Like the Packers vs. the Bears or the Cowboys vs. the Redskins, pro football's economic gridiron hosted the classic struggle of labor vs. management. It's important to stress that while this book quotes several stout opinions regarding NFL owners and the NFLPA, those aren't necessarily the opinions of all players, nor are they necessarily the opinions of each player within these pages. Like with any controversial topic, opinions and perspectives differ.

The owners' aggressive resistance to a free-market employment system and the players' lack of a muscular union kept player salaries to a minimum. Imagine what Bob Griese, who quarterbacked his team to three consecutive Super Bowls and back-to-back championships, might have commanded in today's free agency system. Instead he worked an off-season real estate job.

Today's NFL player not only collects a higher salary than the men you've read about, but he also receives better post-career health care and a greater pension.

Benefits change with each Collective Bargaining Agreement, so blanket statements assessing the gaps are difficult to make. Carl Eller's benefits differ from John Elway's, whose benefits will differ from Peyton Manning's when he retires. It's easier to provide real-life illustrations of the scenarios that NFL retirees face.

Elvin Bethea receives cortisone shots every ninety days to manage severe pain in his right arm and hand, a direct result of NFL injuries. Every time he goes he's on the hook for the cost due to the absence of health care benefits available to him. This adds up to a considerable amount per year, and that's just dealing with one specific issue. The reality of retirees not being provided medical benefits forces another Hall of Famer's wife to keep working rather than retire, simply to maintain an insurance plan to cover his football-related medical costs.

Individual workers' compensation claims do get filed, but these claims can get bogged down. One Hall of Fame player is in his seventh year of the process; another is in his third.

Retired players seem most concerned about those who haven't fared well in a secondary career. Some point to a business earning billions of dollars per year and ask why people have to fully absorb medical costs related to working for that business—occasionally causing financial distress—when it appears to be within the league's means to make a real difference without sacrificing a substantial percentage of wealth. They note today's benchwarmer making a high six- or seven-figure income while former stars who helped build the league, making that benchwarmer's salary possible, aren't taken care of.

Sadly one man contacted for this book, an NFL champion and Pro Bowl–caliber player, was unable to interview because of dementia. I learned that another well-known player I'd hoped to interview had trouble remembering how to open his car door. I decided not to pursue contacting him. We've yet to learn the depth to which these tragedies exist, but they are very real.

Virtually every player with whom I spoke experienced some sort of permanent physical consequence from pro football. Still the vast majority concluded the NFL experience was well worth the side effects, and most seemed to enjoy their post-career lives. Many simply stated injuries were "just part of the game."

The game changed over time, as did its popularity. One

generation of fathers shared their love of pro football with their sons, who followed the NFL with their sons, who now watch with their sons and daughters. Through this timeline the league once known as the sputtering American Professional Football Association accumulated an enormous number of fans. As a result its gross receipts top the Gross Domestic Products (GDP) of many first-world countries simply because of the sheer number of enthusiasts. The Dallas Cowboys alone generated $280 million in 2009, a sum larger than the GDP of Finland—*by over $40 million*. At the time this was written, *Forbes* assessed the value of the Cowboys at over $2 billion. The average NFL franchise was estimated to be worth over $1 billion, with the Oakland Raiders deemed lowest at $825 million.

None of this could've been achieved without men like Al Wistert, George Taliaferro, Bart Starr, Irv Cross, Jack Youngblood, and thousands of others toiling between the hash marks, building brick by brick, yard by yard, season by season, the entity our nation couldn't imagine autumn Sundays without.

These men played, and placed, the game before the money.

ACKNOWLEDGMENTS

I can't express enough thanks to the men who donated their time and stories to this project. Getting to meet and chat with NFL legends is a dream come true for any fan, and I feel blessed and privileged to have compiled this anthology. I sincerely hope I've represented each individual and his era well.

Gaylord Armstrong, a former co-worker, played a key role in this book's beginning. An avid newspaper reader, Gaylord often clipped interesting sports articles from the *New York Times* and *Wall Street Journal* for me to read. One of those articles introduced me to the baseball classic *The Glory of Their Times*, by Lawrence Ritter, and the seeds for this book were planted. I thought, "Somebody needs to do this for football players."

A few years later sports artist Robert Hurst and I puffed cigars poolside in our mutual friend Jim Raup's backyard. Robert mentioned he'd been friends with Dick "Night Train" Lane, helping raise money for Night Train in his later years. I lamented that the lives of football players hadn't been well documented and offhandedly mentioned that I thought the world needed a football version of *The Glory of Their Times*. Robert said, "That sounds great. Would you like to go to Bob Lilly's golf tournament?"

Robert served as the project's catalyst. The player connections he had were invaluable toward bringing this idea to life, and his role is impossible to forget. His sports and music art can be viewed and purchased at www.ADamn FineArtist.com.

The importance of David Henry Sterry's and Arielle Eckstut's help regarding publishing matters cannot be overstated. David walked me through the entire process from writing a proposal, to contacting and communicating with publishers, to selecting which offer to accept. Before receiving his professional guidance my proposal basically read, "Dude, I've got this really cool football thing I'm doing." You can seek their assistance at www.TheBookDoctors.com.

The only participant I'd met before these interviews was Dan Reeves, and that was after a Packers-Broncos game my dad took me to for my seventeenth birthday. I appreciate the many people who connected me with players: Robert Hurst, Steve Turner, Bruce Lawrence (the best guitar player you've never heard), Michael and Alexis Kabat, Ted King, Garland Boyette Jr., Russell McHargue and Jo Ann Carothers, Leigh Ann Nelson, Lane Convey, Gloria Ashcraft, John and Pat Cherundolo, Ed Miller at the *Virginian-Pilot*, and Tammy Owens at the Pro Football Hall of Fame. Some players put me in touch with other players, and extra thanks go to Walt Garrison, Louie Kelcher, and Buddy Lex.

This work introduced me to many great people in the sports memorabilia industry, and several lent invaluable assistance to *The Game before the Money*. I'd like to thank Bill Mattis of AllStarInc, Jeff Wilson of J&T Sports, Ryan Fiterman of Fiterman Sports Group, Larry Dluhy of Sports Collectibles of Houston, Jay Willett of Diamonds in the Rough, and Tristar Productions.

Like a winning football team, no art project reaches its potential without teammates making plays. My appreciation goes to (in no particular order): Rob Taylor and the University of Nebraska Press; John Eisenberg; Joe Nick Patoski; the Richard family; Anne Pratt; Karl Anderson; Chris Potter; Glen Grunberger; Jason Rathman; Justin Bomberg; Cara Duryea; Hod Eckel; W. K. Stratton; Lisa Losasso; D. J. Stout; Lana McGilvray; the Texas Sports Hall of Fame; Jim and Mark Raup; Josh Leventhal; Andy Grooms and Bev and Mike Thom; Earl, Tyler, and Christian Campbell; Robert Kahler; Don Jakeway; Paul Wimmer; Chris McBurney; Gary Stebnitz; Laudine Luhn; the Virginia Sports Hall of Fame; the North Carolina Sports Hall of Fame; M. J. Bogatin; Bojana Ristich; Lawrence Glass; Willie Lanier; Don Talbert; Dave Parks; Jane Arnett; Jill Driban; Dixie Beale; Lisa Grueneberg; Katie Vine; Mike Renfro; Bob and Ann Lilly; Mel Renfro; the Houston International Hostel; Lynn Swann; Diane Flowers; Bill Bently; Gail Vetere; Andrew Kennelly; Mark Meloon; Randy Davenport; Alex Celestino; Walt Michaels; Eddie Fernandez; Michael Gillette; Todd Moye; Christen Karniski; Bruce Stave; Linda Shopes; Chris Chappel; and the lifelong support of many friends and family.

APPENDIX

## Monetary Figures Historically and in 2013 Dollars (in Order of Appearance, Rounded to Nearest Dollar)

| Year/Name | Historical | 2013 |
|---|---|---|
| 1925 Red Grange per game, pay | $50,000 | $667,417 |
| 1925 | $35,000 | $467,192 |
| 1935 Stan Kostka | $5,000 | $85,254 |
| 1936 Riley Smith per game pay | $250 | $4,201 |
| 1936 Average full-time wage | $1,184 | $19,898 |
| 1946 MLB minimum | $5,000 | $59,896 |
| 1936 Chuck Cherundolo tuition | $17 | $286 |
| 1942 Per game pay | $150 | $2,150 |
| 1945 Annual salary | $12,000–15,000 | $155,000–195,000 |
| 1945 Wine sales commission | $0.15 | $1.95 |
| 1946 Bill Dudley | $500 | $5,990 |
| 1949 Buddy Lex stipend | $20 | $196 |
| 1946 Nolan Luhn Chevrolet | $1,500 | $17,969 |
| 1947 Charley Trippi | $100,000 | $1,047,515 |
| 1947 Trippi annual salary | $25,000 | $261,879 |
| 1948 Johnny Lujack | $17,000 | $164,777 |
| 1949 | $18,500 | $181,576 |
| 1950 | $20,000 | $193,856 |
| 1951 | $20,000 | $179,689 |
| 1957 NFL minimum | $5,000 | $41,565 |
| 1957 Median male income | $5,601 | $46,561 |
| 1958 NHL minimum | $7,000 | $56,580 |

| | | |
|---|---|---|
| 1958 Median male income with college | $6,710 | $54,236 |
| 1959 Packers profit | $72,612 | $582,882 |
| 1959 Packers TV deal | $75,000 | $602,052 |
| 1952 Yale Lary | $6,500 | $57,297 |
| 1952 | $1,200 | $10,578 |
| 1952 Frank Gifford | $8,500 | $74,927 |
| 1952 Gifford bonus | $250 | $2,204 |
| 1954 Johnny Lattner | $10,000 | $86,839 |
| 1954 | $3,500 | $30,394 |
| 1957 Sonny Jurgensen | $9,000 | $74,817 |
| 1961 | $14,000 | $109,376 |
| 1958 Jim Taylor | $9,500 | $76,788 |
| 1960 Rozelle contract | $50,000 | $394,588 |
| 1960 AFL minimum | $6,500 | $51,296 |
| 1960 Average U.S. male income | $6,343 | $50,057 |
| 1961 Median male income with college | $7,586 | $59,266 |
| 1961 NFL Champ. TV | $615,000 | $4,804,734 |
| 1962 NFL Champ. TV | $615,000 | $4,757,005 |
| 1962 CBS contract | $9.3 million | $71,935,192 |
| 1963 AFL Champ. TV | $926,000 | $7,068,951 |
| 1964 CBS contract | $14 million | $105,494,968* |
| 1964 CBS NFL Champs. | $3.6 million | $27,127,277 |
| 1964 AFL contract | $36 million | $271,272,774* |
| 1965 Joe Namath | $427,000 | $3,166,524 |
| 1965 Donny Anderson | $600,000 | $4,449,448 |
| 1968 NFL minimum/rookies | $9,000 | $60,413 |
| 1968 NFL minimum/vets | $10,000 | $67,125 |
| 1968 Median male income with college | $10,866 | $72,938 |
| 1968 6-year pension | $7,800 | $52,357 |
| 1968 10-year pension | $12,000 | $80,550 |
| 1962 New CBS contract | $300,000 | $2,320,490 |
| 1960 Carroll Dale bonus | $500 | $3,946 |

| | | |
|---|---|---|
| 1960 Carroll Dale salary | $8,000 | $63,134 |
| 1960 D. Jones bet | $5 | $39 |
| 1965 NFL Champ. payout | $7,000-8,000 | $52,000-59,000 |
| 1965 | $10,000 | $74,157 |
| 1967 Super Bowl 1 winner | $15,000 | $104,908 |
| 1967 Super Bowl 1 loser | $7,500 | $52,454 |
| 1968 Super Bowl 2 winner | $15,000 | $100,688 |
| 1968 Super Bowl 2 loser | $7,500 | $50,344 |
| 1965 rookie salaries | $12,000-14,000 | $89,000-104,000 |
| 1965 rookie bonuses | $3,000-5,000 | $22,000-37,000 |
| 1960 Guino Gonsoulin | $8,500 | $67,080 |
| 1960 Gonsoulin bonus | $780 | $5,919 |
| 1960 Dick Frey | $6,500 | $51,296 |
| 1961 Irv Cross | $10,000 | $78,126 |
| 1962 Garland Boyette | $500 | $3,867 |
| 1962 Mick Tingelhoff | $18,000 | $139,229 |
| 1964 Johnny Unitas | $100,000 | $753,535 |
| 1964 Colts | $12,000 | $90,424 |
| 1964 Colts | $15,000 | $113,030 |
| 1965 Playoff money | $10,000 | $74,157 |
| 1965 Dan Reeves | $10,000 | $74,157 |
| 1965 Dan Reeves bonus | $1,000 | $7,416 |
| 1966 Walt Garrison | $15,000 | $108,146 |
| 1966 Trailer cost | $3,000 | $21,629 |
| 1972 Skoal offer | $18,000 | $100,592 |
| 1972 Super Bowl 6 winner | $15,000 | $83,826 |
| 1968 Ken Houston | $500 | $3,356 |
| 1968 Elvin Bethea | $15,000 | $100,687 |
| 1968 Dodge Charger | $8,000 | $53,700 |
| 1968 Per diem | $50 | $335 |
| 1968 Per diem after taxes | $43 | $289 |
| 1968 Tax on per diem | $7 | $47 |
| 1969 | $16,000 | $101,840 |
| 1970 Pro bowl "if clause" | $1,500 | $9,031 |
| 1970 Raise/Pro Bowl winner | $1,000 | $6,020 |

| | | |
|---|---|---|
| 1970 Pro Bowl loser | $750 | $4,515 |
| 1970 Cle/Bal/Pitt | $3 million | $18,061,546 |
| 1970 TV contracts | $185 million | $1.1 billion* |
| 1970 NFL minimum/rookies | $12,500 | $75,256 |
| 1970 NFL minimum/vets | $13,000 | $78,267 |
| 1970 Median male income with college | $12,144 | $73,113 |
| 1974 TV contracts | $269 million | $1.2 billion* |
| 1976 Reggie Jackson | $3 million | $12,316,134 |
| 1976 Bobby Grich | $1.5 million | $6,158,067 |
| 1976 MLB free agents | $200,696 | $823,933 |
| 1976 MLB average | $52,300 | $214,711 |
| 1977 Super Bowl 11 winner | $15,000 | $57,821 |
| 1977 Super Bowl 11 loser | $7,500 | $28,910 |
| 1977 Average NFL salary | $30,000 | $115,642 |
| 1977 Median male income with college | $17,391 | $67,037 |
| 1978 Fran Tarkenton | $275,000 | $985,259 |
| 1978 Larry Hisle | $3 million | $10,748,282 |
| 1987 TV contract | $1.4 billion | $2.88 billion* |
| 1980 Louie Kelcher | $400 | $1,135.33 |
| 1975 Doug English | $40,000 | $173,886.25 |
| 1976 | $25,000 | $102,757.91 |
| 1977 | $30,000 | $115,780.69 |
| 1978 | $35,000 | $125,574.47 |
| 1976 Chris Bahr | $29,000 | $119,199.17 |
| 1976 | $42,000 | $172,633.29 |
| 1980 Playoffs | $36,000 | $102,179.27 |
| 1980 | $33,000 | $93,664.33 |

*Calculated using the CPI Inflation Calculator on the U.S. Bureau of Labor Statistics website, reflecting differences in the Consumer Price Index in historical dollars vs. July 2013 dollars. The CPI calculator only handles figures up to $10 million. Higher quantities were calculated by multiplication. For example, the calculator stated $10 million in 1970 equaled $60,205,154.64 in 2013 dollars. Multiplying the 2013 amount by 18.5 produced the $1.1 billion figure regarding 1970 television contracts.

## AUTHOR'S NOTE CONCERNING SOURCES

Factual information regarding number of All-Pro seasons, post-season awards such as the MVP, and various career and game statistics came from *The ESPN Pro Football Encyclopedia*, 1st ed. Occasionally individual game statistics not found in the aforementioned encyclopedia were skimmed from box scores contained in the Pro-Football-Reference.com database.

Historical collegiate football scores and statistics were gleaned from *The ESPN College Football Encyclopedia: A Complete History of the Game* and *The USA Today College Football Encyclopedia: A Comprehensive Modern Reference to America's Most Colorful Sport, 1953–Present.*

*Extra Points*

Bethea, Elvin, and Mark Adams. *Smashmouth: My Football Journey from Trenton to Canton*. Champaign IL: Sports Publishing LLC, 2005.

Bleier, Rocky, and Terry O'Neil. *Fighting Back*. New York: Stein and Day, 1975.

Cooper, D. W. *Because It Was Sunday: The Legend of Jack Youngblood*. Authorized biography. Chandler AZ: Bravda Velo, 2011.

DeLamielleure, Joe, and Michael Benson. *Joe DeLamielleure's Tales from the Buffalo Bills*. Champaign IL: Sports Publishing LLC, 2007.

Dobler, Conrad. *Pride and Perseverance: A Story of Courage, Hope, and Redemption*. Chicago: Triumph Books, 2009.

Dobler, Conrad, and Vic Carucci. *They Call Me Dirty*. New York: Putnam Adult, 1988.

Garrison, Walt, and Mark Stallard. *Then Landry Said to Staubach: The Best Dallas Cowboys Stories Ever Told*. Chicago: Triumph Books, 2007.

Garrison, Walt, and John Tullius. *Once a Cowboy*. New York: Random House, 1988.

Gifford, Frank, and Peter Richmond. *The Glory Game: How the 1958 NFL Championship Changed Football Forever*. New York: HarperCollins, 2008.

Gifford, Frank, and Harry Waters. *The Whole Ten Yards*. New York: Random House, 1993.

Griese, Bob, and Dave Hyde. *Perfection: The Inside Story of the 1972 Miami Dolphins' Perfect Season*. Hoboken NJ: John Wiley and Sons, 2012.

Griese, Bob, Brian Griese, and Jim Denney. *Undefeated: How Father and Son Triumphed over Unbelievable Odds Both on and off the Field*. Nashville TN: Thomas Nelson, 2000.

Helyar, John. *The Lords of the Realm: The* Real *History of Baseball*. New York: Ballantine Books, 1994.

Hornung, Paul, and William F. Reed. *Golden Boy*. New York: Simon and Schuster, 2004.

Hornung, Paul, and William F. Reed. *Lombardi and Me: Players, Coaches, and Colleagues Talk about the Man and the Myth*. Chicago: Triumph Books, 2006.

Knight, Dawn. *Taliaferro: Breaking Barriers from the* NFL *Draft to the Ivory Tower*. Bloomington: Indiana University Press, 2007.

Maynard, Don, and Matthew Shepatin. *You Can't Catch Sunshine*. Chicago: Triumph Books, 2010.

Reeves, Dan, and Dick Connor. *Reeves: An Autobiography*. Chicago: Bonus Books, 1988.

Ritter, Lawrence. *The Glory of Their Times: The Story of the Early Days of Baseball Told by the Men Who Played It*. New York: Harper Perennial Modern Classics, 2010.

Starr, Bart, and Murray Olderman. *Starr: My Life in Football*. New York: William Morrow, 1987.

Taylor, Jim, and Kristine Setting Clark. *The Fire Within*. Chicago: Triumph Books, 2010.

Whittingham, Richard. *What a Game They Played: An Inside Look at the Golden Era of Pro Football*. (Oral history of the generation previous to *The Game before the Money*, featuring interviews with Sammy Baugh, Red Grange, and Don Hutson.) Lincoln NE: University of Nebraska Press, 2002.

# INDEX

344; free agents and, 140, 173, 270-73; for Frank Gifford, 63, *342*; for Austin "Goose" Gonsoulin, 136-37, 140, 144, *343*; for Stan Kostka, 3, *341*; for Yale Lary, 59, *342*; for Johnny Lattner, 68, *342*; for Johnny Lujack, 39, *341*; negotiations for, 3, 33, 39, 68, 119, 132, 136-37, 140, 169-70, 239, 244; for Dan Reeves, 197, *343*; for rookies, 3, 119, 239, 306; for Pete Rozelle, 119, *342*; for Jim Taylor, 105, *342*; concerning television, 57, 118-19, 120, 271, 272-73, *342*, *344*; for Mick Tingelhoff, 173, *343*; for Charley Trippi, 3, 33, *341. See also* salaries

Copper Bowl, 136, 117

Coryell, Don, 287, 288, 290, 291, 320-21

Cotton Bowl, 48, 87

court cases, 54, 56, 118, 120, 270, 271

coverage, 179, 197-98, 288-89

crackback blocks, 254

Creekmur, Lou, 16, 17

Cross, Irv, 153-59, *343*

Dale, Carroll, 123-34, *342-43*

Dallas Cowboys: in Championship Games, 83, 89, 90, 120-21, 130-31, 177, 199-200, 214; football drafts and, 177, 196, 205, 229; founding of, 119, 177; friendships and rivalries with, 178, 197, 200, 215, 218, 222; at Ice Bowl, 89, 90, 120-21, 130-31, 177; players for, 130, 154-55, 177-79, 196-202, 205-18, 222, 263, 277; in playoff games, 177, 183, 212; preseason games and, 94, 198; profits concerning, 336; in Super Bowls, 120-21, 177, 200, 212-13, *213*, 216, 245, 262-64; training camps for, 197-98, 206-8; wins and losses for, 83, 130-31, 177, 183, 199-200, 212, 245, 263-64. *See also* Landry, Tom

Dallas Texans, 48, 74-76, 136-37, 147-48. *See also* Kansas City Chiefs

Davidson, Cotton, 71-79, *78*

Davis, Al, 76-77, 141, 180, 181, 282, 296, 319, 328-29

Davis, Clarence, 281

Davis, Willie 163

DeBartolo, Eddie, 324

defense: blitzes for, 77, 165, 197-98, 207, 262; "Bruise Brothers" as, 321; Fearsome Foursome as, 155; formations and game plays for, 63, 111-12, 155, 162, 173-74, 178, 209, 276-77; Purple People Eaters as, 192, 261; safeties as, 119, 138, 211, 220-25, 303, 329; *See also* defensive backs; defensive ends; defensive tackles; linebackers

defensive backs: Irv Cross as, 154-55; Frank Gifford as, 62; Austin "Goose" Gonsoulin as, 135-44; Sonny Jurgensen as, 96; Yale Lary as, 60; Johnny Lattner as, 68; Johnny Lujack as, 38, 40; Don Maynard as, 108-9, 110, 141-42; Mel Renfro as, 198; safeties as, 211, 220-25, 329; Bart Starr as, 87; George Taliaferro as, 49; Charley Trippi as, 35

defensive ends: George Andrie as, 211; Al "Bubba" Baker as, 308, 309; Elvin Bethea as, 230-31, 232-40, *236*, *241*; Carl Eller as, 191-93; Dick Frey as, 147-50, *149*; Dave Pureifory as, 308; Otis Sistrunk as, 281-82; Jack Youngblood as, 114, 275-78

defensive tackles: Doug English as, 303-14, *304*, *315*; game plays concerning, 90, 94, 261; Louie Kelcher as, 261-62, 318-24; Nolan Luhn as, 25-26; Otis Sistrunk as, 281-82; Al "Ox" Wistert as, 21

Grange, Red, 3, *341*
"the Greatest Game Ever Played,"
109–10
Green, Cornell, 211
Green Bay Packers: in Championship Games, 83–84, 89–90, 128, 130–31, 177, 183, 199; coaches for, 16, 25, 26–28, 29–30, 35, 132; football drafts by, 25, 81, 82, 88, 94–95, 105; players for, 16, 25–31, 81–85, 87–90, 94–95, 104–6, 128–32; in playoff games, 129, 183, 187, 212; profits concerning, 57, *342*; rivalries with, 29; in Super Bowls, 78, 84, 120–21, 131, 199; television contracts and, 57, *342*; training camps for, 128–29; wins and losses for, 78, 82, 83, 84, 105, 120–21, 129–31, 177, 199. *See also* Lombardi, Vince
Grich, Bobby, 272, *344*
Gridiron Greats, 114
Griese, Bob, 243–47
Griese, Brian, 247
Griffin, Dean, 137, 139
Grim, Allan, 54, 56, 118, 120

Halas, George, 28–29, 39, 50, 61
halfbacks, 35, 62, 65–66, 68, 109, 211
Halls of Fame. *See* College Football Hall of Fame; Pro Football Hall of Fame
Hanratty, Terry, 251, 262–63
Harris, Franco, 259–60, 262, 264, 266, 281
Hayes, Bob, 179, 198
Heidi Bowl, 112
Heisman Trophy, 33, 39, 65, 67–68, 70, 93–94
helmets: chinstraps on, 287–88; facemasks on, 17, 27, 35–36, 66, 126, 290; interiors of, 142, 237; of leather and plastic, 17, 22, 35; rookies and, 98
high school stadiums, 28, 75

Hill, Calvin, 201, 212, 278, 296
Hisle, Larry, 272, *344*
hits: after snaps, 8; by defensive linemen, 73, 97–98; by Austin "Goose" Gonsoulin, 142, 144; by Ken Houston, 222–23; injuries from, 99–100, 106, 129, 142–43, 247, 251, 283; by Tony Lorick, 184, 185; by Bronko Nagurski, 6; by Jim Taylor, 105–6. *See also* tackles
Hornung, Paul, 92–95
Houston, Ken, 219–26, *343*
Houston Oilers: in Championship Games, 148–50, 232–33; coaches for, 148, 221, 232, 239; football drafts by, 229, 301; players for, 148–50, *149, 162*, 169, 170–71, *171*, 220–21, 229–40, *241*, 301–2; preseason games and, 230; training camps for, 230, 239; wins and losses for, 148–50, 232–33
huddles, 97, 99, 113, 183–84, 199, 263
Hughes, George, 16
Hunt, Lamar, 74–75, 119
Hutson, Don, 25, 120

Ice Bowl, 84, 89–90, 120–21, 130–31, 177
I formation, 254
incomes. *See* bonuses; contracts; salaries
Indiana University, 45, 51, 81
injuries: of All-Americans, 251; to arms, 223, 235, 247; arthritis from, 18, 51, 61, 190; to chests and sternums, 26, 76, 235; concussions as, 17, 129, 158, 171, 215, 237, 290; dementia and memory loss from, 9, 17, 190, 335; to hands and thumbs, 193, 235, *236*; from hits and tackles, 99–100, 106, 129, 247, 251, 278–79, 283, 311–12; to knees, 17, 61, 69, 190, 193, 201, 214–15, 223–25, 252, 292, 293, 313; to legs, 26, 102–3, 114, 235, 245, 277,

320; to necks, 144, 237–38, 311–12; to noses, 9, 17, 26, 35–36, 60; concerning players, 6, 114, 127, 183, 185–86, 302, 334–35; retirement and, 225, 247, 282–83, 311–14, 334–35; rules about, 66, 287; to shoulders, 41, 77, 103, 236, 278, 293, 313; team cuts and, 143, 144, 148, 287; concerning tongues, 126, 142–43; from wars, 256–58

integration, 3, 48–49, 120, 295–96, 298

interceptions, 40, 93, 98, 129, 130, 137–38, 178, 183, 204, 211, 221, 222, 263–64, 281, 329

jackets, 59, 61, 241, 242

Jackson, Reggie, 171, 111

Jimmy the Greek, 157–58

jobs: in acting and broadcasting, 63, 156–58, 247, 268; advertising as, 28, 215–17; in banking and insurance, 267; board memberships as, 50, 145; coaching as, 30, 36, 41–42, 70, 79, 147, 155, 156, 225; in construction, 145; in education, 182, 225; in industry, 3; law enforcement as, 17; in sales, 42, 59, 88, 128, 148, 182, 190, 231, 294, 341; in service and repair, 30, 114, 171

Johnson, Billy "White Shoes," 300–302

Jones, Deacon, 127, 155, 242, 276 343

Jordan, Lee Roy, 176–79, 205, 209

judges, 54, 56, 118, 120

Jurgensen, Sonny, 96–103, 342

Kansas City Chiefs, 205, 220, 245, 265–67, 305. See also Dallas Texans

Kardiac Kids. See Cleveland Browns

Kearney, Jim, 220

Kefauver, Estes, 55

Kelcher, Louie, 261–62, 317–25, 344

Kerkorian, Gary, 73

Kezar Stadium, 192

kickers, 14–15, 93, 113, 244, 322, 327–31

kickoffs, 26, 49, 68, 93, 109, 207, 208, 329

kicks, 14–15, 264, 327–28. See also punts

Klein, Gene, 319, 320, 324

Korean War, 56, 59–60, 69

Kostka, Stan, 3, 341

Kunz, Cal, 139–40

Lambeau, Curly, 25, 26–28, 29–30, 35, 120

Lambeau Field, 82

Landry, Tom: as coach, 119, 156, 177, 178–79, 197, 198, 200–202, 208–9, 215; friendships and rivalries with, 217–18, 222; regarding mistakes, 213; with New York Giants, 63, 209

L.A. Rams. See Los Angeles Rams

Lary, Yale, 59–61, 342

Lattner, Johnny, 64–70, 342

laws. See antitrust laws

Layne, Bobby, 6, 16, 40, 60, 61

leaders. See records

leagues: All-American Football Conference (AAFC) as, 3, 46, 47, 56, 57; Canadian Football League (CFL) as, 72, 168–70, 190; National Hockey League (NHL), 56–57, 341. See also American Football League (AFL); National Football League (NFL)

Leahy, Frank, 37, 38, 41, 64, 65, 67, 69, 93

legislation. See antitrust laws

Lex, Joseph "Buddy," 12–18, 341

Lilly, Bob, 94

linebackers: Chuck Bednarik as, 22, 98; Garland Boyette as, 165–66, 167–71; Dick Butkus as, 174, 187; Chuck Cherundolo as, 5–7; Dave Edwards as, 211; hook passes and, 111–12; Lee Roy Jordan as, 178–79, 209

linemen: centers as, 7-8, 173-75;
offensive guards as, 19-21, 146,
148-50, *149*, 184, 286-90, 291-
93, 296-97; offensive tackles as,
16, 17, 21, 80-85, 184, 230, 288-
89, 294. *See also* defensive backs;
defensive ends; defensive tackles
Lombardi, Vince: as coach and
disciplinarian, 57, 82-84, 88-90,
94, 97, 100-01, 103, 105-6, 209;
death of, 102; as general manager, 132-33; during practices,
100-102, 125; quotations and
slogans of, 82, 88-89, 90, 101,
133-34; retirement of, 78, 84-85
long passes, 21-22, 38, 75, 112-13, 179
Lorick, Tony, 180-90
Los Angeles Dons, 46-47
Los Angeles Raiders, 329-30. *See also*
Oakland Raiders
Los Angeles Rams, 126-28, 129, 155,
187, 205, 276-79
losses: for Baltimore Colts, 129-30,
131, 182, 183; bonuses for, 131, 231,
272, *343*, *344*; at bowl games, 15,
33, 67, 71; for Chicago Cardinals,
35; for Cleveland Browns, 59, 60,
130, 328; crowds and fans concerning, 75; for Dallas Cowboys,
83, 130-31, 177, 183, 199-200, 212,
245, 263-64; for Detroit Lions,
313; for Green Bay Packers, 82,
83; for Houston Oilers, 232-33;
for Kansas City Chiefs, 245; for
Miami Dolphins, 321-22; for
Minnesota Vikings, 192, 246, 261,
281-82; for New York Giants, 83,
110; for Oakland Raiders, 78,
84, 112-13, 282; for Philadelphia
Eagles, 21, 34; for Pittsburgh
Steelers, 246; for San Diego
Chargers, 148; for San Francisco
49ers, 60
Louisiana State University, 104

Luhn, Nolan, 24-31, *341*
Lujack, Johnny, 37-42, *341*

Madden, John, 75, 282
Major League Baseball (MLB). *See*
baseball
managers, 21, 126-27, 132-33, 137,
139, 239
man-to-man coverage, 179, 197-98,
288-89
Marshall, George Preston, 2, 48
Marshall, Jim, 186-87, 191-92
Matte, Tom, 129, 183
Maxwell Award, 32, 65, 68
Maynard, Don, 63, 107-15, 141-42
Mazur, Johnny, 65
Meredith, Don, 130, 179, 198, 199,
209
mergers, 47, 56, 118-19, 120, 133,
270, 271
Miami Dolphins: coaches for, 50-51,
182, 188, 244-46; players for,
244-47; in playoff games, 245,
281, 321-22; in Super Bowls, 212,
245, 246, 324
Michigan State University, 249-51,
295-96
middle linebackers, 165-66, 167-71,
178-79, 209
military drafts, 2, 12, 45-46, 69, 73-
74, 79, 255-56
military service: during Korean War,
59-60, 69; in Reserve Officers'
Training Corps (ROTC), 69, 82,
255; United Service Organizations (USO) and, 154-55; during
Vietnam War, 210, 255-58; volun-
teers for, 38, 147, 280, 283; during
World War II, 7, 12-13, 20, 24, 33
Minnesota Vikings: coaches for, 132,
173; drafts by, 191; friendships
among, 175; losses for, 192, 246,
261, 281-82; players for, 132, 173-
75, 191-93, 261, 281-82; in Super

North Carolina Agricultural and Technical State University, 228–29

North Carolina A&T. *See* North Carolina Agricultural and Technical State University

Northwestern University, 153

notebooks. *See* playbooks

Oakland Coliseum, 319–20

Oakland Raiders: in Championship Games, 282; coaches and owners for, 76–77, 141, 180, 181, 282, 296, 319, 328–29; football drafts by, 126, 280, 328–29; players for, 76–79, *78*, 141, 280–83, 328–29; in playoff games, 328, 329; profits concerning, 336; rivalries with, 280, 319–20; in Super Bowls, 78, 84, 281–82, 328, 329; trades and, 76, 77, 79, 280; in wild card games, 329; wins and losses for, 76, 77, 78, 84, 112–13, 328, 329. *See also* Los Angeles Raiders

occupations. *See* jobs

offense: centers as, 7–8, 173–75; formations and stances for, 14, 37–38, 178–79, 197–98, 209, 253–54; offensive guards for, 19–21, 146, 148–50, *149*, 184, 286–90, 291–93, 296–97; offensive tackles for, 16, 17, 21, 80–85, 184, 230, 288–89, 294. *See also* fullbacks; game plays; quarterbacks; running backs; wide receivers

offensive tackles, 16, 17, 21, 80–85, 184, 230, 288–89, 294

officials, 73, 75, 126, 131, 174, 183

off-season jobs. *See* jobs

offside, 21–22, 214

Oklahoma State University, 203–5

onside kicks, 264

operations, 103, 214, 235, 252, 258, 283, 312. *See also* surgeries

Orange Bowl, 15–16, 24–25, 67, 71, 111

overtime games, 110, 129, 245

owners: of Baltimore Colts, 120, 186, 270; regarding benefits and pensions, 55, 56, 61, 193; of Chicago Bears, 28–29, 39, 50, 61; of Denver Broncos, 139–40, 145; concerning free agents, 334; of Los Angeles Rams, 126–27; of Oakland Raiders, 76–77, 141, 180, 181, 282, 296, 319, 328–29; of Philadelphia Eagles, 3; of Pittsburgh Steelers, 7, 9, 257; of San Diego Chargers, 319, 320, 324; of San Francisco 49ers, 324; concerning strikes, 272, 311; of Washington Redskins, 2, 48

painkillers. *See* shots

Parker, Clarence "Ace," 10–12, 96

Parker, Jim, 94, 184, 189

Parseghian, Ara, 153, 249, 250, 251, 253–54

passes: during Championship Games and Super Bowls, 21–22, 112–13, 130–31, 262–64; Hail Mary as, 179; hook passes as, 111–12, 113; interceptions of, 40, 98, 137–38, 221, 222, 263–64; long passes as, 21–22, 38, 75, 112–13, 179; play-action passes as, 290; punts and, 7, 263; records concerning, 15, 16, 40, 86, 96, 108, 243; routes for, 113, 138, 141; rushing and, 155, 276–77, 307; for touchdowns, 15, 16, 27, 40, 75, 77, 98–99, 112–13, 198. *See also* game plays

payouts. *See* bonuses

Payton, Walter, 222–23, 310

penalties, 66, 96

Penn State University. *See* Pennsylvania State University

Pennsylvania Military College (PMC). *See* Widener University

players (*cont.*)
215, 222, 233, 320; for San Diego
Chargers, 261-62, 319-24, 330-31;
for San Francisco 49ers, 135, 144,
324-25; for Seattle Seahawks,
193; for St. Louis Cardinals, 107,
164-68, 285-92; strikes by, 258,
272, 310, 311; team cuts and, 139,
143, 144, 148, 168, 188-89, 287;
for Washington Redskins, 100-
102, 120, 127, 221-25, 300. *See also*
All-Americans; All-Pros; football
drafts; friendships; injuries; jobs;
pensions
playing fields, 41, 82, 98, 110-11. *See
also* stadiums
playoff games: for American Football Conference (AFC), 245, 281,
285, 329; Baltimore Colts in, 129,
131, 177, 183; bonuses for, 183,
329, *343, 344*; Dallas Cowboys in,
177, 183, 212; Detroit Lions in, 60;
Green Bay Packers in, 129, 183,
187, 212; Kansas City Chiefs in,
245; Los Angeles Raiders in, 330;
Miami Dolphins in, 245, 281, 321-
22; Oakland Raiders in, 328, 329;
as overtime games, 129, 245; San
Diego Chargers in, 321-22; San
Francisco 49ers in, 60
Polo Grounds, 110, 111
post pattern, 138, 141
practices, 100-102, 125-26, 233, 245-
46, 250
Prairie View A & M University, 219-20
preseason games: Baltimore Colts
and, 97-98; in Canton OH, 182;
Dallas Cowboys and, 94, 198;
exhibition games as, 29, 105, 137,
140-41, 255, 259; Houston Oilers
and, 230; Philadelphia Eagles
and, 97-98; salaries for, 230
Pro Bowls: George Andrie in, 211;
Elvin Bethea in, 231; bonuses and

clauses for, 220, 231, *343-44*; Garland Boyette in, 160; Irv Cross in,
153; Carroll Dale in, 123; Cotton
Davidson in, 71; Joe DeLamiel-
leure in, 295; Conrad Dobler
in, 284; Carl Eller in, 191; Doug
English in, 303; Walt Garrison in,
215; Frank Gifford in, 62; Austin
"Goose" Gonsoulin in, 140; Bob
Griese in, 243; Paul Hornung in,
92; Ken Houston in, 220; Billy
"White Shoes" Johnson in, 300;
Lee Roy Jordan in, 176; Sonny
Jurgensen in, 96; Louie Kelcher
in, 321; Yale Lary in, 60; Johnny
Lattner in, 64; Johnny Lujack in,
37; Don Maynard in, 107; Otis
Sistrunk in, 280; Bob Skoronski
in, 80; Bart Starr in, 86; George
Taliaferro in, 47; Jim Taylor in,
104; Mick Tingelhoff in, 173; Al
"Ox" Wistert in, 19; Jack Young-
blood in, 275
profits, 57, 336, *342*
Pro Football Hall of Fame: Elvin
Bethea in, 240-42, *241*; Lou
Creekmur in, 16; Joe DeLamiel-
leure in, 295; Carl Eller in, 191;
Dan Fouts in, 324; funds concern-
ing, 298, 299; Frank Gifford in,
62; Bob Griese in, 243; Paul Hor-
nung in, 95; Ken Houston in, 225;
inductees and players in, 95, 106,
120; Sonny Jurgensen in, 96; Yale
Lary in, 59; Don Maynard in, 107;
Joe Montana in, 324; Clarence
"Ace" Parker in, 12; Bart Starr in,
86; Charley Taylor in, 220; Jim
Taylor in, 104; Charley Trippi in,
32; Al "Ox" Wistert and, 22; Jack
Youngblood in, 275
Prothro, Tommy, 276, 319-20
punters: Canadian Football League
(CFL) and, 168-69; Cotton David-

returners. *See* punt returners

returns, 77, 168–69, 221

reverse plays, 130, 143, 255, 330

Rice University, 107–8

Ring of Fame, 145, 211

Ring of Honor. *See* Ring of Fame

rings, 59, 150, 283, 297, 324

rivalries: with Chicago Bears, 29, 35, 40–41; with Chicago Cardinals, 35, 40–41; with Cleveland Browns, 297; with Dallas Cowboys, 178, 215, 222; with Green Bay Packers, 29; between leagues, 3; with Oakland Raiders, 280, 319–20; with Pittsburgh Steelers, 280, 297; with San Diego Chargers, 319–20; with Washington Redskins, 178, 215, 222

Robinson, Eddie, 160–63

rodeos, 208–9, 215–16

rookies: awards for, 47, 201; Al "Bubba" Baker as, 308, 309; bonuses for, 137, 197, 229–30, 306, *343, 344*; contracts for, 3, 119, 239, 306; helmets and, 98; salaries for, 97, 121, 294, *342, 343, 344*. *See also* training camps

Rooney, Art, 7, 9, 257

Rose Bowl, 13, 32–33, 191, 244, 247

Rosenbloom, Carroll, 120, 186, 189, 270

ROTC. *See* Reserve Officers' Training Corps (ROTC)

Rote, Kyle, 109

Rote, Tobin, 60

Rozelle, Pete, 119, 126, 270–71, *342*

rules: about catches, 281; for clotheslining, 126, 143; for crackback blocks, 254; about facemasks, 27, 126, 290; about fights, 189; about injuries, 66, 287; for positions, 234–35, 287; referees and officials regarding, 73, 75, 126, 174; about retirement, 217; "Rozelle Rule"

as, 270–71; about substitutions, 26, 125

running backs: Marcus Allen as, 330; Rocky Bleier as, 251–55, 258–67; Earl Campbell as, 304–5; halfbacks as, 35, 62, 65–66, 68, 109, 211; Calvin Hill as, 201, 212, 278, 296; Paul Hornung as, 93; Walter Payton as, 222–23, 310; Dan Reeves as, 130, 154–55, 197–201, 208; Mel Renfro as, 198; Don Shy as, 255; O.J. Simpson as, 296, 297; tailbacks as, 11, 14, 161; George Taliaferro as, 48, 49; Jim Taylor as, 104–6; Charley Trippi as, 35; Steve Van Buren as, 21, 22; Buddy Young as, 73. *See also* fullbacks

running plays, 182, 187–88, 191–92, 261–62, 266–67, 305

rushing, 41, 104, 155, 276–77, 296, 307

sacks. *See* hits; tackles

safeties, 138, 211, 220–25, 329

salaries: for Chris Bahr, 327, *344*; for Baltimore Colts, 182–83, *343*; for baseball players, 270, 272, 310, *341, 344*; for Elvin Bethea, 229, 231, *343*; bonuses and raises regarding, 126, 231, 327, 342, *344*; for Garland Boyette, 164, *343*; Canadian Football League (CFL) and, 168; for Chuck Cherundolo, 6, *341*; for Carroll Dale, 126, 133, *343*; for football veterans, 121, 271, 325, *342, 344*; for free agents, 173, 270–73, 310–11, 334, *344*; for Dick Frey, 148, *343*; for Sonny Jurgensen, 103, *342*; for Johnny Lattner, 68, *342*; male median income as, 56–57, 120, 121, 271, 272, 333, *341–42, 344*; mergers and, 118–19, 120; negotiations for, 33–34, 55, 56, 68, 121, 270–71; per diems as, 230, *343*;

University of Wyoming, 285
USC. *See* University of Southern California (USC)
USO. *See* United Service Organizations (USO)
U.S. Tobacco Company. *See* United States Tobacco Company

Van Brocklin, Norm, 40, 99
Van Buren, Steve, 21, 22
Varrichione, Frank, 66–67
Vessels, Billy, 65
veterans. *See* football veterans
Vietnam War, 154, 210, 255–58
Virginia Polytechnic Institute and State University, 124–26
Virginia Tech. *See* Virginia Polytechnic Institute and State University

wages. *See* bonuses; contracts; salaries
wars: injuries from, 256–58; Korean War as, 56, 59–60, 69; military drafts for, 2, 12, 45–46, 69, 73–74, 79, 255–56; Vietnam War as, 210, 255–58; World War II as, 2, 3, 7, 12–13, 20, 24, 33, 45–46
Washington Redskins: coaches for, 8, 97, 100, 102, 178, 221, 222, 224–25, 290; owners of, 2, 48; players with, 100–102, 120, 127, 221–25, 300; rivalries with, 178, 215, 222
watches, 127
Waterfield, Bob, 127, 128
weather: blizzards and snowstorms as, 29, 34–35, 66, 138; during Championship Games, 34–35, 84, 89–90, 232; temperatures and, 15, 29, 41, 323, 328
Widener University, 300–301
wide receivers: Lance Alworth as, 211–12; Chris Burford as, 75;

Carroll Dale as, 127–32; Frank Gifford as, 62; Bob Hayes as, 179, 198; Billy "White Shoes" Johnson as, 300–302; Nolan Luhn as, 25, 26–27, 28–29; Don Maynard as, 111–13; George Taliaferro as, 49
wild card teams, 232, 329
wins: for Baltimore Colts, 110, 177, 183, 212; bonuses for, 131, 132, 150, 183, 231, 272, *343*, *344*; at bowl games, 15, 33, 71, 244; for Chicago Cardinals, 21, 34; for Cleveland Browns, 47, 59, 177, 182; crowds and fans concerning, 75, 98–99; for Dallas Cowboys, 177, 200, 245; for Denver Broncos, 282; for Detroit Lions, 59, 60; for Green Bay Packers, 78, 83, 84, 105, 120–21, 129–31, 177, 183, 199; for Houston Oilers, 148–50, 232; for Los Angeles Raiders, 330; for Los Angeles Rams, 127, 277; for Miami Dolphins, 245; for "mythical national championship," 251–52; for New Orleans Saints, 292; for Oakland Raiders, 76, 77, 328, 329; for Philadelphia Eagles, 21, 34–35, 98–99; for Pittsburgh Steelers, 261–67; for San Diego Chargers, 320, 321–22; for St. Louis Cardinals, 288
Wistert, Al "Ox," 19–23
World War II, 2, 3, 7, 12–13, 20, 24, 33, 45–46
Wrigley Field, 41
wrong way run, 191–92

Yankee Stadium, 102, 110
Young, Buddy, 48, 73
Youngblood, Jack, 114, 275–79

zone coverage, 179, 288–89